# Textbook A

# Level 5

**Siegfried Engelmann**
**Jean Osborn**
**Steve Osborn**
**Leslie Zoref**

A Division of The McGraw·Hill Companies

Columbus, Ohio

## Acknowledgments

Grateful acknowledgment is made for permission to use the following material.

"Open Range" Courtesy of Golden Books Publishing Company, Inc. *Open Range* from *Tenggren's Cowboys and Indians* by Kathryn and Byron Jackson © 1968, 1996 Golden Books Publishing Company, Inc. Used by permission. All rights reserved.

Harry Behn, "Trees." From The Little Hill Poems & Pictures by Harry Behn. Copyright 1949 by Harry Behn, renewed © 1977 by Alice L. Behn. All rights reserved. Reprinted by permission of Marian Reiner.

"In Time of Silver Rain" From COLLECTED POEMS by Langston Hughes. Copyright © 1994 by the Estate of Langston Hughes Reprinted by permission of Alfred A. Knopf, a Division of Random House Inc.

## Illustration Credits

Jan Benham, Rose Mary Berlin, Barbara Couseller, John Edwards Studio, Len Epstein, Meryl Henderson, Rachel Iramyi, Susan Jerde, Stephanie Pershing, Karen Tafoya

## Photo Credits

**1** © PhotoDisc; **2** © Corbis; **151** © The Bridgeman Art Library; **248** © Brock May/Photo Researchers; **249 (t)** © Bill Beatty/Animals Animals Earth Scenes, **(c)** © Bill Dyer/Photo Researchers, **(b)** © Bill Dyer/Photo Researchers; **251** © Francois Gohier/Photo Researchers; **255** © Leonard Lee Rue III/ Photo Researchers; **256** © Rod Planck/ Photo Researchers; **281 (t)** © Stephen J. Krasemann/ DRK Photo, **(bl)** © Nigel J Dennis/ Photo Researchers, **(br)** © Tim Davis/ Photo Researchers; **283** © Renee Lynn/Photo Researchers; **286** © Kevin Schafer/Corbis; **287** © Wayne Lynch/DRK Photo.

**www.sra4kids.com**

*SRA/McGraw-Hill*

*A Division of The McGraw-Hill Companies*

Send all inquiries to:
SRA/McGraw-Hill
8787 Orion Place
Columbus, OH 43240-4027

Printed in the United States of America.

ISBN 0-07-569159-0

7 8 9 RRW 06

# Table of Contents

# Unit 1

# No Place like Home

Your home is where you live. Some homes are small apartments in crowded cities. Others are big houses way out in the country. But no matter what their size or location, homes are special places.

In this unit, you will read a short story and a famous novel about children who travel far away from their homes. Their journeys are exciting, frightening, and full of wonder. Yet something is missing. Travel may be fun, but at the end of the journey, there's no place like home.

Ron's Summer Vacation

The Wonderful Wizard of Oz

# 1

## A WORD LISTS

| 1<br>*State Names* | 2<br>*Compound Words* | 3<br>*New Vocabulary* |
|---|---|---|
| 1. Florida | 1. sketchbook | 1. vacation |
| 2. Colorado | 2. weekend | 2. poster |
| 3. Maine | 3. homework | 3. kayak |
| 4. Indiana | 4. backyard | 4. kayaking |
| | | 5. instead |
| | | 6. sketchbook |
| | | 7. assignment |

# Ron's Summer Vacation

### *by Ozzie Reid*

## Chapter 1

Summer vacation was over, and the first day of school was almost over. Ron sat at his new desk in Ms. Brown's fifth-grade classroom, waiting for the school bell to ring. He had already finished reading the story in his textbook, and he didn't have any homework yet, so he just looked around the room.

Ms. Brown had hung several travel posters on the wall behind her desk. One poster showed kids playing in the ocean next to a big, sandy beach. "Visit Florida!" the poster said. ✿

Another poster showed a boy and a girl standing on top of a mountain, looking all around. "Colorado has great views!" it said. A third showed a boy paddling a kayak down a swiftly moving river, under the words, "For a real vacation, paddle up to Maine!"

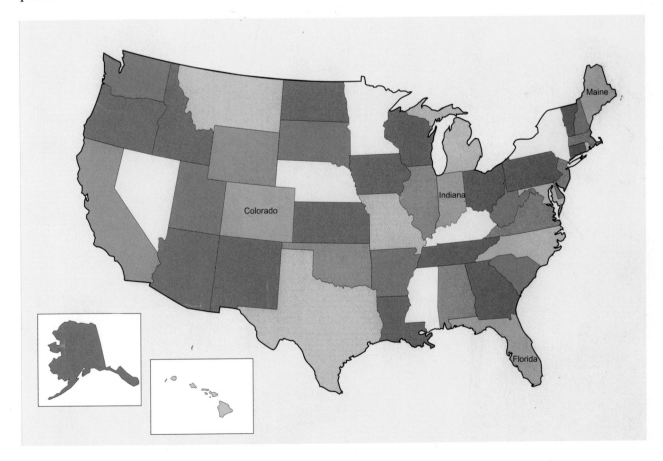

Vacation! The word made Ron's eyes light up. It sounded so great, so full of promise. Then Ron remembered. Ever since his father died in a car wreck six years ago, his family hadn't taken a single summer vacation. They had spent every one of those summers at home in Flatville, Indiana, not doing much of anything.

Oh, sure, on some weekends Ron's mother would drive him and his sister Debby to Flatville State Park, where they'd hike around in the woods for a few hours. But Ron didn't think those weekend trips counted as real vacations. For him, vacations were when you spent two weeks climbing mountains in Colorado or a month relaxing on a beach in Florida or the whole summer kayaking down a wild river in Maine. Now *those* were vacations. They were fun. They were exciting. They cost a lot of money.

Money! The word made Ron frown. He didn't know much about money, but he did know that his mom never seemed to have any. At the beginning of every year, his mom said, "Maybe we'll have enough money to take a real vacation this summer." But by the time summer rolled around, she wasn't talking about vacations anymore. Instead, she said, "Sorry, Ron, we'll have to stay in Flatville this summer. Maybe next year."

Every summer she said that. She said it in the summer after Ron finished kindergarten and when he finished first, second, third, and fourth grades. He'd spent every one of those summers hanging around Flatville. Now here he was at the beginning of fifth grade, looking at the posters on his classroom wall and dreaming of a real vacation. ◆

The posters made Ron think about his sister Debby, who was three years older than he was. Sometimes Ron wished he had a brother instead—a brother he could play sports with, a brother who liked to fool around and have fun. But he didn't have a brother. All he had was Debby, and Debby was no fun at all.

Ever since their father died, Debby's idea of fun was to draw pictures. Every day, she sat by her bedroom window with a sketchbook and drew whatever she saw. Some days she drew the trees in the backyard. Some days she drew clouds. Some days she drew robins hunting in the grass for worms.

Ron had to admit that Debby was a pretty good artist. She was only in eighth grade, but she could already draw pictures that looked just like the real thing. Her trees looked like real trees, with branches, leaves, blossoms, and fruit. Her clouds looked fluffy or full of rain, with different areas of light and dark. Even her robins seemed ready to fly off the page.

Compared with other kids her age, Debby was miles ahead in art. Of course, she did spend more time drawing than other kids—a lot more time. In fact, Debby spent almost every spare hour of the day drawing in her room. She had started a few years ago by drawing simple pictures of objects in the house, such as cups, chairs, and books. But she got tired of drawing those objects, so she started looking out her window.

Ron wondered how much longer Debby would be happy with her window. Although she could see a lot from there, it wasn't like being out in the country. If she were out in the country, she could be drawing pictures of forests or mountains or swiftly moving rivers. But the only way she could draw those pictures was to look at the real thing. And the only way to see the real thing was to take a vacation.

Vacation! There was that awful word again! Ron tried to put it out of his mind. Suddenly, he noticed Ms. Brown talking to the class.

"Because this is the first day of school," she said, "I'm going to give you a really easy homework assignment. I'd like you to write a paragraph or two about your summer vacation. Describe the places you visited. Tell about all the wonderful times you had. I'm sure it will be very easy since it's so fresh in your mind."

Then Ms. Brown called on several students to describe their summer vacations. A lot of the students hadn't done much, but Natalie Smith had played on a beach in Michigan. Kiko Meyer had climbed Pike's Peak in Colorado. Fred Arnsworth had gone kayaking in Alaska.

Ron sank lower in his chair. He hoped Ms. Brown wouldn't call on him. What would he say if she did? That he'd spent the whole summer in Flatville? That he hadn't had a vacation in six years? That his sister drew pictures of their backyard? He didn't want to tell her any of those things. The other students would only laugh.

Just then, the bell rang.

"Oh, dear, we're out of time," said Ms. Brown. "Remember to bring me your vacation stories by tomorrow morning. Now close your desks and line up by the door. The sooner you're ready, the sooner we can leave."

---

# C COMPREHENSION

Write the answers.
1. How do you know that Ron is the main character in the story?
2. Why do you think the word *money* made Ron frown?
3. How do you think Ron felt when other kids talked about their vacations? Why did he feel that way?
4. Why did Ron think that Debby was a good artist?
5. Why was Ron worried about his homework assignment?

# D WRITING

If you could take a vacation anywhere in the world, where would you go? Why?
• Write a paragraph that explains your answer. Be sure the paragraph answers the following questions:
  - Where would you go?
  - What does that place look like?
  - What kinds of things would you do there?
• Make your paragraph at least three sentences long.

## A WORD LISTS

**1**

*Word Practice*
1. CD player
2. cell phone
3. computer
4. Internet
5. e-mail

**2**

*Compound Words*
1. notebook
2. backpack
3. classroom
4. hallway
5. driveway
6. downtown

**3**

*Word Endings*
1. really
2. swiftly
3. slowly
4. usually

**4**

*New Vocabulary*
1. cashier
2. usual
3. expecting
4. rapids
5. vanish
6. startled
7. kayaking
8. instead

## B READING

# Ron's Summer Vacation

## Chapter 2

Ron threw his notebook into his backpack and stood in line, waiting to leave the classroom. He didn't say anything to anybody, because he was worried about his homework assignment. When Ms. Brown finally opened the classroom door, Ron walked through with his eyes to the ground.

Out in the hallway, students were laughing and shoving each other and making noise. But Ron just kept on walking, right down the hallway and out the front door.

Outside, he could see parents waiting for their children. Some were standing near the front door, but others just stayed in their cars in the parking lot, listening to their radios or CD players. ✿

One woman in an expensive car was talking on a cell phone and looking at her gold watch. Ron figured her car had air conditioning, because all her windows were closed. He wondered what it would be like to drive home in an expensive, air-conditioned car while talking on the phone. His mom's car was a rusty older model that only got air-conditioned in the winter, when the heater didn't work.

Right now, his mom's car was parked at her job. She worked as a cashier in a grocery store several miles from their house. She worked from nine o'clock in the morning to six o'clock in the evening, so she never picked up Ron from school. Instead, he usually went home in a school bus. If he didn't take the bus, he had to walk.

Ron looked over at the school buses lined up in the driveway. Students were standing next to the doors, waiting to get on. Somehow, Ron didn't feel like riding the bus today. He didn't want to talk to anybody, and he wasn't in a hurry to get home. So he decided to walk.

Ron's house was about a mile from school. Usually he could walk home in a half hour or less. He would go east on Center Street for three blocks, then south on Oak Street for five blocks, then east again for a half block on Shady Lane. His address was 367 Shady Lane.

Today, Ron set off on Center Street as usual. But when he got to Oak Street, he decided to head north instead of south. He hadn't walked on this part of Oak Street much before, but he knew that it went downtown. He thought that he might look at some of the store windows in the downtown mall or the posters outside the movie theater. ♦

As Ron walked, he kept thinking about his homework assignment. What was he going to write? He couldn't think of anything to say except that he'd spent the whole summer in Flatville, going to the state park, watching TV, and hanging out with his friends.

Just then, Ron looked up and saw

that he was passing the library. He remembered that the library had several computers in a special room. People used the computers to surf the Internet, write e-mail, and work on projects.

Ron stopped walking and thought about going into the library. Why not? He could write his homework assignment on one of the computers. His story might be boring to read, but at least he'd be done with it. If he finished the story this afternoon, he'd have the evening free to watch TV, play outside, or read a book.

When Ron entered the library, he looked around for the computer room. He couldn't find it right away, but he did see a clock. It was just a few minutes after four. Suddenly, Ron remembered that Debby was expecting him to be home by four. His mom usually called around four-thirty to make sure that Ron and Debby were safe.

Ron thought about running home as fast as he could, but then he saw a pay phone on the wall. He had some change in his pocket, so he called Debby and told her that he'd be home by six, after he'd finished working in the library. That was fine with Debby. She said she was already sitting in her room, drawing a picture of the neighbors' swing set.

Ron hung up and found the computer room in a corner of the library. When he walked into the room, a woman at the desk showed him how to use the writing program on the computer. Ron had already used the same program at school, so it didn't take him long to get ready.

Except for the woman at the desk, Ron was the only person in the room. He stared at the computer screen, wondering how to begin. "I spent my

summer vacation in one of the hottest vacation spots in America" was his first sentence. Then he wrote another sentence: "It's called Flatville, Indiana."

Ron laughed at what he had written. What a joke. Flatville was hot all right, but Ron didn't think that anyone had ever taken a vacation there. What would a person do? Flatville didn't have any mountains or beaches, and the only river was the Little Muddy, a small creek that flowed slowly through the middle of town. It was called the Little Muddy because the water was almost always brown with mud.

The first two sentences of Ron's story weren't really true, but at least they were a good beginning. He decided to write some more sentences that weren't really true. Why not? The real story was so boring that he got tired just thinking about it.

Ron stared at the screen for a minute and then started writing again. "I did something new and exciting every day," he wrote. "But the most exciting event was when I paddled my kayak down the swiftly moving rapids of the Little Muddy."

Ron laughed again. He could almost see himself floating down the Little Muddy in a kayak. The water flowed so slowly that he would have to paddle like crazy just to move a few feet. He might even get stuck in the mud.

If only the Little Muddy was a wild river, with dangerous rapids and huge rocks—just like the river in the poster of Maine. Ron closed his eyes and imagined what it would be like to paddle down a wild river in Maine. He would have to grip the paddle as hard as he could and keep switching it from side to side to guide the kayak. If he made one slip, he might crash into the rocks and flip over.

Ron closed his eyes tighter and made a picture of the river in his mind. He could almost hear the roar of the rapids and feel the cold, clear water spraying in his face. His arms were moving as fast as they could, and the wind was whistling by his ears.

That was a great picture. Ron thought he'd describe it for his story, so he opened his eyes and looked at the computer screen. But instead of words, the screen showed a picture of a wild river in Maine.

Ron couldn't believe what he saw. He reached out to touch the screen, but it vanished in front of his hand. Instead of hitting the screen, his hand just waved in the air. And then it got wet.

Startled, Ron looked around. He wasn't in the computer room anymore. He was sitting in a kayak, paddling down a wild river in Maine.

## C COMPREHENSION

Write the answers.
1. Why did Ron decide to walk instead of taking the bus?
2. How do you think Ron felt about the woman in the air-conditioned car?
3. Why did Ron write sentences that weren't true?
4. Why wouldn't people want to kayak in the Little Muddy?
5. Name at least two ways that the Little Muddy was different from the wild river.

## D WRITING

Pretend that the last sentence of Ron's story says, "But the most exciting event was when I paddled my kayak down the swiftly moving rapids of a wild river in Maine."

• Write a paragraph that continues Ron's story. Be sure your paragraph answers the following questions:
  – What is the river like?
  – How do you feel as you paddle down the river?
  – What exciting things happen to you on the river?
• Make your paragraph at least four sentences long.

## A WORD LISTS

| 1<br>*Word Practice* | 2<br>*Word Endings* | 3<br>*New Vocabulary* | 4<br>*Vocabulary Preview* |
|---|---|---|---|
| 1. blue jay | 1. instantly | 1. boulder | 1. cupboard |
| 2. cardinal | 2. quickly | 2. supplies | 2. sober |
| 3. robin | 3. closely | 3. lack | 3. celebration |
| 4. wildflower | 4. completely | 4. notice | 4. budge |
| 5. bobcat | 5. suddenly | 5. shrug | 5. bounding |
| | 6. hardly | | |
| | 7. swiftly | | |

## B VOCABULARY FROM CONTEXT

1. The room contained a rusty stove and a **cupboard** for the dishes.
   • cup • ceiling • cabinet
2. The sun and wind had taken the sparkle from her eyes and left them a **sober** gray.
   • serious • happy • red
3. They had a great **celebration** after winning the game.
   • school • party • sleep
4. He tried to pull the post out of the ground, but the post would not **budge.**
   • glisten • disappear • move
5. The animals were **bounding** swiftly down the tunnel.
   • sitting • running • walking

## C WORD ENDINGS

Complete each item by adding the correct ending to the word in bold type.

1. The picture was **perfect,** so it was painted ____.
2. When he was hungry, he would get **anxious,** so he waited for dinner ____.
3. The young man was **polite,** so he acted ____.
4. She had a **loud** voice, so she talked ____.
5. The noise was **sudden,** so we heard it ____.
6. The car was very **slow,** so it went very ____.

# Ron's Summer Vacation

## Chapter 3

Ron still couldn't believe that he was really paddling a kayak down a wild river in Maine. He looked around again. He was surrounded by a forest of pine trees that stretched as far as he could see. Many different kinds of birds flew from tree to tree or sat in the branches, whistling and chirping. Some were red, some were blue, and others were black, brown, or gray. Ron thought that some of the birds were cardinals, blue jays, and robins, but he wasn't sure about the others.

The forest floor was covered with pinecones, pine needles, bushes, and wildflowers. ✿

Far away, Ron saw a group of deer grazing. He wondered if there were other animals in the woods, like bears or bobcats or snakes. Thinking about those animals made Ron afraid for a second, but he soon forgot his fear and looked at the river around his kayak.

The water was as clear as glass. It seemed to be several feet deep, and Ron could see rocks of many shapes and sizes at the bottom of the river. Swimming above the rocks were dozens of fish. They looked so close that Ron thought he might be able to reach out and grab one. He put his hand in the water and instantly took it out. Boy, was that water cold!

Ron noticed that he was wearing just a life jacket, a T-shirt, a swimming suit, and a pair of sneakers without socks. He also noticed that the water was moving quickly, even though the river was fairly calm. There weren't any rapids or boulders in the water, and Ron's kayak just kept moving forward in a straight line.

Ron looked down the river to see where he was headed. He couldn't see very far ahead, because a bend in the river blocked his view. But Ron could hear the sound of roaring rapids. He guessed that the rapids started soon after the bend in the river.

The sound of the rapids made Ron's heart beat faster, and it also made him a little afraid. He wondered how well he could paddle through the rapids, so he examined his kayak closely. It was a small plastic kayak, with just one seat in the middle, where Ron was sitting. The inside of the kayak was completely empty: no food, no maps, no supplies of any kind. For a moment, the lack of supplies made Ron glad because nothing would get wet or lost if the kayak tipped over.

The next moment, however, Ron started to worry about his lack of supplies. What if he got hungry? What if he got lost? What if night fell and he

didn't have any light or anywhere to sleep? What if there were bears?♦

Those questions bothered Ron, but he didn't want to think about them. Instead, he tried to find out how well he could guide the kayak. He looked at his paddle, which had a wide blade at each end. The two blades were connected by a long handle that Ron held in the middle. When Ron stroked the paddle through the water on the right side of the kayak, the kayak turned a little bit left. When he stroked the paddle on the left side, the kayak turned a little bit right.

When Ron wanted to go straight, he made a right stroke, then a left stroke, then another right stroke, then another left stroke, and so on. As long as he made equal numbers of left and right strokes, the kayak went straight.

To turn the kayak, Ron had to make strokes on just one side of the kayak. First he practiced turning right by making several strokes on the left side. Then he practiced turning left by making strokes on the right side.

Ron crossed from one side of the river to the other, and then back again. After a while, he decided to go straight as fast as he could. Left, right, left, right went his paddle as Ron put his head down and picked up speed. He was having so much fun that he didn't notice that the kayak had gone around the bend in the river. He also didn't notice that someone was yelling his name.

"Ron!" the voice yelled.

Ron kept paddling.

"Ron! Ron! Over here!" the voice yelled even louder.

Ron looked around. Who was calling his name?

"RON!" the voice yelled at the top of its lungs.

Ron followed the sound of the voice and saw a girl standing on the left bank of the river, waving her arms up and down and yelling his name. He looked more closely, and he couldn't believe what he saw. It was his sister Debby. What was she doing here? And what did she want?

"Ron!" she yelled again. "You have to come out! We have to go home!"

Home? What was she talking about? Ron was just starting to have fun. He didn't want to go home. He'd only been on vacation in Maine for a few minutes, and he didn't want it to end so soon.

Ron pretended he couldn't hear Debby. He laid the paddle on his lap and cupped his hands behind his ears. Then he shrugged his shoulders as if to say, "I can't hear you."

Debby started yelling again. Ron saw that she was standing next to a kayak just like his own. Behind her was a little shed filled with kayaks. A man was in the shed, working on one of the kayaks. Ron wondered who the man was and what he was doing with all those kayaks.

"Ron!" Debby yelled again. "Get out right now! You can't go any farther! You have to stop here!"

Ron thought fast. He knew that Debby wanted him to get out, but she was only his sister. If his mother had been there, he would have stopped. But Debby was just, well, Debby. Why should he listen to her? Besides, he was having too much fun.

While Ron was turning these ideas over in his mind, he suddenly noticed that the water was moving much faster.

Debby kept yelling at him, but he was moving farther and farther away from her, at a faster and faster rate.

Ron looked back over his shoulder and could hardly see Debby anymore. Then he looked forward. There, just a few hundred feet in front of him, the river narrowed into swiftly moving rapids between huge boulders. Ron could hear the roar and see the water pounding against the rocks again and again, spraying into the air.

Ron began to feel afraid. The roar got louder and louder. The kayak moved faster and faster. He had to decide what to do. He wanted to try the rapids, but he didn't know if he was good enough.

At the last second, he made up his mind to head for the left bank of the river. But it was too late. The kayak was moving too quickly, and he couldn't turn it or make it stop. He was headed into the rapids. He couldn't go anywhere else.

## E COMPREHENSION

Write the answers.
1. Why was Ron afraid when he thought about the animals that lived in the woods?
2. Why did Ron worry about his lack of supplies?
3. How did Ron feel about the rapids when he first heard them? Why did he feel that way?
4. Why didn't Ron want to come out of the river?
5. Why didn't Ron obey Debby?

## F WRITING

What do you think will happen to Ron if he enters the rapids?
- Write a paragraph that explains your answer. Be sure your paragraph answers the following questions:
  - What will happen to Ron's paddle?
  - What will happen to Ron's kayak?
  - How will Ron feel?
  - Where will Ron end up?
- Make your paragraph at least four sentences long.

# 4

## A WORD LISTS

### 1
*Compound Words*
1. playground
2. waterfall
3. slingshot

### 2
*Word Endings*
1. loudly
2. furiously
3. probably
4. quickly
5. tightly
6. barely

### 3
*Vocabulary Preview*
1. dangerous
2. current
3. disappeared
4. approach
5. ignored
6. manager

## B VOCABULARY FROM CONTEXT

1. It's **dangerous** to ride your bike on a street with lots of traffic.
   - easy  - safe  - not safe
2. Near the rapids, the **current** got faster.
   - flow of water  - raisin  - riverbank
3. We thought the book had **disappeared**, but then we found it under the couch.
   - vanished  - dismissed
   - reappeared

4. They couldn't **approach** the fire because it was too hot.
   - put out  - see  - come close to
5. The man **ignored** his ringing telephone.
   - paid no attention to  - copied
   - obeyed
6. At the store, the **manager** told the other workers what to do.
   - customer  - boss  - cashier

# Ron's Summer Vacation

## Chapter 4

Ron knew he had made some mistakes. He should have listened to Debby. He should have stopped when she called to him. He should have known that the river was too dangerous. But he didn't have time to worry about all that right now, because he was headed straight into the rapids. He had to use every muscle in his body to guide the kayak, and he had to think fast.

The water was moving so quickly that Ron could hardly steer. He could only go with the current and hope that he didn't crash into any boulders. He held his paddle tightly with both hands. ✿

The first few feet of the rapids weren't that bad. Ron's kayak stayed in the middle, far from the rocks along the edge. But then the rapids narrowed and the water moved even faster. Ron looked ahead and saw a huge boulder sticking out of the middle of the river. Half the river flowed around the right side of the boulder, and the other half flowed around the left.

Both sides looked dangerous, with the water spraying high into the air and roaring loudly. Ron decided to try for the right side of the boulder. Using all his strength, he made several quick strokes on the left side of the kayak. Nothing happened. He was still going in a straight line, and he was headed directly toward the boulder!

Ron quickly moved his paddle over to the right. He was only a few feet from the boulder, and he had to turn fast. He grabbed the handle as hard as he could, and he paddled furiously. At the last second, the kayak turned left and swept around the left side of the boulder, with only inches to spare.

Now Ron was really frightened. He was going many times faster than when he had started, back in the calm part of the river. His kayak was filling with cold water, and he was soaking wet from all the spray. He could just barely see the boulder as he swept around it, carried along by the current.

Ron felt as if he were zooming down a huge, curving playground slide. But the slide didn't seem to have any end, and Ron had no idea where he was headed.

Suddenly, Ron could no longer see the boulder, so he figured that he must have passed it safely. But he didn't dare to look back, because he was too afraid of what might be coming next. ♦

Ron stared down the river as far as he could. He didn't see any more boulders, just fast-moving rapids with rocks on both sides. If he stayed in the middle of the river, he should be all right.

But just when Ron thought he might be safe for a little while, he noticed that the river seemed to disappear a few hundred yards away. He could hear a really loud roar coming from that spot, and he could see spray shooting into the air.

Ron wondered why the river disappeared so suddenly. Could it be going into a big hole? Or did it just stop all of a sudden? Then the answer struck Ron like a bolt of lightning. That must be a waterfall! The river must come to a certain point and then drop down, down to the rocks below!

Time was running out. Ron knew that he couldn't kayak over the waterfall, no matter how high or low it was. He had to get out of the river. But how? The current was moving faster and faster, and try as he might, Ron couldn't make the kayak turn. He paddled backwards and forwards, then forwards and backwards. He tried turning right. Then he tried turning left. Nothing worked.

Ron thought about jumping out of the kayak, but that would be even worse. He wouldn't be able to swim against the current, and the water would smash him against the rocks. At least the kayak protected him a little.

Meanwhile, the edge of the waterfall came closer and closer. As Ron approached, he saw a boulder sticking just a few feet out of the water right at the edge of the waterfall. His only chance was to smash the kayak against the boulder and hope that it would stop him from going over. Besides, the current was taking him straight toward the boulder, so he had no other choice.

This time, Ron didn't try to turn the kayak. He just kept his eyes on the boulder and waited to see what would happen. He was only ten feet away, five, four, three, two, one.

The kayak hit the boulder straight on. Then the kayak flipped into the air. Ron shot out of the kayak like a rock from a slingshot. The world was spinning so fast that Ron couldn't even see where he was going. All of a sudden, he hit water—deep, cold water. Thanks to the life jacket, he floated back up to the surface of the water.

Ron saw that he had flown over the waterfall, which was only about twenty feet high, and landed in a large, round pool. He could see the kayak lying upside down at the edge of the pool. The front part was smashed, and the sides didn't look too good either. The paddle was nowhere in sight. At the far end of the pool, the river kept flowing, but Ron couldn't even bear to look at it.

Ron swam to the edge of the pool and pulled himself out onto a rocky beach. He was shivering from the cold water, but he didn't seem to have any broken bones. He just sat on the ground for a while and caught his breath. Then he took off his wet life jacket, shirt, and shoes. He figured the warm sun would quickly dry both him and his clothes.

Ron poured the water out of his shoes. Then he wrung out his life jacket and shirt and laid them on top of some rocks to dry. After that, he found a smooth spot on top of a small boulder and sat down to think.

Ron figured that Debby and the man from the kayak shed would soon come looking for him. Debby had probably run over to the man and told him that Ron

had paddled into the rapids. Now the two of them were probably running along the riverbank, looking for Ron.

He felt like such a fool. What was he going to say to Debby when she found him at the bottom of the waterfall, with the kayak smashed and his clothes soaking wet? How was he going to explain why he had just ignored her as he paddled by?

As Ron thought about these questions, he noticed that he was getting very sleepy. Kayaking was hard work. His arms were tired, and his legs were sore. He stood up and walked to a sandy spot where he could lie down. The life jacket was already pretty dry, so he used it as a pillow.

Ten seconds later, Ron was fast asleep.

## D COMPREHENSION

Write the answers.
1. Why did the water seem to disappear at the waterfall?
2. When Ron was in the rapids, why didn't he jump out of the kayak?
3. What did Ron hope would happen when he smashed into the second boulder?
4. Why was Ron worried about Debby at the end of the chapter?
5. What do you think Ron will dream about while he's asleep? Why will he have that dream?

## E WRITING

What do you think Debby will say to Ron if she finds him?
- Write the speech that you think Debby will make. Be sure your speech answers the following questions:
  - How does Debby feel about what Ron did when he passed the kayak shed?
  - How does Debby feel about the risks Ron took?
  - What does Debby think could have happened to Ron?
  - What kind of person does Debby think Ron is?
- Make your speech at least four sentences long.

# A WORD LISTS

### 1
*Hard Words*
1. cyclone
2. prairie
3. Dorothy
4. aunt
5. Toto
6. horizon

### 2
*Word Endings*
1. cackle
2. candle
3. tunnel
4. sparkle
5. incredible
6. startle
7. twinkle

### 3
*Word Practice*
1. whirl
2. whirlwinds
3. electric
4. surround
5. surroundings
6. orphan
7. rough
8. deliver

### 4
*Word Practice*
1. sure
2. pressure
3. fun
4. funnel
5. anxious
6. usual
7. anxiously

### 5
*New Vocabulary*
1. in spite of
2. attic
3. rust
4. horizon
5. snarling
6. lanterns

### 6
*Vocabulary Preview*
1. merrily
2. mass
3. cradle
4. wail
5. sober

# B VOCABULARY FROM CONTEXT

1. The dog was happy and his eyes twinkled **merrily**.
   • sadly • happily • meanly
2. The sun had baked the plowed land into a gray **mass**.
   • house • ice floe
   • area with no shape
3. She felt as if she were being rocked gently, like a baby in a **cradle**.
   • truck • small bed • pillow
4. From the far north, they heard the low **wail** of the wind.
   • sea animal • howl • squeak
5. His expression was sad and **sober**.
   • eager • happy • serious

# Ron's Summer Vacation

## Chapter 5

"Ron!" said the voice. "Ron!"

Ron was dreaming about Flatville. Strangely, the dream was so pleasant that he didn't want to wake up.

"Ron!" said the voice again. "Are you okay?"

He knew that voice. It was Debby's. Ron thought it was the sweetest voice he'd ever heard. He woke up.

"I'm fine," Ron said as he opened his eyes.

Debby and the man from the kayak shed were standing over him. They both looked out of breath and worried.

Ron stood up slowly and kept his eyes on the ground. He didn't know what Debby would say, but he figured she would be plenty mad at him. ✿

Much to Ron's surprise, Debby reached out and gave him a big hug that seemed to last forever. Then she pulled back and asked again, "Are you sure you're okay?"

Ron nodded his head yes, even though he felt really ashamed. He couldn't believe how stupid he'd been.

"We've been looking for you for a long time," Debby said. "We didn't know if you were dead or alive. It's a good thing that Mr. Mason was able to help me."

Ron turned to look at Mr. Mason. He had gray hair and glasses, and he didn't look too happy. "You're a very lucky boy," he said. "You could easily have been killed. Only the best kayakers can go down these rapids. It's no place for a beginner."

"I know," Ron said, and the three of them looked over at the damaged kayak on the rocks.

Debby said, "Didn't you hear me back at Mr. Mason's kayak rental shed? I kept calling your name, but you didn't answer. Don't you remember that Mom told us to get out of the river at the shed? That's where we were supposed to return the kayaks to Mr. Mason."

Ron hung his head. He didn't know what to say. Of course he had heard Debby. Of course he should have left the river while it was safe. But he didn't do any of those things. Instead, he had just kept on going, right into the rapids.

Then Ron remembered something strange. Only a few hours ago, he was sitting in the library, writing about his summer vacation. After that, he was suddenly here in Maine, paddling a kayak. Should he tell Debby and Mr. Mason about the library? Or should he just keep it to himself? ♦

Ron decided not to mention the library, at least for now. After a moment, he lifted up his head and said, "I'm sorry, Debby, I don't know what came over me. I just wanted to stay in the kayak and make the vacation last a little longer."

Debby looked at Ron strangely. "Longer?" she laughed. "Ron, we've already been in Maine for three weeks. Mom's waiting for us back at the cabin. We're driving home first thing tomorrow morning."

Ron hung his head again. Now he was really confused. How could they have been here for three weeks? All he could remember was the last few hours.

"Well, at least your body is okay," Debby said, "even if your mind is on vacation."

"Let's go back to the shed," said Mr. Mason. "I'll come back and get the kayak tomorrow."

Debby, Ron, and Mr. Mason began walking back up the riverbank toward the shed. As they walked, Ron told them his story. He didn't want to tell them about the library, so he started with the part about paddling past the shed. He told them about the first boulder in the middle of the rapids and how he had gone to the left. Then he told them about the second boulder at the edge of the waterfall. Finally, he described how he had flown through the air and landed in the pool.

"You're a lucky boy," Mr. Mason kept saying. Ron could tell that Mr. Mason wasn't happy, and then he figured out why. Mr. Mason's kayak was badly damaged, and it was Ron's fault.

When the three of them got back to the shed, Ron asked Mr. Mason, "What about the kayak? Do we have to pay you for that?"

"Well," Mr. Mason began, "let me talk to your mother. I think we can work something out."

"I have an idea!" Debby said suddenly. "Just wait here!"

Ron and Mr. Mason watched as Debby ran over to one of the kayaks. She reached in, pulled out her sketchbook, and came back.

Debby opened the sketchbook to the first page and showed a drawing to Mr. Mason. "How do you like this picture?" she asked. "Do you think it's worth one kayak?"

Mr. Mason looked at the drawing and let out a gasp. "Why, that's beautiful!" he said. "It looks just like the river!"

Ron peeked over Mr. Mason's shoulder to look at the picture. Debby had drawn the river and the forest near the shed, just the way they were. The picture showed the sunlight sparkling on the water and the birds flying through the trees. Coming down the river was a boy paddling a kayak.

"That's just beautiful!" Mr. Mason said again. "I'll take it!"

Debby blushed and said, "I've been working on it all vacation. It's so great to be outdoors, instead of just looking at the world through my window."

Ron smiled at Debby. He was really proud of her. Then he looked at the picture again. He thought he'd seen the picture somewhere before, but he didn't know where. Then he remembered. It was the same picture that he'd seen on the computer screen when he was in the library.

He looked at the picture harder and harder and then reached out to touch it. But instead of touching paper, his fingers

touched glass. He looked again and saw that the picture was on the computer screen. He was back in the library, back where he had begun his vacation.

Ron let out a startled cry. The woman at the desk smiled at him and said, "You've been sleeping at the computer. Did you finish your story?"

"I . . . I don't know," Ron answered. He looked at the screen again. Instead of the picture of the river, the screen showed the first few sentences of Ron's story. He read the first sentence, the one that said, "I spent my summer vacation in one of the hottest vacation spots in America."

Ron thought about that first sentence. Then he wrote a new second sentence. It said, "That spot is called the library."

After he'd written that sentence, the rest was easy. He explained how he'd gone to the library and dreamed that he was paddling a kayak in Maine. Then he told everything that had happened in his dream. It wasn't a real vacation, but it was almost as good as the real thing.

When he finished his story, Ron raced home just in time to meet his mother coming home from work.

"Ron! Debby!" she said, as she walked through the front door. "I have wonderful news! They've made me a manager at the store, and I'm going to make a lot more money! I think I can finally take us on a real vacation! How would you like to go to Maine next summer?"

"I'd love to," said Ron. "I hear it's a beautiful place."

# D COMPREHENSION

Write the answers.
1. Why could Debby have been mad at Ron?
2. Why do you think Debby wasn't mad at Ron when she found him?
3. Why do you think Ron didn't mention the library to Debby and Mr. Mason?
4. How was the picture that Debby showed Mr. Mason different from her other pictures?
5. Why did Ron think the library was one of the hottest vacation spots in America?

# E WRITING

Finish the story that Ron started in the computer room, beginning with these sentences: "I spent my summer vacation in one of the hottest vacation spots in America. That spot is called the library."

- Make sure your story answers the following questions:
  - What happened when Ron was in the first part of the river?
  - What happened when Ron passed the kayak shed?
  - What happened in the rapids?
  - How did Ron go over the waterfall?
  - How did Ron get back to the computer room?
- Make your story at least ten sentences long.

# 6

## A WORD LISTS

### 1
*Word Endings*
1. people
2. terrible
3. tinkle
4. sprinkle

### 2
*Word Practice*
1. pressure
2. shriek
3. whirlwinds
4. grown-ups
5. surroundings

### 3
*Vocabulary Review*
1. sober
2. mass
3. merrily
4. wail
5. cradle

### 4
*Vocabulary Review*
1. in spite of
2. attic
3. rust
4. horizon

### 5
*Word Endings*
1. happy
2. happi • ly
3. angry

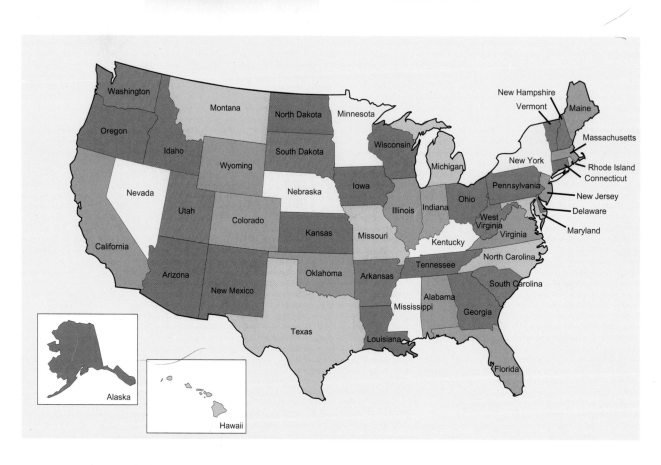

STORY BACKGROUND

# From Kansas to Oz

Today you will start reading a famous novel called *The Wonderful Wizard of Oz*. The version you will read is a little shorter than the original book, but the story remains the same.

*The Wonderful Wizard of Oz* begins in the state of Kansas more than a hundred years ago. At that time, people had almost none of the machines that we use today. They didn't have cars or televisions. They didn't have radios or CD players, computers or telephones. They used candles to light their houses, and they kept warm in the winter by building fires in their fireplaces.

The map on page 26 shows where Kansas is located. Kansas is a prairie, which is a flat grassland with almost no trees.

More than a hundred years ago, many people moved to Kansas to become farmers. But life was hard for the early farmers in Kansas because the winters were cold and the summers were hot and dry. During the summer, the hot sun would turn the green grass gray, and the land would dry up and crack. The streams and ponds would also dry up, and the wind would blow great clouds of dust.

# The Wonderful Wizard of Oz
## *by L. Frank Baum**

*Adapted for young readers

# Chapter 1
# Kansas

Dorothy lived in the middle of the great Kansas prairies with Uncle Henry, who was a farmer, and Aunt Em, who was Uncle Henry's wife. Their house was small, for the lumber to build it had to be carried many miles by wagon. There were four walls, a floor, and a roof, which made one room. This room contained a rusty cooking stove, a cupboard for the dishes, a table, four chairs, and the beds. Uncle Henry and Aunt Em had a big bed in one corner, and Dorothy had a little bed in another corner. ✿

There was no attic at all and no cellar—except a small hole, dug in the ground, called a cyclone cellar. The family could go into the cellar in case one of those great whirlwinds arose, mighty enough to crush any building in its path. The cellar was reached by a trapdoor in the middle of the floor. A ladder inside led down into a small, dark hole.

When Dorothy stood in the doorway and looked outside, she could see nothing but the great, gray prairie on every side. No trees or houses could be seen on the flat country that reached the edge of the sky in all directions.

The sun had baked the plowed land into a gray mass with little cracks running through it. Not even the grass was green, for the sun had burned the tops of the grass blades until they were the same gray color as the land. Once, the house had been painted white, but the sun blistered the paint and the rains washed it away, and now the house was as dull and gray as everything else.

When Aunt Em came here to live, she was young and pretty. The sun and wind had changed her, too. They had taken the sparkle from her eyes and left them a sober gray. They had taken the red from her cheeks and lips, and they were gray also. She was thin and she never smiled, now. ♦

Dorothy was an orphan, which was why she had come to live with her aunt and uncle. At first, Aunt Em had been so startled by Dorothy's laughter that she would scream and press her hand upon her heart whenever Dorothy laughed. Aunt Em was still amazed that Dorothy could find anything to laugh about.

Uncle Henry never laughed. He worked hard from morning till night and did not know what joy was. He was gray also, from his long beard to his rough boots. He looked stern, and he rarely spoke.

It was Toto who made Dorothy laugh and kept her from growing as gray as her surroundings. Toto was not gray. He was a little black dog, with long, silky hair and small black eyes that twinkled merrily on either side of his funny, small nose. Toto played all day long, and Dorothy played with him and loved him dearly.

Today, however, Dorothy and Toto were not playing. Uncle Henry sat on the doorstep and looked anxiously at the sky, which was even grayer than usual. Dorothy stood in the door with Toto in her arms and looked at the sky, too. Aunt Em was washing the dishes.

---

## D COMPREHENSION

Write the answers.
1. Why was Dorothy's house small?
2. Why were the land, the grass, and the house gray?
3. How had Aunt Em changed? What made her change?
4. Why do you think Aunt Em was startled by Dorothy's laughter?
5. Why do you think Uncle Henry was looking anxiously at the sky?

## E WRITING

Write a paragraph that describes Dorothy's house.
- Be sure your paragraph answers the following questions:
  - What is the house made of?
  - What color is the house?
  - How many rooms does the house have?
  - What furniture does the house have?
- Make your paragraph at least four sentences long.

# A WORD LISTS

**1**
*Hard Words*
1. accidents
2. dismally
3. gorgeous
4. sorceress
5. magician
6. deaf

**2**
*Hard Words*
1. bowed
2. danger
3. hollow

**3**
*Word Endings*
1. hungry
2. angry

**4**
*New Vocabulary*
1. for
2. prairie
3. cyclone
4. orphan
5. rubies

**5**
*Vocabulary Preview*
1. deaf
2. ripples
3. brilliant
4. bondage
5. dismally

# B VOCABULARY FROM CONTEXT

1. The wind shrieked so loudly that she nearly became **deaf.**
   • happy   • unable to hear   • blind
2. The wind made waves and **ripples** in the grass.
   • small waves   • bricks
   • dandelions
3. The **brilliant** feathers of the birds were every color you could imagine.
   • gray   • bright and colorful
   • unhappy
4. We are grateful because you set us free from **bondage.**
   • slavery   • riches   • having fun
5. The lonely dog put his cold little nose into her face and whined **dismally**.
   • sadly   • eagerly   • rapidly

# Cyclones

Chapter 2 of *The Wonderful Wizard of Oz* tells about a cyclone. Here are some facts about cyclones.

A cyclone is a strong wind that spins around and around. One kind of cyclone looks like a giant funnel. This kind of cyclone is also called a tornado or a twister. A tornado moves forward quickly and destroys almost everything in its path.

The wind that forms a cyclone may spin as fast as three hundred miles an hour.

The middle of the cyclone is called the eye of the cyclone. Most eyes are narrow, but some are wider than a house. The air in the eye is still, but it is surrounded by the spinning wind.

The picture below shows the parts of a cyclone.

# Chapter 2
# The Cyclone

Uncle Henry and Dorothy kept looking at the sky. After a while, they heard a low wailing wind from the north. They could see where the long grass bent in waves before the coming storm.

There now came a sharp whistling from the south. As Uncle Henry and Dorothy turned their eyes that way, they saw ripples in the grass coming from that direction also.

Suddenly Uncle Henry stood up.

"There's a cyclone coming, Em," he called to his wife. "I'll go look after the animals." Then he ran toward the sheds where the cows and horses were kept. ✿

Aunt Em dropped her work and came to the door. One glance told her of the danger close at hand.

"Quick, Dorothy!" she screamed. "Run for the cellar!"

Toto jumped out of Dorothy's arms and hid under the bed inside the house, and the girl went after him. Aunt Em was badly frightened. She threw open the trapdoor in the floor and climbed down the ladder into the small, dark hole.

Dorothy caught Toto at last and started to follow her aunt. When she was halfway across the room, there came a great shriek from the wind, and the house shook so hard that Dorothy lost her footing and sat down suddenly on the floor.

Then a strange thing happened.

The house whirled around two or three times and rose slowly through the air. Dorothy felt as if she were going up in a balloon.

The north and south winds met where the house stood and made it the exact center of the cyclone. In the middle of a cyclone the air is generally still, but the great pressure of the wind on every side of the house raised it higher and higher until the house was at the very top of the cyclone. The house stayed at the top, and then it was carried miles and miles away as easily as you could carry a feather.

It became very dark, and the wind howled horribly, but Dorothy found she was riding quite easily. After the first few whirls and one other time when the house tipped badly, she felt as if she were being rocked gently, like a baby in a cradle.

Toto did not like it. He ran about the room, here and there, barking loudly. But Dorothy sat quite still on the floor and waited to see what would happen.

Once Toto got too near the open trapdoor and fell in. At first, Dorothy thought she had lost him, but soon she saw one of his ears sticking up through the hole. The strong pressure of the air

was keeping him from falling. ♦

Dorothy crept to the hole, caught Toto, and dragged him into the room again. Then she closed the trapdoor so that no more accidents could happen.

Hour after hour passed away, and slowly Dorothy got over her fright. She still felt quite lonely, and the wind shrieked so loudly that she nearly became deaf. At first she wondered if she would be smashed to pieces when the house fell again. But as the hours passed and nothing terrible happened, she stopped worrying and decided to wait calmly and see what would happen. At last she crawled over the swaying floor to her bed and lay down on it. Toto followed and lay down beside her.

In spite of the swaying of the house and the wailing of the wind, Dorothy soon closed her eyes and fell fast asleep.

## E COMPREHENSION

Write the answers.
1. Why did Uncle Henry run toward the animals before the cyclone hit?
2. At first, why didn't Dorothy follow Aunt Em to the cyclone cellar?
3. Why do you think Dorothy waited calmly while the cyclone carried the house?
4. How did Toto behave differently from Dorothy when the cyclone lifted the house?
5. What would you do if the place you live in was lifted up by a cyclone? Why would you do that?

## F WRITING

Write a paragraph about the brave things Dorothy did.
- Be sure your paragraph answers the following questions:
  - What did Dorothy do when Toto ran away?
  - How did Dorothy act while the house was spinning around?
  - What did Dorothy do when Toto fell through the hole?
- Make your paragraph at least four sentences long.

# 8

## A WORD LISTS

### 1
*Hard Words*
1. wizard
2. messenger
3. gracious
4. civilized
5. leather
6. balanced
7. calmly

### 2
*Word Practice*
1. bowed
2. magician
3. jolt
4. handkerchief
5. sunbonnet

### 3
*Word Practice*
1. grown-ups
2. polished
3. Munchkins
4. paused
5. magic
6. magical

### 4
*Vocabulary Review*
1. ripples
2. deaf
3. dismally
4. brilliant
5. bondage
6. inquired

### 5
*New Vocabulary*
1. cheering
2. balanced
3. for
4. rubies
5. emeralds
6. diamonds

### 6
*Vocabulary Preview*
1. messenger
2. civilized
3. gorgeous
4. brook
5. sprinkled
6. sorceress

## B VOCABULARY FROM CONTEXT

1. A **messenger** came to me and brought me the news.
   - thought
   - person who delivers messages
   - person who can't move

2. There are no witches in the great **civilized** countries.
   - well-mannered
   - make-believe
   - unimportant

3. Everything was beautiful, especially the **gorgeous** flowers.
   - very pretty
   - very loud
   - very ugly

4. The **brook** was filled with bubbling, sparkling water that rushed along.
   - small croak
   - small stream
   - small puddle

5. Her white dress was **sprinkled** with bright little stars.
   - dotted
   - blackened
   - rough

6. She was such a powerful witch that people said she was the greatest **sorceress** in the land.
   - tree
   - magician
   - man

# Chapter 3
# The Munchkins

A sudden jolt awakened Dorothy. It was so sudden that it might have hurt her if she had not been lying on the soft bed. The jolt made her catch her breath and wonder what had happened. Toto put his cold little nose into her face and whined dismally.

Dorothy sat up and noticed that the house was not moving; nor was it dark, for bright sunshine came in the window, filling the little room. She sprang from her bed, and with Toto following at her heels, she ran across the room and opened the door. ❀

Then she looked around and gave a cry of amazement. Her eyes grew bigger and bigger at the wonderful sights she saw. The cyclone had set the house down in a country of marvelous beauty. There were lovely patches of green grass all around, with large trees bearing rich fruits. Gorgeous flowers were everywhere, and birds with brilliant feathers sang and fluttered in the trees and bushes. A small brook was close by, rushing and sparkling along between green banks. The sound of the brook was very cheering to the girl who had lived so long on the dry, gray prairies.

While Dorothy stood looking eagerly at the beautiful sights, she noticed a group of strange people coming toward her. They were not as big as the grown-ups Dorothy was used to, but neither were they very small. In fact, they seemed about as tall as Dorothy, who was tall for her age, although they looked many years older.

The group consisted of three men and one woman, and all were oddly dressed. They wore round hats that rose to a small point a foot above their heads. Little bells around the hat brims tinkled sweetly when the people moved. The hats of the men were blue. The woman's hat was white, and she wore a white gown that was sprinkled with little stars that glistened in the sun like diamonds.

The men were dressed in blue, of the same shade as their hats, and they wore well-polished boots with blue bands at the tops. The men, Dorothy thought, were about as old as Uncle Henry, for two of them had beards. But the woman looked much older: her face was covered with wrinkles, her hair was nearly white, and she walked rather stiffly.

When the men came near where Dorothy was standing, they paused and whispered among themselves. They acted as if they were afraid to come closer. But the old woman walked up to Dorothy, made a low bow, and said in a sweet voice, "You are welcome, most noble

Sorceress, to the Land of the Munchkins. We are grateful to you for having killed the Wicked Witch of the East and for setting our people free from bondage."

Dorothy listened to this speech with wonder. What could the woman possibly mean by calling her a sorceress and saying that she had killed the Wicked Witch of the East? She was just a harmless little girl who had been carried by a cyclone many miles from home, and she had never killed anything in her life.

But the old woman seemed to expect an answer, so Dorothy said, "You are very kind, but there must be some mistake. I have not killed anyone."

"Your house did, anyway," replied the old woman with a laugh. "Look!" she continued, pointing to the corner of the house. "There are her two feet, still sticking out from under your house."

Dorothy looked and gave a little cry of fright. There, indeed, under the corner of the house, two feet were sticking out, wearing silver shoes with pointed toes.

"Oh, dear! Oh, dear!" cried Dorothy, clasping her hands together. "The house must have fallen on her. What shall we do?"

"There is nothing to be done," said the woman calmly.

"But who was she?" asked Dorothy.

"She was the Wicked Witch of the East, as I said," answered the woman. "She has held all the Munchkins in bondage for many years, making them slave for her night and day. Now they are all set free, and we are grateful to you."

"Who are the Munchkins?" inquired Dorothy.

"They are the people who live in this Land of the East, where the Wicked Witch ruled."

"Are you a Munchkin?" asked Dorothy.

"No, but I am their friend, although I live in the Land of the North. When the Munchkins saw that the Witch of the East was dead, they sent a swift messenger to me, and I came at once. I am the Witch of the North." ◆

"Oh, gracious!" cried Dorothy. "Are you a real witch?"

"Yes, indeed," answered the woman. "But I am a good witch, and the people love me. I am not as powerful as the Wicked Witch was; if I had been, I would have set the Munchkins free myself."

"But I thought all witches were wicked," said the girl, who was half-frightened at facing a real witch.

"Oh, no, that is not true. There were only four witches in all the Land of Oz, and two of them, those who live in the North and the South, are good witches. I know this is true, for I am one of them myself and cannot be mistaken. The witches who lived in the East and the West were, indeed, wicked witches. But now that you have killed one of them, there is only one wicked witch in all the Land of Oz—the one who lives in the West."

"But," said Dorothy, after a moment's thought, "Aunt Em told me that the witches all died years and years ago."

"Who is Aunt Em?" inquired the old woman.

"She is my aunt who lives in Kansas, where I came from," said Dorothy.

The Witch of the North seemed to think for a time, with her head bowed and her eyes upon the ground. Then she looked up and said, "I do not know where Kansas is, for I have never heard of that country. But tell me, is it a civilized country?"

"Oh, yes," replied Dorothy.

"Then that explains it. In the civilized countries, I believe there are no witches left—nor wizards nor sorceresses nor magicians. But, you see, the Land of Oz has never been civilized, for we are cut off from all the rest of the world.

Therefore, we still have witches and wizards."

"Who are the wizards?" asked Dorothy.

"Oz himself is the Great Wizard," answered the Witch, sinking her voice to a whisper. "He is more powerful than all the rest of us together. He lives in the Emerald City."

---

# D COMPREHENSION

Write the answers.
1. Describe how the Land of Oz looked different from Kansas.
2. Why did the Witch of the North think Dorothy was a sorceress?
3. Why were the Munchkins grateful to Dorothy?
4. How were civilized countries different from the Land of Oz?
5. What kind of powers do you think the Witch of the North has?

# E WRITING

Write a paragraph that compares Kansas with the Land of Oz.
- Be sure the paragraph answers the following questions:
  - What does Kansas look like?
  - What does the Land of Oz look like?
  - What kind of people live in Kansas?
  - What kind of people live in Oz?
- Make your paragraph at least four sentences long.

# A WORD LISTS

### 1
*Hard Words*
1. desert
2. Quadlings
3. Gillikins
4. solemn
5. delicious
6. journey
7. gingham

### 2
*Word Practice*
1. gracious
2. handkerchief
3. exactly
4. magical
5. Winkies
6. sunbonnet

### 3
*Vocabulary Review*
1. gorgeous
2. messenger
3. civilized
4. sprinkled
5. brook

### 4
*New Vocabulary*
1. gingham
2. velvet
3. silk
4. leather

### 5
*New Vocabulary*
1. balanced
2. delicious
3. slate
4. pave
5. apparent

### 6
*Vocabulary Preview*
1. solemn
2. charm
3. sob
4. injured
5. journey
6. trot
7. brisk

# B VOCABULARY FROM CONTEXT

1. She looked very grim as she counted in a **solemn** voice.
   - clear • serious • happy
2. Her shoes had a secret **charm** that kept her out of danger.
   - shoelaces • magic power
   - hat band
3. Dorothy began to **sob**, and large tears fell from her eyes.
   - cry • smile • listen
4. She fell down and **injured** her knee.
   - hurt • tickled • listened to

5. It was a long **journey** through the forest and past the fields.
   - turkey • moment • trip
6. The dog's legs were so short that he had to **trot** to keep up with his master.
   - sleep • run slowly • eat
7. She walked at such a **brisk** pace that she arrived at the city an hour before the others.
   - slow • happy • fast

# Chapter 4
# The Yellow Brick Road

Dorothy was going to ask another question, but just then the Munchkins, who had been standing silently by, gave a loud shout and pointed to the corner of the house where the Wicked Witch had been lying.

"What is it?" asked the good witch. She looked and began to laugh. The feet of the dead witch had disappeared entirely and nothing was left but the silver shoes.

"She was so old," explained the Witch of the North, "that she dried up quickly in the sun. That is the end of her. But the silver shoes are yours, and you shall have them to wear." ✿

The Witch of the North reached down and picked up the shoes. After shaking out the dust, she handed them to Dorothy. "The Witch of the East was proud of these silver shoes," said the old woman. "They have some kind of magical charm, but I do not know what it is."

Dorothy carried the shoes into the house and placed them on the table. Then she came out again to the Munchkins and said, "I am anxious to get back to my aunt and uncle, for I am sure they will worry about me. Can you help me find my way?"

The Munchkins and the witch first looked at one another, and then at Dorothy, and then they shook their heads.

"I am afraid," said the witch, "that a great desert surrounds the whole Land of Oz, and no one can live to cross it."

Then she reached behind her back and pulled out a slate. A map of the Land of Oz suddenly appeared on it.

One Munchkin pointed to the Land of the East and said, "This is where we are now. You can see that the desert is not far from here."

The second Munchkin pointed to the Land of the South. "The South is where the Quadlings live," he said. "They have the same desert, for I have been there and seen it."

"I am told," said the third Munchkin, "that the West also has the same desert. And that country, where the Winkies live, is ruled by the Wicked Witch of the West. She would make you her slave if you passed her way."

"The North is my home, and the Gillikins live there," said the witch. "This same great desert is also at its edge. I am sorry, my dear, but it appears that you will have to live with us, because you cannot cross the desert."

Dorothy began to sob at this, for she felt lonely among all these strange people. Her tears seemed to make the

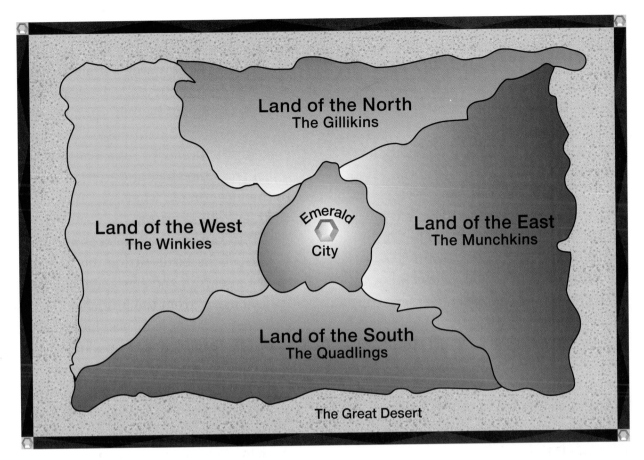

Land of the North
The Gillikins

Land of the West
The Winkies

Emerald City

Land of the East
The Munchkins

Land of the South
The Quadlings

The Great Desert

kindhearted Munchkins sad, for they immediately took out their handkerchiefs and also began to weep.

As for the witch, she put the slate on the ground, took off her round hat, turned it upside down, and balanced the point on the end of her nose. Then she counted "One, two, three" in a solemn voice.

All at once, the map on the slate faded away, and big white letters appeared in its place. The letters said: LET DOROTHY GO TO THE EMERALD CITY.

The old woman read the words on the slate and asked, "Is your name Dorothy, my dear?"

"Yes," answered the child, looking up and drying her tears.

"Then you must go to the Emerald City. Perhaps Oz will help you."

"Where is this city?" asked Dorothy.

"It is in the exact center of the country, and it is ruled by Oz, the Great Wizard I told you about."

"Is Oz a good man?" inquired the girl, anxiously.

"He is a good wizard. Whether he is a man or not I cannot tell, for I have never seen him."

"How can I get there?" asked Dorothy.

"You must walk. It is a long journey, through a country that is sometimes pleasant and sometimes dark and terrible. However, I will use all the magic arts I know to keep you from harm."

"Won't you go with me?" pleaded the girl, who had begun to think that the old woman was her only friend.

"No, I cannot do that," she replied. "But I will give you my kiss, and no one will dare injure a person who has been kissed by the Witch of the North."

She came close to Dorothy and kissed her gently on the forehead. Her lips left a round, shining mark on Dorothy's skin.

"The road to the Emerald City is paved with yellow brick," said the witch, "so you cannot miss it. When you get to Oz, do not be afraid. Just tell your story and ask the wizard to help you. Goodbye, my dear."

The three Munchkins bowed low to Dorothy and wished her a pleasant journey, after which they walked away through the trees. The witch gave Dorothy a friendly little nod, whirled around on her left heel three times, and disappeared, much to the surprise of little Toto. ♦

But Dorothy, who knew that the woman was a witch, had expected her to disappear in just that way and was not surprised in the least.

When Dorothy was left alone, she began to feel hungry. So she went into the house and cut herself some bread, which she spread with butter. She gave some of the bread to Toto. Then she took a pail from the shelf and carried it down to the little brook, where she filled it with clear, sparkling water.

Toto ran over to the trees and began to bark at the birds sitting there. Dorothy went to get him and saw such delicious fruit hanging from the branches that she gathered some of it. It was just what she wanted to complete her breakfast.

Then Dorothy went back to the house. She helped herself and Toto to a good drink of the cool, clear water, and she started to prepare for the journey to the Emerald City.

Dorothy had only one other dress,

but that happened to be clean and was hanging on a peg beside her bed. It was gingham, with checks of white and blue; and although the blue was somewhat faded, it was still a pretty dress. The girl washed herself carefully, dressed herself in the clean gingham, and put her pink sunbonnet on her head. She took a little basket and filled it with bread from the cupboard and laid a white cloth over the top. Then she looked down at her feet and noticed how old her shoes were.

"They surely will never do for a long journey, Toto," she said. And Toto looked up into her face with his little black eyes and wagged his tail to show that he knew what she meant.

At that moment, Dorothy saw the Wicked Witch's silver shoes lying on the table.

"I wonder if they will fit me," she said to Toto. "They would be just the thing to take a long walk in."

She took off her old leather shoes and tried on the silver ones. They fit her just as well as if they had been made for her.

Finally, she picked up her basket.

"Come along, Toto," she said. "We will go to the Emerald City and ask the Great Oz how to get back to Kansas."

She closed the door, locked it, and put the key carefully in the pocket of her dress. And so, with Toto trotting along behind her, she started on her journey.

There were several roads nearby, but it did not take her long to find the one paved with yellow brick. Within a short time, she was walking briskly toward the Emerald City, her silver shoes tinkling merrily on the hard yellow roadbed. The sun shone brightly and the birds sang sweetly. Dorothy did not feel at all sad, even though she had been taken from her home and set down in a strange land.

## D COMPREHENSION

Write the answers.
1. What do you think the charm of the silver shoes might be?
2. Why couldn't Dorothy leave the Land of Oz?
3. Give at least two examples of the good witch's magical powers.
4. Why wasn't Dorothy surprised when the witch suddenly disappeared?
5. Why was Dorothy happy at the end of the chapter?

## E WRITING

Where would you rather live, in Kansas or in the Land of Oz?
- Write a paragraph that explains your answer. Be sure the paragraph answers the following questions:
  - What is good about each place?
  - What is bad about each place?
  - Where would you rather live and why?
- Make your paragraph at least four sentences long.

# 10

## A WORD LISTS

### 1
*Hard Words*
1. curiosity
2. Boq
3. clumsiness

### 2
*Word Endings*
1. earnestly
2. politely
3. gratefully
4. apparently

### 3
*Word Practice*
1. secret
2. scarecrow
3. embarrassed
4. uncomfortable

### 4
*Vocabulary Review*
1. brisk
2. injured
3. solemn
4. trot
5. journey

### 5
*New Vocabulary*
1. field of grain
2. apparent
3. crops
4. dome
5. fiddlers

### 6
*Vocabulary Review*
1. leather
2. velvet
3. gingham
4. silk

### 7
*Vocabulary Preview*
1. hearty
2. amused
3. resolved
4. represented
5. earnestly
6. husky
7. suspected

## B VOCABULARY FROM CONTEXT

1. Dorothy was so hungry that she ate a **hearty** supper.
   • tiny • late • large
2. The dog looked so funny that she **amused** all of us.
   • saddened • bit • entertained
3. Although he felt like crying, he **resolved** to keep the tears back.
   • made his bed • made up his mind
   • made a mistake
4. The mask that she wore **represented** the face of a gorilla.
   • looked like • sounded like

5. She wanted them to understand, so she told about her problem very **earnestly**.
   • sincerely • happily • timidly
6. He was a big man and he spoke in a **husky** voice.
   • small • high • deep or thick
7. He wasn't sure, but he **suspected** that she was a witch.
   • thought • suspended • knew

# Chapter 5
# The Scarecrow

Dorothy was surprised, as she walked along, to see how pretty the country was. There were neat fences, painted a blue color, at the sides of the road, and beyond them were fields of grain and vegetables. Apparently, the Munchkins were good farmers and knew how to raise large crops.

Once in a while, Dorothy would pass a house, and the people would come out to look at her. They would bow low as she went by, for everyone knew she had destroyed the Wicked Witch and set them free from bondage. ❧

The houses of the Munchkins were odd looking. Each was round, with a big dome for a roof. All were painted blue, for in this country of the East, blue was the favorite color.

Toward evening, when Dorothy was tired from her long walk and was beginning to wonder where she should pass the night, she came to a house that was larger than the rest. Many men and women were dancing on the green lawn in front of the house. Five little fiddlers played as loudly as possible, and the people were laughing and singing. A big table nearby was loaded with delicious fruits, nuts, cakes, and many other good things to eat.

The people greeted Dorothy kindly and invited her to dinner. Then they asked her to spend the night with them. The home belonged to one of the richest Munchkins in the land, and his friends were gathered with him to celebrate their freedom from the bondage of the Wicked Witch.

Dorothy ate a hearty supper and was waited on by the rich Munchkin himself, whose name was Boq. Then she sat down on a bench and watched the people dance.

When Boq saw her silver shoes, he said, "You must be a great sorceress."

"Why?" asked the girl.

"Because you wear silver shoes and have killed the Wicked Witch. Besides, you have white in your dress, and only witches and sorceresses wear white."

"My dress is blue and white checked," said Dorothy, smoothing out the wrinkles in it.

"It is kind of you to wear that," said Boq. "Blue is the color of the Munchkins, and white is the witch color, so we know you are a friendly witch."

Dorothy did not know what to say to this, for all the people seemed to think that she was a witch. But she knew very well that she was only an ordinary little girl.

When Dorothy grew tired of watching the dancing, Boq led her into the house, where he gave her a room with a pretty bed in it. The sheets were made of blue cloth, and Dorothy slept soundly on them till morning, with Toto curled up on the blue rug beside her.

She ate a hearty breakfast and watched a small Munchkin baby, who played with Toto and pulled his tail and laughed in a way that greatly amused Dorothy. Toto was a curiosity to all the people, for they had never seen a dog before.

"How far is it to the Emerald City?" the girl asked.

"I do not know," answered Boq solemnly. "I have never been there. It is better for people to keep away from Oz unless they have business with him. But it is a long way to the Emerald City, and the journey will take many days. The country here is rich and pleasant, but you must pass through rough and dangerous places before you reach the end of your journey."

Boq's statement worried Dorothy a little, but she knew that only the Great Oz could help her get to Kansas again, so she bravely resolved not to turn back.

She said goodbye to her friends and again started along the yellow brick road. When she had gone several miles, she wanted to rest, so she climbed to the top of the fence beside the road and sat down. There was a large cornfield beyond the fence, and not far away she saw a Scarecrow, placed high on a pole to keep the birds away from the ripe corn.

Dorothy leaned her chin upon her hand and gazed thoughtfully at the Scarecrow, whose head was a small sack stuffed with straw. Eyes, nose, and mouth were painted on it to represent a face.

The Scarecrow had an old blue pointed Munchkin hat on his head, and he wore a faded blue suit of clothes, which was also stuffed with straw. On his feet were some old boots with blue tops, just like those that Munchkin men wore. The Scarecrow was raised above the stalks of corn by a pole stuck up his back.

While Dorothy was looking earnestly into the strange painted face of the Scarecrow, she was surprised to see one of the eyes slowly wink at her. She thought she was seeing things at first, for none of the scarecrows in Kansas ever winked at her. Then the Scarecrow

nodded his head to her in a friendly way. She climbed down from the fence and walked up to him while Toto ran around the pole and barked.

"Good day," said the Scarecrow in a rather husky voice.

"Did you speak?" asked the girl in wonder.

"Certainly," answered the Scarecrow. "How do you do?"

"I'm pretty well, thank you," replied Dorothy politely. "How do you do?"

"I'm not feeling well," said the Scarecrow, with a smile, "for it is very boring to be stuck up here night and day to scare away crows."

"Can't you get down?" asked Dorothy.

"No, for this pole is stuck up my back. If you will please take away the pole, I will be very grateful to you."

Dorothy stretched her arms and easily lifted the Scarecrow off the pole. Because he was stuffed with straw, the Scarecrow was quite light. "Thank you very much," said the Scarecrow when he had been set down on the ground. "I feel like a new man."

Dorothy thought it was odd to hear a stuffed man speak and to see him bow and walk along beside her. ♦

"Who are you?" asked the Scarecrow when he had stretched himself and yawned. "And where are you going?"

"My name is Dorothy," said the girl, "and I am going to the Emerald City to ask the Great Oz to send me back to Kansas."

"Where is the Emerald City?" he inquired. "And who is Oz?"

"Why, don't you know?" she answered in surprise.

"No, indeed. I don't know anything. You see, I am stuffed with straw, so I have no brains at all," he said sadly.

"Oh," said Dorothy, "I'm awfully sorry for you."

The Scarecrow asked, "Do you think that if I go to the Emerald City with you, Oz would give me some brains?"

"I do not know," she answered, "but you may come with me if you like. If Oz will not give you any brains, you will be no worse off than you are now."

"That is true," said the Scarecrow. "You see," he continued, "I don't mind my legs and arms and body being stuffed, because I cannot get hurt. If anyone steps on my toes or sticks a pin into me, it doesn't matter, for I can't feel it. But I do not want people to call me a fool, and if my head stays stuffed with straw instead of with brains, how am I ever to know anything?"

"I understand how you feel," said the girl, who was truly sorry for him. "If you will come with me, I'll ask Oz to do all he can for you."

"Thank you," he answered gratefully.

They walked back to the road. Dorothy helped him over the fence, and they started along the yellow brick road for the Emerald City.

Toto did not like the Scarecrow at first. He sniffed around the stuffed man as if he suspected there might be a nest of rats in the Scarecrow's straw, and he often growled at the Scarecrow in an unfriendly way.

"Don't mind Toto," said Dorothy to her new friend. "He never bites."

"Oh, I'm not afraid," replied the Scarecrow. "He can't hurt the straw. Do let me carry that basket for you. I won't mind it, for I can't get tired. I'll tell you a secret," he continued as he walked along. "There is only one thing in the world that I am afraid of."

"What is that?" asked Dorothy. "The Munchkin farmer who made you?"

"No," answered the Scarecrow. "The only thing I fear is a lighted match."

---

## D COMPREHENSION

Write the answers.
1. Why did Boq think that Dorothy was a sorceress?
2. What would make you think that someone was a sorceress?
3. What purpose do scarecrows serve?
4. Does the Scarecrow act like somebody who doesn't have any brains? Explain your answer.
5. Why do you think the Scarecrow is afraid of a lighted match?

## E WRITING

Write a paragraph that explains how the Scarecrow could help Dorothy on her journey.
- Be sure your paragraph answers the following questions:
  - How could the Scarecrow entertain Dorothy?
  - What could the Scarecrow do if Dorothy were in danger?
  - How else could the Scarecrow help Dorothy?
- Make your paragraph at least four sentences long.

# 11

## A WORD LISTS

### 1
*Hard Words*
1. shoulder
2. inconvenient
3. one-legged
4. fortunate

### 2
*Word Endings*
1. husky
2. hearty
3. ordinary
4. curiosity
5. dreary

### 3
*New Vocabulary*
1. people of flesh and blood
2. spoil
3. husky
4. earnestly
5. suspected
6. hearty
7. represent
8. resolved

### 4
*Vocabulary Preview*
1. clumsiness
2. fortunate
3. dreary

## B VOCABULARY FROM CONTEXT

1. Because of his **clumsiness,** he kept falling down.
   - gracefulness  • awkwardness
   - skill
2. After they were saved from the witch, they all felt **fortunate** to be alive.
   - lucky  • sober  • disappointed

3. Our homes were gray and very **dreary** looking.
   - dull  • happy  • beautiful

# Chapter 6
# The Road Gets Rough

After a few hours, the road began to get rough, and the walking became so difficult that the Scarecrow often stumbled over the yellow bricks, which were now very uneven. Sometimes, indeed, the bricks were broken or missing altogether, leaving holes that Toto jumped across and Dorothy walked around. But the Scarecrow, who had no brains, walked straight ahead and stepped into the holes and fell down on the yellow bricks. These falls never hurt him, however, and Dorothy would pick him up and set him on his feet again, while he joined her in laughing merrily at his own clumsiness. ❀

The farms were not nearly so well cared for here as they had been farther back. There were fewer houses and fewer fruit trees, and the farther the travelers went, the more dismal and lonesome the country became.

At noon, Dorothy and the Scarecrow sat down by the roadside, near a little brook, and Dorothy opened her basket and took out some bread. She offered a piece to the Scarecrow, but he refused.

"I am never hungry," he said, "and it is a lucky thing that I am not. For my mouth is only painted, and if I were to cut a hole in it so I could eat, the straw I am stuffed with would come out, and that would spoil the shape of my head."

Dorothy saw at once that this was true, so she only nodded and went on eating her bread.

When Dorothy had finished her dinner, the Scarecrow said, "Tell me something about yourself and the country you came from."

So she told him all about Kansas and how gray everything was there and how the cyclone had carried her to this strange Land of Oz. The Scarecrow listened carefully and said, "I cannot understand why you want to leave this beautiful country and go back to the dry, gray place you call Kansas."

"That is because you have no brains," answered the girl. "No matter how dreary and gray our homes are, we people of flesh and blood would rather live there than in any other country, no matter how beautiful it is. There is no place like home."

The Scarecrow sighed.

"Of course I cannot understand it," he said. "If your heads were stuffed with straw, like mine, you would probably all live in the beautiful places, and then Kansas would have no people at all. It is fortunate for Kansas that you have brains." ♦

# D COMPREHENSION

Write the answers.
1. Why did the Scarecrow walk straight into the holes in the road?
2. Why wasn't the Scarecrow hurt when he fell down?
3. Name at least three ways that the country changed as Dorothy went farther down the road.
4. Why did the Scarecrow think that Dorothy might want to stay in Oz?
5. Why did Dorothy want to go back to Kansas?

# E WRITING

Do you think the Scarecrow is smart? Write a paragraph that explains your answer. Be sure the paragraph answers the following questions:
- Why does the Scarecrow think he's stupid?
- In what ways is the Scarecrow stupid?
- In what ways is the Scarecrow smart?

# A WORD LISTS

### 1
*Hard Words*
1. comrade
2. passage
3. companions
4. coward
5. astonished
6. mystery

### 2
*Word Practice*
1. fastened
2. embarrass
3. embarrassed
4. lifted
5. uplifted

### 3
*Word Practice*
1. comfort
2. comforted
3. luck
4. luckily
5. uncomfortable

### 4
*Vocabulary Review*
1. fortunate
2. clumsiness
3. dreary

### 5
*New Vocabulary*
1. ray of sunshine
2. maiden
3. satisfaction
4. inconvenient
5. desert
6. companions
7. mystery

### 6
*Vocabulary Preview*
1. declared
2. motionless
3. comforted

# B VOCABULARY FROM CONTEXT

1. The Scarecrow **declared,** "I can see quite well."
   • asked   • said   • wondered
2. She stood so still that she seemed to be **motionless.**
   • without movement   • without arms
   • without a voice
3. When she rocked the baby and sang to it, the baby stopped crying and felt **comforted.**
   • calm   • irritated   • worse

# Chapter 7
# The Forest

Dorothy and the Scarecrow were still sitting by the roadside. Dorothy said, "Won't you tell me a story while we are resting?"

The Scarecrow seemed a little embarrassed at first, but then he told her the story of his life, as follows:

*My life has been so short that I really don't know anything. I was only made the day before yesterday. What happened in the world before that time is all unknown to me. Luckily, when the farmer made my head, one of the first things he did was to paint my ears, so I heard what was going on.* ✿

*There was another Munchkin with the farmer, and the first thing I heard was the farmer saying, "How do you like those ears?"*

*"They aren't straight," answered the other Munchkin.*

*"Never mind," said the farmer. "They are ears just the same," which was true.*

*"Now I'll make the eyes," said the farmer. So he painted my right eye, and as soon as it was finished, I found myself looking at him and at everything around me with a great deal of curiosity, for this was my first glimpse of the world.*

*"That's a rather pretty eye," remarked the other Munchkin. "Blue paint is just the color for eyes."*

*"I think I'll make the other eye a little bigger," said the farmer. When the second eye was done, I could see much better than before. Then the farmer made my nose and my mouth, but I did not speak.*

*I had fun watching them make my body and my arms and legs. And when they fastened on my head, at last, I felt very proud, for I thought I was just as good a man as anyone.*

*"This fellow will scare the crows," said the farmer. "He looks just like a man."*

*"Why, he is a man," said the other.*

*The farmer carried me under his arm to the cornfield and set me up on a tall stick. Then he and his friend walked away and left me alone.*

*I did not like to be deserted in this way, so I tried to walk after them. But my feet would not touch the ground, and I was forced to stay on that pole. It was a lonely life, and I had nothing to think of, since I had just been made a little while before. Many crows and other birds flew into the cornfield, but as soon as they saw me, they flew away again, thinking I was a Munchkin. This pleased me and made me feel that I was quite an important person.*

*After a while, an old crow flew near me. He looked at me carefully, landed on my shoulder, and said, "I wonder if that farmer thought he could fool me by putting you here. Any smart crow can see that you are only stuffed with straw." Then he hopped down at my feet and ate all the corn he wanted.*

*When the other birds saw that I did not harm the old crow, they also came to eat the corn; and in a short time, there was a great flock of them around me.*

*I felt sad because it seemed that I was not such a good Scarecrow after all. But the old crow comforted me, saying, "If you only had brains in your head, you would be as good a man as any of them and a better man than some of them. Brains are the only things worth having in this world, whether you are a crow or a man."*

*After the crows had gone, I thought about what the old crow had said. I decided I would try hard to get some brains. Then you came along and pulled me off the stake, and from what you said, I am sure the great Oz will give me brains as soon as I get to the Emerald City.*

"I hope the Wizard will help you," said Dorothy earnestly, after the Scarecrow had finished his story. "You seem very anxious to have brains."

"Oh, yes, I am anxious," returned the Scarecrow. "It is such an uncomfortable feeling to know that I am a fool."

"Well," said the girl, "let's go." And she handed the basket to the Scarecrow.

There were no fences at all by the roadside now, and there were no farms. Toward evening, Dorothy and the Scarecrow came to a great forest, where the trees grew so big and close together that their branches met over the road. It was almost dark under the trees, for the branches shut out the daylight.

"If this road goes in, it must come out," said the Scarecrow. "And since the Emerald City is at the other end of the road, we must go wherever it leads us."

"Anyone would know that about the road," said Dorothy.

"Certainly. That is why I know it," answered the Scarecrow. "If I had needed brains to figure it out, I never could have said it." ♦

After an hour or so, the light faded away, and they found themselves stumbling along in the darkness. Dorothy could not see at all, but Toto could, for some dogs see very well in the dark. The Scarecrow declared that he could also see well, so Dorothy took hold of his arm and managed to get along.

She said, "If you see any house or any place where we can pass the night, you must tell me. It is very uncomfortable to walk in the dark."

Soon the Scarecrow stopped.

"I see a little cottage to the right of us," he said. "It is built of logs and branches. Shall we go there?"

"Yes, indeed," answered the girl. "I am all tired out."

So the Scarecrow led her through the trees until they reached the cottage, and Dorothy entered and found a bed of dried leaves in one corner. She lay down at once with Toto beside her and soon fell into a sound sleep. The Scarecrow, who was never tired, stood up in another corner and waited until morning came.

When Dorothy awoke, the sun was shining through the trees, and Toto was outside chasing birds. The Scarecrow was still standing in his corner, waiting for her.

"We must go and search for water," she said to him.

"Why do you want water?" he asked.

"To wash the road dust off my face, and to drink, so the dry bread will not stick in my throat."

"It must be inconvenient to be made of flesh," said the Scarecrow thoughtfully. "You must sleep and eat and drink. However, you have brains, and it is worth a lot of trouble to be able to think properly."

They left the cottage and walked through the trees until they found a little spring of clear water, where Dorothy drank and bathed and ate her breakfast. The girl saw that there was not much bread left in the basket, and she was thankful that the Scarecrow did not have to eat anything, for there was barely enough for herself and Toto for the day.

When Dorothy had finished her meal, she was startled to hear a deep groan nearby.

"What was that?" she asked.

"I don't know," replied the Scarecrow, "but we can go and see."

Just then another groan reached their ears. The sound seemed to come from behind them. They turned and walked through the forest a few steps, and Dorothy saw something shining in a ray of sunshine. She ran to the place and then stopped short with a cry of surprise.

One of the big trees had been partly chopped through, and standing beside it, with an uplifted axe in his hands, was a man made entirely of tin. He stood perfectly motionless, as if he could not move at all.

Dorothy looked at him in amazement, and so did the Scarecrow, while Toto barked sharply and made a snap at the tin legs, which hurt his teeth.

"Did you groan?" asked Dorothy.

"Yes," answered the tin man, "I did. I've been groaning for more than a year, and no one has ever heard me before or come to help me."

# D COMPREHENSION

Write the answers.
1. Why did the Scarecrow feel proud when the farmer first made him?
2. Why wasn't the old crow scared of the Scarecrow?
3. The old crow said, "Brains are the only things worth having in this world." Do you agree with the old crow? Explain your answer.
4. What did the Scarecrow mean when he said, "It must be inconvenient to be made of flesh"?
5. Why do you think the tin man could not move?

# E WRITING

Write a paragraph that tells the story of the Scarecrow's life. Be sure the paragraph answers the following questions:
- Who made the Scarecrow and why?
- When did the Scarecrow begin to see and hear the world?
- What did the old crow tell the Scarecrow?
- What did the Scarecrow decide to do?

# 13

## A WORD LISTS

**1**

*Hard Words*
1. shiver
2. jagged
3. sorrow
4. courage
5. guide
6. approve
7. awkward

**2**

*Word Practice*
1. marriage
2. cruel
3. halves
4. alas

**3**

*Vocabulary Review*
1. comforted
2. motionless
3. inconvenient
4. declared
5. deserted
6. maiden
7. satisfaction

**4**

*New Vocabulary*
1. courage
2. awkward
3. jagged
4. moved

**5**

*Vocabulary Preview*
1. shouldered his axe
2. comrade
3. passage
4. misfortune

## B VOCABULARY FROM CONTEXT

1. The woodman **shouldered his axe** and marched through the forest.
   • brought his axe to his shoulder
   • thought his axe was his shoulder
   • made his axe look like a shoulder

2. They met a **comrade**, who joined them on their journey.
   • enemy   • tree   • friend

3. The woodman cleared a **passage** through the thick shrubs and bushes.
   • passenger   • idea   • path

4. The woman had the **misfortune** of cutting her leg with her axe.
   • good luck   • bad luck   • blade

# Chapter 8
# The Tin Woodman

Dorothy was startled to hear the tin man speak, and she was moved by his sad voice.

"What can I do for you?" she inquired softly.

"Get an oilcan and oil my joints," he answered. "They are rusted so badly that I cannot move them at all. But if I am well oiled, I will soon be all right again. You will find an oilcan on a shelf in my cottage."

Dorothy at once ran back to the cottage and found the oilcan. Then she returned and asked anxiously, "Where should I begin?"

"Oil my neck joint first," replied the Tin Woodman. ✿

So she oiled his neck. Because the neck was quite badly rusted, the Scarecrow took hold of the man's head and moved it gently from side to side until it turned freely.

"Now oil the joints in my arms," said the Tin Woodman. So Dorothy oiled them, and the Scarecrow bent them carefully until they were quite free from rust and as good as new. Then the woodman gave a sigh of satisfaction and lowered his axe, which he leaned against the tree.

"This is a great comfort," he said. "I have been holding that axe in the air ever since I rusted, and I'm glad to be able to put it down at last. Now, if you will oil the joints of my legs, I shall be all right."

So they oiled his legs until he could move them freely. The Tin Woodman thanked the travelers again and again for saving him, for he seemed a very polite man and very grateful.

"I might have stood there always if you had not come along," he said. "You have certainly saved my life. But how did you happen to be here?"

"We are on our way to the Emerald City to see the great Oz," Dorothy answered. "We stopped at your cottage to pass the night."

"Why do you wish to see Oz?" the Tin Woodman asked.

"I want him to send me back to Kansas, and the Scarecrow wants him to put a few brains into his head," she replied.

The Tin Woodman appeared to think deeply for a moment. Then he said, "Do you suppose Oz could give me a heart?"

"Why, I guess so," Dorothy answered. "It would be as easy as giving the Scarecrow brains."

"True," the Tin Woodman replied. "If you will allow me to join your party, I will also go to the Emerald City and ask Oz to help me."

"Come along," said the Scarecrow, and Dorothy said that she would be pleased to have him join them.

So the Tin Woodman shouldered his axe and asked Dorothy to put the oilcan in her basket. "For," he said, "if I should get caught in the rain and rust again, I would need the oilcan badly." Then they all walked through the forest until they came to the yellow brick road.

It was a bit of good luck to have the Tin Woodman, for soon after the comrades had begun their journey, they came to a place where the trees and branches grew so thickly over the road that they could not pass.

But the Tin Woodman set to work with his axe and chopped so well that he soon cleared a passage.

Dorothy was thinking so earnestly as they walked along that she did not notice when the Scarecrow stumbled into a hole and rolled over to the side of the road. Indeed, he had to call to her to help him up again.

"Why didn't you walk around the hole?" asked the Tin Woodman.

"I don't know enough," replied the Scarecrow cheerfully. "My head is stuffed with straw, you know, and that is why I am going to Oz to ask him for some brains."

"Oh, I see," said the Tin Woodman. "But, after all, brains are not the best things in the world."

"Do you have any?" inquired the Scarecrow.

"No, my head is quite empty," answered the Tin Woodman. "But I once had brains, and also a heart. Having tried them both, I would much rather have a heart."

"And why would you rather have a heart?" asked the Scarecrow.

"I will tell you my story, and then you will know."

So while they were walking through the forest, the Tin Woodman told the following story:

*I was born the son of a woodman who chopped down trees in the forest and sold the wood for a living. When I grew up, I too became a woodchopper, and after my father died, I took care of my old mother as long as she lived. Then I made up my mind that instead of living alone I would marry, so that I would not become lonely.*

*There was a Munchkin girl who was so beautiful that I soon grew to love her with all my heart. She promised to marry me as soon as I could earn enough money to build a better house for her; so I set to work harder than ever. But the girl lived with an old woman who did not want her to marry anyone, for the woman was so lazy that she wanted the girl to remain with her and do the cooking and the housework.*

*So the old woman went to the Wicked Witch of the East and promised the witch two sheep and a cow if she would prevent the marriage. The Wicked Witch agreed to help, and she put a spell on my axe. One day, when I was chopping away, the axe slipped and cut off my left leg.*

*At first, this seemed a great misfortune, for I knew a one-legged man could not do very well as a woodchopper. So I went to a tinsmith and had him make me a new leg out of tin. The leg worked very well, once I was used to it; but my action angered the Wicked Witch because I could still marry the pretty Munchkin girl.* ♦

When I began chopping again, my axe slipped and cut off my right leg. Again I went to the tinsmith, and again he made me a leg out of tin. After this, the axe cut off my arms, one after the other, but I had them replaced with tin arms. The Wicked Witch then made the axe slip and cut off my head, and at first I thought that was the end of me. But the tinsmith happened to come along, and he made me a new head out of tin.

I thought I had tricked the Wicked Witch then, and I worked harder than ever. But I did not know how cruel my enemy could be. She thought of a new way to kill my love for the beautiful Munchkin maiden and made my axe slip again so that it cut right through my body, splitting me into halves.

Once more the tinsmith came to my aid and made me a body of tin. He fastened my tin arms and legs and head to my tin body, by means of joints, so that I could move around as well as ever. But, alas! Now I had no heart, so I lost all my love for the Munchkin girl and did not care whether I married her or not. I suppose she is still living with the old woman, waiting for me to come after her.

My body shone so brightly in the sun that I felt very proud of it; and it did not matter now if my axe slipped, for it could not cut me. There was only one danger—my joints could rust. But I kept an oilcan in my cottage and took care to oil myself whenever I needed it. However, one day I forgot to oil myself. I got caught in a rainstorm, and before I knew it, my joints had rusted, so I was forced to stand in the woods until you came to help me. Standing there for a year was terribly hard, but while I stood there, I had time to think that the greatest loss I had known was the loss of my heart.

When I was in love, I was the happiest man on Earth. But you cannot love if you do not have a heart, and so I am resolved to ask the Wizard of Oz to give me one. If the Wizard gives me a heart, I will go back to the Munchkin maiden and marry her.

Both Dorothy and the Scarecrow were greatly interested in the story of the Tin Woodman, and now they knew why he was so anxious to get a new heart.

"All the same," said the Scarecrow, "I will ask for brains instead of a heart, for a fool would not know what to do with a heart if he had one."

"I shall take the heart," answered the Tin Woodman. "Brains do not make you happy, and happiness is the best thing in the world."

Dorothy did not say anything, for she did not know which of her two friends was right, and she wondered if she would ever get back to Kansas and Aunt Em.

What worried her most was that the bread was nearly gone, and another meal for herself and Toto would empty the basket. To be sure, neither the Tin Woodman nor the Scarecrow ever ate anything, but she was not made of tin or straw, and she could not live unless she was fed.

# D COMPREHENSION

Write the answers.
1. What kind of weather would make the Tin Woodman stop working? Why?
2. How did the Tin Woodman help the travelers as they walked through the forest?
3. Why did the Tin Woodman think that a heart was more important than brains?
4. Why did the Scarecrow think that brains were more important than a heart?
5. Which do you think is more important: brains or a heart? Explain your answer.

# E GLOSSARY

Find the following words in your glossary. Copy what the glossary says about each word.
1. ledge
2. budge

# F WRITING

Write a paragraph that explains how the Woodman became the Tin Woodman. Be sure your paragraph answers the following questions:
- Whom did the Woodman want to marry?
- Who put a spell on the Woodman's axe and why?
- What did the axe do to the Woodman?
- Who repaired the Woodman?

# 14

## A WORD LISTS

### 1
*Word Practice*
1. peculiar
2. manage
3. Kalidahs
4. fierce
5. relief
6. adventure
7. disease

### 2
*Word Endings*
1. hinges
2. places
3. fences
4. cottages
5. manages

### 3
*Word Practice*
1. here
2. hereafter
3. bearable
4. unbearable

### 4
*Word Practice*
1. guide
2. welcome
3. ashamed
4. dangerous

### 5
*Vocabulary Review*
1. comrade
2. passage
3. misfortune

### 6
*Vocabulary Preview*
1. approve of
2. sorrow
3. unbearable
4. astonished
5. remarkable
6. shiver
7. coward
8. strides

## B VOCABULARY FROM CONTEXT

1. Toto did not **approve of** the new comrade and tried to bite him.
   • smell   • look at   • like

2. When his friends left, he felt great **sorrow** and started to cry.
   • happiness   • anger   • sadness

3. When she couldn't stand being alone anymore, she cried, "This is **unbearable**."
   • something I don't mind
   • something I can't stand
   • something I like

4. When she saw the Scarecrow wink at her, she was **astonished**.
   • not interested   • surprised   • hopeful

5. The dog was **remarkable** because it had a coat of seven different colors.
   • ordinary   • boring   • unusual

6. When she went outside without a coat on, she began to **shiver** from the cold.
   • tremble   • run   • sweat

7. He was such a **coward** that he was afraid of everybody.
   • brave person   • fearful person
   • nice person

8. The Lion's **strides** were so long that he took one step each time Dorothy took three steps.
   • steps   • windows   • hooves

# Chapter 9
# The Cowardly Lion

All this time, Dorothy and her companions had been walking through the thick woods. The road was still paved with yellow brick, but the bricks were covered by dried branches and dead leaves from the trees, and it was difficult to walk.

There were very few birds in this part of the forest, for the birds of Oz love the open country, where there is plenty of sunshine. Now and then the travelers would hear a deep growl from some wild animal hidden among the trees. These sounds made Dorothy's heart beat fast, for she did not know what made the sounds. But Toto knew, and he walked close to Dorothy's side and did not even bark. ❀

"How long will it be," Dorothy asked the Tin Woodman, "before we are out of the forest?"

"I cannot tell," he answered, "for I have never been to the Emerald City. My father went there once when I was a boy, and he said it was a long journey through a dangerous country. But I am not afraid so long as I have my oilcan, and nothing can hurt the Scarecrow. As for you, you have the mark of the good Witch's kiss on your forehead, and that will protect you from harm."

"But Toto!" said Dorothy anxiously. "What will protect him?"

"We must protect him ourselves if he is in danger," replied the Tin Woodman.

Just as he spoke, a terrible roar came from the forest, and the next moment, a great Lion bounded into the road. With one blow of his paw, he sent the Scarecrow spinning over and over to the edge of the road, and then he struck at the Tin Woodman with his sharp claws. But, to the Lion's surprise, he could make no dent in the tin, although the Tin Woodman fell over in the road and lay still.

Little Toto, now that he had an enemy to face, ran barking toward the Lion, and the great beast opened his mouth to bite the dog. But Dorothy, fearing Toto would be killed, rushed forward and slapped the Lion on his nose as hard as she could while she cried out, "Don't you dare bite Toto! You ought to be ashamed of yourself, a big beast like you, to bite a poor little dog!"

"I didn't bite him," said the Lion as he rubbed his nose with his paw where Dorothy had hit it.

Dorothy said, "No, but you tried to. You are nothing but a big coward."

"I know that I am a coward," said the Lion, hanging his head in shame. "I've always known it. But how can I help it?"

"I don't know, I'm sure. To think of

your striking a stuffed man, like the poor Scarecrow!"

"Is he stuffed?" asked the Lion in surprise, as he watched her pick up the Scarecrow, set him on his feet, and pat him into shape again.

"Of course he's stuffed," replied Dorothy, who was still angry.

"So that's why he went over so easily," remarked the Lion. "It astonished me to see him whirl around like that. Is the other one stuffed, too?"

"No," said Dorothy. "He is made of tin." And she helped the Tin Woodman up.

"That's why he nearly ruined my claws," said the Lion. "When they scratched against the tin, it made a cold shiver run down my back. What is that little animal you are so fond of?"

"He is my dog," answered Dorothy.

"Is he made of tin, or stuffed?" asked the Lion.

"Neither. He's just a dog," said the girl.

"Oh! He's a curious animal and seems remarkably small, now that I look at him. No one would think of biting such a little thing except a coward like me," continued the Lion sadly.

"What makes you a coward?" asked Dorothy, looking at the great beast in wonder, for he was as big as a small horse.

"It's a mystery," replied the Lion. "I suppose I was born that way. All the other animals in the forest naturally expect me to be brave, for the Lion is supposed to be the King of Beasts. I soon learned that if I roared very loudly every living thing was frightened and got out of my way."

The Lion continued, "But whenever I've met people, I've been awfully scared. But I just roared at them, and they have always run away as fast as they could go. If the elephants and the tigers and the bears had ever tried to fight me, I would have run myself—I'm such a coward. But just as soon as they hear me roar, they all try to get away from me, and of course I let them go."

The Scarecrow said, "But that isn't right. The King of Beasts shouldn't be a coward."

"I know it," answered the Lion, wiping a tear from his eye with the tip of his tail. "It is my great sorrow and makes my life very unhappy. But whenever there is danger, my heart begins to beat fast."

"Perhaps you have heart disease," said the Tin Woodman.

"It may be," said the Lion.

"If you have," continued the Tin Woodman, "you ought to be glad, for it proves you have a heart. As for me, I have no heart, so I cannot have heart disease." ♦

Thoughtfully, the Lion said, "Perhaps if I had no heart I would not be a coward."

"Do you have brains?" asked the Scarecrow.

"I suppose so. I've never looked to see," replied the Lion.

"I am going to the great Oz to ask him to give me some brains," remarked the Scarecrow, "for my head is stuffed with straw."

"And I am going to ask him to give me a heart," said the Tin Woodman.

"And I am going to ask him to send me back to Kansas," added Dorothy.

"Do you think Oz could give me courage?" asked the cowardly Lion.

"Just as easily as he could give me brains," said the Scarecrow.

"Or give me a heart," said the Tin Woodman.

"Or send me back to Kansas," said Dorothy.

"Then, if you don't mind, I'll go with you," said the Lion, "for my life is simply unbearable without a bit of courage."

"You will be very welcome," answered Dorothy, "for you will help to keep away the other wild beasts. It seems to me they must be more cowardly than you are if they let you scare them so easily."

"They really are," said the Lion. "But that doesn't make me any braver, and as long as I know that I am a coward, I will be unhappy."

So once more the little party set off on their journey, the Lion walking with proud strides at Dorothy's side. Toto did not approve of this new comrade at first. He could not forget how he had almost been crushed between the Lion's great jaws, but after a time, he became more relaxed. Soon, Toto and the cowardly Lion became good friends.

The group traveled peacefully for the rest of that day. Once, the Tin Woodman stepped on a beetle that was crawling along the road and killed the poor little thing. This made him very unhappy, for he was always careful not to hurt any living creature; and as he walked along, he wept several tears of sorrow. These tears ran slowly down his face and over the hinges of his jaw, and they rusted the hinges.

When Dorothy asked him a question, the Tin Woodman could not open his mouth, for his jaws were tightly rusted together. He became greatly frightened at this and made many motions to Dorothy to help him, but she could not understand, nor could the Lion. But the Scarecrow took the oilcan from Dorothy's basket and oiled the Woodman's jaws, so after a few moments, he could talk as well as before.

"This will teach me a lesson," he said, "to look where I step. For if I should kill another bug or beetle, I would surely cry again, and crying rusts my jaws so that I cannot speak."

After that, the Tin Woodman walked very carefully, with his eyes on the road, and when he saw a tiny ant going by, he would step over it, so as not to harm it. He knew very well that he had no heart, and therefore, he took great care never to be cruel or unkind to anything.

"You people with hearts," he said, "have something to guide you and need never do wrong. But I have no heart, and so I must be very careful. When Oz gives me a heart, of course, I won't have to be so careful."

## D COMPREHENSION

Write the answers.
1. Why did Dorothy slap the Lion on the nose and yell at him?
2. Why do you think the lion is called the King of Beasts?
3. Why do you think other animals were scared by the Lion's roar?
4. Do you think the Tin Woodman needs a heart? Why or why not?
5. Do you think the Scarecrow needs brains? Why or why not?

## E GLOSSARY

Find the following words in your glossary. Copy what the glossary says about each word.
1. tussle
2. reserve

## F WRITING

Write a paragraph that describes the Lion. Be sure your paragraph answers the following questions:
- Is the Lion brave or cowardly?
- How does the Lion scare other animals?
- What would happen if the other animals tried to fight the Lion?
- What does the Lion want and why?

# A WORD LISTS

### 1
*Word Endings*
1. distances
2. edges
3. cottages
4. fences
5. places

### 2
*Word Practice*
1. adventure
2. delight
3. delightful
4. fierce

### 3
*Word Practice*
1. faintest
2. shaggy
3. relief
4. Kalidahs

### 4
*Vocabulary Review*
1. approve of
2. sorrow
3. unbearable
4. strides
5. astonished
6. remarkable
7. awkward
8. jagged

### 5
*New Vocabulary*
1. snug
2. crouch
3. gloomy

### 6
*Vocabulary Preview*
1. splendid
2. peculiar
3. dreadful

# B VOCABULARY FROM CONTEXT

1. Dorothy built a **splendid** fire that made large flames and gave off a lot of heat.
   • ugly   • marvelous   • small

2. They saw **peculiar** looking people who had three eyes and four arms.
   • ordinary   • regular   • strange

3. When she saw the awful things the tigers did, she said, "Those beasts are **dreadful**."
   • horrible   • great   • silly

# Chapter 10
# The Kalidahs

The travelers had to camp out that night under a large tree in the forest, for there were no houses near. The tree made a good shelter, and the Tin Woodman chopped a great pile of wood with his axe. Dorothy built a splendid fire that warmed her and made her feel less lonely. She and Toto ate the last of their bread, and now she did not know what they would do for breakfast.

"If you wish," said the Lion, "I will go into the forest and kill a deer for you. You can roast it by the fire, since your tastes are so peculiar that you prefer cooked food, and then you will have a very good breakfast." ✿

"Don't, please don't," begged the Tin Woodman. "I would certainly weep if you killed a poor deer, and then my jaws would rust again."

But the Lion went away into the forest and found his own supper, and no one ever knew what it was, for he didn't mention it.

The Scarecrow found a tree full of nuts and filled Dorothy's basket with them so that she would not be hungry for a long time. She thought this was very kind and thoughtful of the Scarecrow, but she laughed heartily at the awkward way in which the poor creature picked up the nuts. His padded hands were so clumsy and the nuts were so small that he dropped almost as many as he put into the basket.

But the Scarecrow did not mind how long it took him to fill the basket. The nut tree was far away from the fire, and he feared a spark from the fire might get into his straw and burn him up. He only came near the fire to cover Dorothy with dry leaves when she lay down to sleep. These kept her very snug and warm, and she slept soundly until morning.

When it was daylight, the girl bathed her face in a little rippling brook, and soon after, they all started toward the Emerald City.

This was to be an important day for the travelers. They had hardly been walking an hour when they saw a great ditch in front of them that crossed the road and divided the forest as far as they could see on either side. It was a very wide ditch, and when they crept up to the edge and looked into it, they could see it was also very deep, with many big, jagged rocks at the bottom.

The sides were so steep that nobody could climb down, and for a moment, it seemed that their journey must end.

"What shall we do?" asked Dorothy despairingly.

"I haven't the faintest idea," said the

Tin Woodman. And the Lion shook his shaggy mane and looked thoughtful.

The Scarecrow said, "We cannot fly, that is certain. Neither can we climb down into this great ditch. Therefore, if we cannot jump over it, we must stop where we are."

"I think I could jump over it," said the cowardly Lion, after measuring the distance carefully in his mind.

"Then we are all right," answered the Scarecrow, "for you can carry us all over on your back, one at a time."

"Well, I'll try it," said the Lion. "Who will go first?"

"I will," declared the Scarecrow. "For if you found that you could not jump over the ditch, Dorothy would be killed, or the Tin Woodman badly dented on the rocks below. But if I am on your back, it will not matter so much, for the fall would not hurt me at all."

"I am terribly afraid of falling myself," said the cowardly Lion, "but I suppose there is nothing to do but try it. So get on my back, and we will make the attempt."

The Scarecrow sat on the Lion's back, and the big beast walked to the edge of the ditch and crouched down.

"Why don't you run and jump?" asked the Scarecrow.

"Because that isn't the way we lions do these things," he replied. Then he sprang forward through the air and landed safely on the other side. They were all greatly pleased to see how easily the Lion had jumped, and after the Scarecrow got down from his back, the Lion sprang across the ditch again.

Dorothy thought she should go next, so she took Toto in one arm and climbed on the Lion's back, holding tightly to his mane with her free hand. The next moment she was flying through the air. And then, before she had time to think about it, she was safe on the other side. The Lion went back a third time and got the Tin Woodman. Then they all sat down for a few moments to give the beast a chance to rest. The Lion's great leaps had made his breath short, and he panted like a big dog that has been running too long.

The forest was very thick on this side, and it looked dark and gloomy. After the Lion had rested, they started along the yellow brick road, silently wondering if they would ever come to the end of the woods and reach the bright sunshine again. To add to their discomfort, they soon heard strange noises coming from the forest, and the Lion whispered to them that the Kalidahs lived in this part of the country. ♦

"What are the Kalidahs?" asked Dorothy.

"They are monstrous beasts with bodies like bears and heads like tigers," replied the Lion. "Their claws are so long and sharp that they could tear me in two as easily as I could kill Toto. I'm terribly afraid of the Kalidahs."

"I'm not surprised that you are," replied Dorothy.

The Lion was about to reply when suddenly they came to another ditch across the road. This ditch was so broad and deep that the Lion knew at once that he could not leap across it.

So they sat down to consider what they should do. After serious thought, the Scarecrow said, "Here is a large tree, standing close to the ditch. If the Tin Woodman can chop it down so that the top falls on the other side, we can walk across it easily."

"That is a first-rate idea," said the Lion. "One would almost think you had brains in your head, instead of straw."

The Tin Woodman set to work at once, and his axe was so sharp that he soon chopped most of the way through the tree. Then the Lion put his strong front legs against the tree and pushed with all his might. The big tree tipped and fell with a crash across the ditch, with its top branches on the other side.

They had just started to cross this tree bridge when a sharp growl made them all look up, and to their horror, they saw two great beasts running toward them. These beasts had bodies like bears and heads like tigers.

"They are the Kalidahs!" said the cowardly Lion, beginning to tremble.

"Quick!" cried the Scarecrow, "Let's cross over."

So Dorothy went first, holding Toto in her arms. The Tin Woodman followed, and the Scarecrow came next. The Lion, although he was certainly afraid, turned to face the Kalidahs, and then he gave a roar that was so loud and terrible that Dorothy screamed and the Scarecrow fell over backward. Even the Kalidahs stopped short and looked at him in surprise.

But seeing they were bigger than the Lion and remembering that there were two of them and only one of him, the Kalidahs again rushed forward. The Lion crossed over the tree and turned to see what they would do next. Without stopping an instant, the fierce beasts also began to cross the tree, and the Lion said to Dorothy, "We will lose, for they will surely tear us to pieces with their sharp claws. But stand close behind me, and I will fight them as long as I am alive."

"Wait a minute!" called the Scarecrow. He had been thinking what to do, and now he asked the Woodman to chop away the end of the tree that rested on their side of the ditch. The Tin Woodman began to use his axe at once, and just as the two Kalidahs were nearly across, the tree fell with a crash into the ditch, carrying the ugly, snarling beasts with it. Both fell onto the sharp rocks at the bottom.

"Well," said the cowardly Lion, heaving a sigh of relief, "I see we are going to live a little while longer, and I am glad, for it must be a very uncomfortable thing not to be alive. Those creatures frightened me so badly that my heart is pounding."

"Ah," said the Tin Woodman, sadly. "If I only had a heart."

# D COMPREHENSION

Write the answers.

1. Pretend you're by yourself in a forest and you run out of food. How would you get food?
2. Explain how the travelers crossed the first ditch.
3. Explain how the travelers crossed the second ditch.
4. Do you think the Lion really needs courage? Why or why not?
5. How did the travelers work together as a team? Give an example.

# E GLOSSARY

Find the following words in your glossary. Copy what the glossary says about each word.

1. gnaw
2. lining

# F WRITING

Do you think the Tin Woodman really needs a heart? Write a paragraph that explains your answer. Be sure your paragraph answers the following questions:

- Why doesn't the Tin Woodman have a heart now?
- What does the Tin Woodman think will happen when he gets a heart?
- Does the Tin Woodman act like someone without a heart? Why or why not?

# A WORD LISTS

**1**
*Word Practice*
1. beckon
2. scent
3. curtsy
4. hurriedly

**2**
*Compound Words*
1. downstream
2. cornfield
3. wildcat
4. indeed
5. hereafter

**3**
*Word Practice*
1. adventure
2. fastened
3. dismal
4. dismally

**4**
*New Vocabulary*
1. raft
2. meadow
3. cozy
4. cluster
5. scarlet
6. dazzle
7. scarcely

**5**
*Vocabulary Preview*
1. delightful
2. refreshed
3. glare

# B VOCABULARY FROM CONTEXT

1. They were pleased to see this **delightful** meadow before them.
   •ugly  •wonderful  •sad

2. The next morning, Dorothy said, "I feel great. The long sleep made me feel **refreshed**."
   •tired  •lonesome  •full of energy

3. The **glare** of the lights almost blinded her.
   •sound  •feeling  •brightness

# Chapter 11
# The River

The adventure with the Kalidahs made the travelers more anxious than ever to get out of the forest. They walked so fast that Dorothy became tired and had to ride on the Lion's back. To their great joy, the trees became thinner the farther they went, and in the afternoon, they suddenly came upon a broad river, flowing swiftly just before them.

On the other side of the water, they could see the yellow brick road running through a beautiful country with green meadows dotted with bright flowers and trees full of delicious fruits. They were greatly pleased to see this delightful land before them. ✿

"How shall we cross the river?" asked Dorothy.

"That is easily done," replied the Scarecrow. "The Tin Woodman must build us a raft so that we can float to the other side."

So the Woodman took his axe and began to chop down small trees to make a raft. While he was busy at this, the Scarecrow found a tree full of fine fruit on the riverbank. This pleased Dorothy, who had eaten nothing but nuts all day, and she made a hearty meal of the ripe fruit.

It takes time to make a raft, even when one is as hard-working as the Woodman, and when night came, the work was not done. So they found a cozy place under the tree, where Dorothy, Toto, and the Lion slept well until morning. Dorothy dreamed of the Emerald City and of the Wizard, who would soon send her back to her own home.

Dorothy and the Lion awakened the next morning, refreshed and full of hope, and Dorothy had a breakfast of peaches and plums from the trees beside the river. Behind them was the dark forest they had passed safely through, but in front of them was a lovely, sunny country that seemed to beckon them on to the Emerald City.

To be sure, the broad river now cut them off from this beautiful land. But the raft was nearly done, and after the Tin Woodman had cut a few more logs and fastened them together with wooden pins, they were ready to start. Dorothy sat down in the middle of the raft and held Toto in her arms. When the Lion stepped upon the raft it tipped badly, for he was big and heavy; but the Scarecrow and the Tin Woodman stood upon the other end to balance it.

The Scarecrow and the Tin Woodman had long poles in their hands to push the raft through the water. They

got along quite well at first, but when they reached the middle of the river, the swift current swept the raft downstream, farther and farther away from the yellow brick road. The water soon grew so deep that the long poles could not touch the bottom.

"This is bad," said the Tin Woodman, "for we are getting farther from the road to the Emerald City. If we lose our way, I couldn't get a heart."

"And I would get no brains," said the Scarecrow.

"And I would get no courage," said the cowardly Lion.

"And I would never get back to Kansas," said Dorothy.

"We must certainly get to the Emerald City if we can," the Scarecrow said. And he pushed so hard on his long pole that it stuck fast in the mud at the bottom of the river. Before he could pull it out again or let go, the raft was swept away, and the poor Scarecrow was left clinging to the pole in the middle of the river.

"Goodbye!" the Scarecrow called after them, and they were very sorry to leave him. Indeed, the Tin Woodman began to cry, but fortunately, he remembered that he might rust, and so he dried his tears.

Meanwhile, the Scarecrow started to think. "I am now worse off than when I first met Dorothy," he thought. "Then, I was stuck on a pole in a cornfield, where I could try to scare the crows. But surely there is no use for a Scarecrow stuck on a pole in the middle of a river. I am afraid I will never have any brains, after all!" ◆

# D STORY DETAILS

Write the answers.
1. Why did the travelers build a raft?
2. What did the travelers use to push the raft at first?
3. In the middle of the river, what made the raft move downstream?
4. In the middle of the river, why didn't the poles reach the bottom anymore?
5. As the raft floated downstream, it went farther and farther from the ▬▬▬.
6. When the Scarecrow pushed extra hard, what happened to the end of his pole?
7. What did the raft keep doing?
8. Where did the Scarecrow end up?
9. Where was the Scarecrow the first time he was on a pole?

# E GLOSSARY

Find the following words in your glossary. Copy what the glossary says about each word.
1. grate
2. attic

# F VOCABULARY

For each item, write a sentence that uses the word.
1. suspected
2. clumsiness
3. fortunate
4. dull
5. inconvenient
6. declared
7. comforted
8. deserted

# G COMPREHENSION

Write the answers.
1. Why do you think Dorothy dreamed about the Emerald City and the Wizard of Oz?
2. What do you think happened in Dorothy's dream?
3. Explain why the Scarecrow thought he was worse off now than when he first met Dorothy.

# H WRITING

The travelers are still floating down the river. Write a story that tells what you think will happen next. Be sure your story answers the following questions:
• What will happen to the Scarecrow?
• What will happen to the other travelers?
• Will the travelers get back together? Why or why not?

## A WORD LISTS

| 1 | 2 | 3 | 4 |
|---|---|---|---|
| *Hard Words* | *Word Practice* | *Vocabulary Review* | *New Vocabulary* |
| 1. spicy | 1. shallow | 1. beckon | 1. fond of |
| 2. odor | 2. blossoms | 2. dazzle | 2. scent, odor |
| 3. mistress | 3. carpet | 3. scarlet | 3. mistress |
| | 4. poison | 4. cluster | 4. shrill |
| | 5. poisonous | 5. scarcely | 5. timid |
| | | 6. dreadful | 6. permit |
| | | 7. refreshed | 7. curtsy |
| | | 8. glare | 8. spicy |
| | | 9. delightful | 9. therefore |

## B READING

## Chapter 12
# The Field of Flowers

The raft floated downstream, and the poor Scarecrow was left far behind. Then the Lion said, "Something must be done to save us. I think I can swim to the shore and pull the raft after me if you will only hold on to the tip of my tail."

So the Lion sprang into the water, and the Tin Woodman caught hold of his tail. Then the Lion began to swim with all his might toward the shore. It was hard work, even though he was so big, but after a while, he pulled them out of the current. When they reached the shallow water, Dorothy took the Tin Woodman's long pole and helped push the raft to the land. ✿

They were all tired when they finally reached the shore and stepped onto the pretty green grass. But their troubles were not over. The current had carried them a long way past the yellow brick road that led to the Emerald City.

"What shall we do now?" asked the Tin Woodman as the Lion lay down on the grass to let the sun dry him.

"We must get back to the road," said Dorothy.

"The best plan would be to walk along the riverbank until we come to the road again," remarked the Lion.

So when they were rested, Dorothy picked up her basket, and they started along the grassy bank, back to the road from which the river had carried them. It was a lovely country, with plenty of flowers and fruit trees and sunshine to cheer them, and if they had not felt so sorry for the poor Scarecrow, they would have been very happy.

They walked along as fast as they could. Dorothy only stopped once to pick a beautiful flower. After a time, the Tin Woodman cried out, "Look!"

Then they all looked at the river and saw the Scarecrow hanging onto his pole in the middle of the water, looking very lonely and sad.

"What can we do to save him?" asked Dorothy.

The Lion and the Woodman both shook their heads, for they did not know. So they sat down on the bank and gazed at the Scarecrow until a Stork flew by.

When the Stork saw them, it stopped to rest at the water's edge.

"Who are you and where are you going?" asked the Stork.

"I am Dorothy," answered the girl. "These are my friends, the Tin Woodman and the cowardly Lion. We are going to the Emerald City."

"This isn't the road," said the Stork

as she twisted her long neck and looked sharply at the strange party.

"I know it," answered Dorothy. "But we have lost the Scarecrow and are wondering how we will get him again."

"Where is he?" asked the Stork.

"Over there in the river," answered Dorothy.

"If he wasn't so big and heavy, I would get him for you," remarked the Stork.

"He isn't a bit heavy," said Dorothy eagerly. "He is stuffed with straw, and if you will bring him back to us, we will thank you ever and ever so much."

"Well, I'll try," said the Stork. "But if I find he is too heavy to carry, I shall have to drop him into the river again."

So the big bird flew into the air and over the water until she came to where the Scarecrow was hanging onto his pole. Then the Stork grabbed the Scarecrow with her great claws and carried him up into the air and back to the bank, where Dorothy and the Lion and the Tin Woodman and Toto were sitting.

When the Scarecrow found himself among his friends again, he was so happy that he hugged them all, even the Lion and Toto. And as they walked along, he sang.

"I was afraid I would have to stay in the river forever," he said, "but the kind Stork saved me, and if I ever get any brains, I shall find the Stork again and return the favor."

"That's all right," said the Stork, who was flying along beside them. "I always like to help anyone in trouble. But I must go now because my babies are waiting for me. I hope you will find the Emerald City and that Oz will help you."

"Thank you," replied Dorothy, and then the kind Stork flew into the air and was soon out of sight.

They walked along listening to the singing of the bright-colored birds and looking at the lovely flowers, which now became so thick that the ground was covered with them. There were big yellow and white and blue and purple blossoms and also great clusters of scarlet flowers, which were so brilliant in color they almost dazzled Dorothy's eyes. ◆

"Aren't they beautiful?" the girl asked as she breathed in the spicy scent of the flowers.

"I suppose so," answered the Scarecrow. "When I have brains, I will probably like them better."

"If I only had a heart, I would love them," added the Tin Woodman.

"I always did like flowers," said the Lion. "They seem so helpless. But there are none in the forest as bright as these."

They now came upon more and more of the big scarlet flowers and fewer and fewer of the other flowers. Soon they found themselves in the middle of a great meadow of scarlet flowers.

Now, when there are many of these flowers together, their odor is so powerful that anyone who breathes them falls asleep; and if the sleeper is not carried away from the flowers, he sleeps on and on forever. But Dorothy did not know this, nor could she get away from the flowers. Her eyes soon grew heavy, and she felt she must sit down to rest and sleep.

But the Tin Woodman would not let her do this.

"We must hurry and get back to the yellow brick road before dark," he said, and the Scarecrow agreed with him. So

they kept walking until Dorothy could stand no longer. Her eyes closed, and she forgot where she was, and she fell among the flowers, fast asleep.

"What shall we do?" asked the Tin Woodman.

"If we leave her here, she will die," said the Lion. "The smell of the flowers is killing us all. I can scarcely keep my eyes open, and the dog is asleep already."

It was true—Toto had fallen down beside his mistress. But the Scarecrow and the Tin Woodman, since they weren't made of flesh, were not troubled by the odor of the flowers.

"Run fast," said the Scarecrow to the Lion, "and get out of this deadly flower bed as soon as you can. We will bring the little girl with us, but if you should fall

asleep, you are too big to be carried."

So the Lion bounded forward as fast as he could go. In a moment, he was out of sight.

"Let us make a chair with our hands and carry her," said the Scarecrow. So they picked up Toto and put the dog in Dorothy's lap. Then they made a chair with their hands for the seat and their arms for the chair's arms, and they carried the sleeping girl between them through the flowers.

On and on they walked, and it seemed that the great carpet of deadly flowers that surrounded them would never end. They followed the bend of the river, and at last came upon their friend the Lion, lying fast asleep among the flowers. They had been too strong for the huge beast, and he had given up at last. He had fallen only a short distance from the end of the field, where the sweet grass spread in beautiful green fields before them.

"We can do nothing for him," said the Tin Woodman, sadly. "He is much too heavy to lift. We must leave him here to sleep on forever, and perhaps he will dream that he has found courage at last."

"I'm sorry," said the Scarecrow. "The Lion was a very good comrade for one so cowardly. But let us go on."

They carried the sleeping girl to a pretty spot beside the river, far enough from the field so that she could not breathe any more of the deadly flowers, and here they laid her gently on the soft grass and waited for the fresh breeze to wake her up.

# C COMPREHENSION

Write the answers.
1. After they escaped the river, how did the travelers plan to get back to the yellow brick road?
2. Why was the Stork able to lift the Scarecrow so easily?
3. Why couldn't the Tin Woodman and the Scarecrow lift the Lion?
4. Would you expect pretty flowers to make you sleepy? Explain your answer.
5. What do you think the Lion is dreaming about while he sleeps?

# D GLOSSARY

Find the following words in your glossary. Copy what the glossary says about each word.
1. flicker
2. century

# E WRITING

Do you think the Lion is brave? Write a paragraph that explains your answer. Be sure your paragraph answers the following questions:
- What brave things has the Lion done since the travelers met him?
- What cowardly things has the Lion done?
- Do you think the Lion could be braver? How?

# 18

## A WORD LISTS

| 1<br>*Hard Words* | 2<br>*Word Practice* | 3<br>*Vocabulary Review* | 4<br>*New Vocabulary* |
|---|---|---|---|
| 1. majesty | 1. beast | 1. fond of | 1. stunned |
| 2. limbs | 2. poisonous | 2. scampered off | 2. drawn |
| 3. introduce | 3. manage | 3. curtsy | 3. dwelled |
| 4. harnessed | 4. under | 4. timid | 4. presence |
| 5. rescued | 5. underneath | 5. shrill | 5. glittered |
| 6. dwelled | 6. hurriedly | 6. therefore | 6. throne |
| 7. presence | 7. exclaimed | 7. permit | 7. oats |

## B READING

## Chapter 13
# The Field Mice

"We cannot be far from the yellow brick road now," remarked the Scarecrow as he stood beside Dorothy. "We have come nearly as far as the river carried us away."

The Tin Woodman was about to say something when he heard a low growl, and turning his head, he saw a strange beast come bounding over the grass toward them. It was, indeed, a great yellow wildcat. The Woodman thought it might be chasing something, for its ears were lying close to its head and its mouth was wide open, showing two rows of ugly teeth, while its red eyes glowed like balls of fire. ✿

As the wildcat came nearer, the Tin Woodman saw that a little gray field mouse was running in front of the beast. Although the Woodman had no heart, he knew it was wrong for the wildcat to try to kill such a pretty, harmless creature. So the Woodman raised his axe, and as the wildcat ran by, he gave it a quick blow that stunned the beast, and it rolled over at his feet.

Now that it was freed from its enemy, the field mouse stopped. Coming slowly up to the Woodman, it said in a squeaky little voice, "Oh, thank you! Thank you ever so much for saving my life."

"Don't speak of it, please," replied the Woodman. "I have no heart, you know, so I am careful to help all those who may need a friend, even if it happens to be only a mouse."

"Only a mouse!" cried the little animal. "Why, I am a Queen—the Queen of all the field mice!"

"Oh, indeed," said the Woodman, making a bow.

The Queen continued, "Therefore, you have done a great deed, as well as a brave one, in saving my life."

At that moment several mice came running up as fast as their little legs could carry them, and when they saw their Queen, they exclaimed, "Oh, Your Majesty, we thought you would be killed! How did you manage to escape the great wildcat?" And they all bowed so low to the little Queen that they almost stood upon their heads.

"This funny tin man," she answered, "stunned the wildcat and saved my life. So hereafter you must all serve him and obey his wishes."

"We will!" cried all the mice in their shrill voices. And then they scampered off in all directions, for Toto had awakened from his sleep. When Toto saw all these mice around him, he gave one bark of delight and jumped right into the middle of the group. Toto had always loved to chase mice.

But the Tin Woodman caught the dog in his arms and held him tightly while he called to the mice, "Come back! Come back! Toto will not hurt you."

When the Woodman said this, the Queen of the Mice stuck her head out from underneath a clump of grass and asked in a timid voice, "Are you sure he will not bite us?"

"I will not let him," said the Woodman. "Do not be afraid."

One by one the mice came creeping back, and Toto did not bark again, although he tried to get out of the Woodman's arms. Finally, one of the biggest mice spoke. "Is there anything we can do," it asked, "to repay you for saving the life of our Queen?"

"I can't think of anything you could do," answered the Woodman.

The Scarecrow, who had been trying to think but could not because his head was stuffed with straw, said quickly, "Oh, yes. You can save our friend, the cowardly Lion, who is asleep in the field."

"A lion!" cried the little Queen. "Why, he would eat us all up."

"Oh, no," declared the Scarecrow. "This lion is a coward."

"Really?" asked the Queen.

"He says so himself," answered the Scarecrow, "and he would never hurt anyone who is our friend. If you will help us to save him, I promise that he will treat you with kindness."

"Very well," said the Queen. "We will trust you. But what shall we do?"

The Scarecrow asked the Queen, "Are there many mice that are willing to obey you?"

"Oh, yes, there are thousands," she replied.

"Then ask them all to come here as soon as possible, and tell each one to bring a long piece of string." ♦

The Queen turned to the mice that were with her and told them to go at once and get all her mice. As soon as they heard her orders, they ran away in every direction as fast as possible.

"Now," said the Scarecrow to the Tin Woodman, "you must go to those trees by the riverside and make a cart that will carry the Lion."

So the Woodman went to the trees and began to work. He cut down the limbs of some trees, and then he chopped away all their twigs and leaves. He made a cart out of the limbs and fastened it together with wooden pegs. Then he sliced four pieces from a big, round tree trunk and used the pieces for wheels. He worked so fast and well that by the time the mice began to arrive, the cart was all ready for them.

They came from all directions, and there were thousands of them—big mice and little mice and middle-sized mice. And each one brought a piece of string in its mouth.

It was about this time that Dorothy woke from her long sleep and opened her eyes. She was greatly astonished to find herself lying on the grass, with thousands of mice standing around and looking at her timidly. But the Scarecrow told her about everything, and turning to the Queen, he said, "Permit me to introduce you to Her Majesty, the Queen."

Dorothy nodded gravely, and the Queen made a curtsy, after which she became quite friendly with Dorothy.

The Scarecrow and the Woodman now began to fasten the mice to the cart, using the strings they had brought. One end of each string was tied around the neck of each mouse, and the other end to the cart. Of course, the cart was a thousand times heavier than any of the mice; but when all the mice had been harnessed, they were able to pull the cart quite easily. Even the Scarecrow and the Tin Woodman could sit on the cart, and they were drawn swiftly by their strange little horses to the place where the Lion lay asleep.

After a great deal of hard work, they managed to get the Lion up on the cart. Then the Queen hurriedly gave her mice the order to start, for she feared that if the mice stayed among the flowers too long, they would also fall asleep.

At first, the little creatures could hardly move the heavy cart. But the Tin Woodman and the Scarecrow both pushed from behind, and they got along better. Soon they rolled the Lion out of the flower bed to the green fields, where he could breathe the sweet, fresh air again, instead of the poisonous odor of the flowers.

Dorothy came to meet them and thanked the little mice warmly for saving her companion from death. She had grown so fond of the big Lion that she was glad he had been rescued.

Then the mice were unharnessed from the cart, and they scampered away through the grass to their homes. The Queen of the Mice was the last to leave. She handed Dorothy a little whistle and said, "If ever you need us again, come out into the field and blow this whistle. We shall hear you and come to help you. Goodbye!"

"Goodbye!" they all answered, and

away the Queen ran. Dorothy held Toto tightly so that he would not run after the Queen and frighten her.

After this, they sat down beside the Lion, waiting for him to wake up. The Scarecrow brought Dorothy some fruit from a tree nearby, which she ate for her dinner.

---

## C COMPREHENSION

Write the answers.

1. Why do you think the Tin Woodman stunned the wildcat instead of killing it?
2. Why did the Queen say that the mice had to obey the Tin Woodman's wishes?
3. Why did the Queen tell the mice to work quickly?
4. Tell about a time when Dorothy might decide to blow the whistle to get help from the mice.
5. What lesson do you think this chapter gives about teamwork? Explain your answer.

## D WRITING

Write a paragraph that explains the Scarecrow's plan for saving the Lion. Be sure your paragraph answers the following questions:

- Who made the cart?
- How were the mice fastened to the cart?
- Why did the mice have to work quickly?
- What made the cart move?

# A WORD LISTS

### 1
*Hard Words*
1. generously
2. cereal
3. basin
4. spectacles
5. apron

### 2
*Word Practice*
1. yawning
2. shadows
3. starved
4. palace
5. arched
6. honest
7. scrambled
8. ceiling

### 3
*Word Practice*
1. silver
2. silvery
3. guard
4. guarded
5. guardian
6. disturbed

### 4
*Vocabulary Review*
1. presence
2. glittered
3. dwelled

### 5
*New Vocabulary*
1. countless
2. tint
3. guardian
4. marble
5. studded
6. admit
7. basin
8. prefer
9. spectacles

# Chapter 14
# The Land of Oz

It was some time before the cowardly Lion awakened, for he had slept among the flowers a long while, breathing in their deadly odor. When he did open his eyes and roll off the cart, he was very glad to find himself still alive.

"I ran as fast as I could," he said, sitting down and yawning. "But the flowers were too strong for me. How did you get me out?"

Then Dorothy and the others told the Lion of the field mice and how the mice had generously saved him from death. ✿

The cowardly Lion laughed and said, "I have always thought that I was very big and terrible; yet such little things as flowers came near to killing me, and such small animals as mice have saved my life. How strange it all is! But, comrades, what shall we do now?"

"We must journey on until we find the yellow brick road again," said Dorothy. "And then we can go on to the Emerald City."

So, when the Lion was fully refreshed and felt like himself again, they all started on the journey. They greatly enjoyed the walk through the soft, fresh grass, and it was not long before they reached the yellow brick road and turned again toward the Emerald City where the Great Oz dwelled.

The road was smooth and well-paved now, and the country was beautiful. The travelers were happy that the forest was far behind, and with it the many dangers they had met in its dark shadows. Once more they could see fences built beside the road; but these were painted green, not blue. They saw a small house, in which a farmer lived, and that was also painted green.

They passed by several of these houses during the afternoon, and sometimes people came to the doors and looked at them as if they would like to ask questions. But no one came near them nor spoke to them, for they were afraid of the great Lion. The people were all dressed in lovely emerald green clothing and wore green hats that were shaped like those of the Munchkins.

"This must be the Land of Oz," said Dorothy, "and we are surely getting near the Emerald City."

"Yes," answered the Scarecrow. "Everything is green here, while in the country of the Munchkins, blue was the favorite color. But the people do not seem to be as friendly as the Munchkins, and I'm afraid we shall be unable to find a place to spend the night."

"I would like something to eat besides fruit," said the girl, "and I'm sure

Toto is nearly starved. Let's stop at the next house and talk to the people."

So when they came to a good-sized farmhouse, Dorothy walked boldly up to the door and knocked. A woman opened it just far enough to look out and said, "What do you want, child, and why is that great Lion with you?"

"We wish to pass the night with you if you will allow us," answered Dorothy. "The Lion is my friend and comrade and would not hurt you for the world."

"Is he tame?" asked the woman, opening the door a little wider.

"Oh, yes," said the girl, "and he is a great coward, too. He will be more afraid of you than you are of him."

"Well," said the woman after thinking it over and taking another peek at the Lion, "if that is the case, you may come in, and I will give you some dinner and a place to sleep."

So they all entered the house. Inside were the woman, two children, and a man. The man had hurt his leg and was lying on a couch in the corner. The people seemed greatly surprised to see so strange a party, and while the woman was busy setting the table, the man asked, "Where are you all going?"

"To the Emerald City," said Dorothy, "to see the Great Oz."

"Oh, indeed!" exclaimed the man. "Are you sure that Oz will see you?"

"Why not?" she replied.

"It is said that he never lets anyone come into his presence. I have been to the Emerald City many times, and it is a beautiful and wonderful place. But I have never been permitted to see the Great Oz, nor do I know of any living person who has seen him." ◆

"Does the Wizard never go out?" asked the Scarecrow.

"Never. He sits day after day in the great throne room of his palace, and even those who serve him do not see him face to face."

"What is he like?" asked Dorothy.

"That is hard to tell," said the man thoughtfully. "You see, Oz is a great Wizard and can take on any form he wishes. Some say he looks like a bird, and some say he looks like an elephant, and some say he looks like a cat. To others, he appears as a beautiful princess or in any other form that pleases him. But no one knows who the real Oz is."

"That is very strange," said Dorothy. "But we must try to see him, or we shall have made our journey for nothing."

"Why do you wish to see the terrible Oz?" asked the man.

"I want him to give me some brains," said the Scarecrow eagerly.

"Oh, Oz could do that easily enough," declared the man. "He has more brains than he needs."

"And I want him to give me a heart," said the Tin Woodman.

"That will not trouble him," continued the man. "Oz has a large collection of hearts, of all sizes and shapes."

"And I want him to give me courage," said the cowardly Lion.

"Oz keeps a great pot of courage in his throne room," said the man. "He covers the pot with a golden plate to keep it from running over. He will be glad to give you some."

"And I want him to send me back to Kansas," said Dorothy.

"Where is Kansas?" asked the man.

"I don't know," replied Dorothy sorrowfully. "But it is my home, and I'm sure it's somewhere."

"Oz can do anything, so I suppose he will find Kansas for you. But first you must get to see him, and that will be a hard task. The Great Wizard does not like to see anyone, and he usually has his own way. But what do you want?" he continued, speaking to Toto. But Toto only wagged his tail, for he could not speak.

The woman now called to them that dinner was ready, so they gathered around the table. Dorothy ate some delicious hot cereal and a dish of scrambled eggs and a plate of nice white bread, and she enjoyed her meal. The Lion ate some of the hot cereal but did not care for it, saying it was made from oats, which is food for horses, not lions. The Scarecrow and the Tin Woodman ate nothing at all. Toto ate a little of everything and was glad to get a good dinner again.

The woman now gave Dorothy a bed to sleep in, and Toto lay down beside her, while the Lion guarded the door of her room so that Dorothy would not be disturbed. The Scarecrow and the Tin Woodman stood up in a corner and kept quiet all night, although of course they could not sleep.

The next morning, as soon as the sun was up, they started on their way and soon saw a beautiful green glow in the sky just in front of them.

"That must be the Emerald City," said Dorothy.

As they walked on, the green glow became brighter and brighter, and it seemed that at last they were nearing the end of their travels. Yet it was afternoon before they came to the great wall that surrounded the city. The wall was high and thick and had a bright green color.

In front of them, at the end of the yellow brick road, was a big gate, all studded with emeralds that glittered so much in the sun that even the painted eyes of the Scarecrow were dazzled by their brightness.

There was a bell beside the gate, and Dorothy pushed the button and heard a silvery tinkling sound on the other side. Then the big gate swung slowly open. They all went through and found themselves in a room with a high arched ceiling. The walls of the room glistened with countless emeralds.

In front of them stood a little man about the size of a Munchkin. He was clothed all in green from his head to his feet, and even his skin had a greenish tint. At his side was a large green box.

## C COMPREHENSION

Write the answers.
1. Why did the Lion think it was strange that flowers nearly killed him and the mice saved his life?
2. Name at least three ways that the road near the Emerald City was different from the road in the forest.
3. Why were the people near the Emerald City afraid to talk to the travelers?
4. Why didn't the man with the bad leg know what Oz really looks like?
5. What do you think Oz really looks like?

## D WRITING

The travelers have seen just a small part of the Emerald City. Write a paragraph that describes what you think the rest of the Emerald City will look like. Be sure your paragraph answers the following questions:
- What color is everything?
- What are the streets like?
- What are the buildings like?

## A WORD LISTS

| 1 | 2 | 3 | 4 |
|---|---|---|---|
| *Compound Words* | *Word Practice* | *Word Practice* | *Vocabulary Review* |
| 1. sunshine | 1. cereal | 1. uniform | 1. guardian |
| 2. wildcat | 2. honest | 2. furniture | 2. prefer |
| 3. woodman | 3. ceiling | 3. whistle | 3. basin |
| 4. scarecrow | 4. lemonade | 4. fountain | 4. studded |
| 5. everything | | | 5. admit |
| 6. therefore | | | 6. marble |

## B READING

# Chapter 15
# The Emerald City

When the little green man saw Dorothy and her companions, he asked, "What do you wish in the Emerald City?"

"We came here to see the Great Oz," said Dorothy.

The man was so surprised at this answer that he sat down to think it over.

"It has been many years since anyone asked me to see Oz," the green man said. "He is powerful and terrible, and if you come here for the foolish reason of bothering the wise thoughts of the great Wizard, he might be angry and destroy you all in an instant." ✿

"But it is not a foolish reason," replied the Scarecrow. "It is important, and we have been told that Oz is a good Wizard."

"So he is," said the green man. "And he rules the Emerald City wisely and well. But to those who are not honest or who approach him out of curiosity, he is most terrible, and few have ever asked to see his face. I am the Guardian of the Gates, and since you demand to see the Great Oz, I must take you to his palace.

But first you must put on these spectacles."

"Why?" asked Dorothy.

"Because if you did not wear spectacles the brightness of the Emerald City would blind you. Even those who live in the City must wear spectacles night and day. The spectacles are all locked on, for Oz so ordered it when the city was first built, and I have the only key that will unlock them."

The green man opened the big green box, and Dorothy saw that it was filled with spectacles of every size and shape. All of them had green glass in them. The Guardian of the Gates found a pair that fit Dorothy and put them over her eyes.

The spectacles had two golden bands fastened to them that passed around the back of Dorothy's head. The Guardian of the Gates locked the bands together with a little key that was at the end of a chain that he wore around his neck. When the spectacles were on, Dorothy could not take them off. Of course, she did not wish to be blinded by the glare of the Emerald City, so she said nothing.

The Guardian of the Gates also put spectacles on the Scarecrow and the Tin Woodman and the Lion and even on little Toto. All were locked with the key. Then he put on his own glasses and told the travelers that he was ready to show them to the palace. Taking a big golden key from a peg on the wall, he opened another gate, and they all followed him through the gate and into the streets of the Emerald City.

Even with their eyes protected by the green spectacles, Dorothy and her friends were at first dazzled by the brightness of the wonderful city. The streets were lined with beautiful houses built of green marble and studded everywhere with sparkling emeralds. The party walked on a sidewalk made of the same green marble. All the pieces of the marble were joined together by rows of emeralds that glittered in the brightness of the sun. The window panes were made of green glass. Even the sky above the city had a green tint, and the rays of the sun were green.

There were many men, women, and children walking around. These people were all dressed in green clothes and had greenish skin. They looked at Dorothy and her strange companions with wondering eyes. The children all ran away and hid behind their mothers when they saw the Lion, and no one spoke to the travelers.

The streets had many shops, and Dorothy saw that everything in them was green. Green candy and green popcorn were for sale, as well as green shoes, green hats, and green clothes of all sorts. At one place, a man was selling green lemonade, and when the children bought it, Dorothy could see that they paid for it with green pennies.

There seemed to be no horses. The men carried things around in little green carts, which they pushed in front of them. Everyone seemed happy and rich.

The Guardian of the Gates led them through the streets until they came to a big building, exactly in the middle of the city, which was the Palace of Oz, the Great Wizard. There was a soldier in front of the door, dressed in a green uniform and with a long green beard.

"Here are some strangers," the Guardian of the Gates said to the soldier.

"They demand to see the Great Oz."

"Step inside," answered the soldier, "and I will carry your message to him."

So they passed through the palace gates and were led to a big room with a green carpet and lovely green furniture studded with emeralds. The soldier made all of them wipe their feet on a green mat before he let them enter this room. When they were inside, he said politely, "Please make yourselves comfortable while I go to the door of the throne room and tell Oz you are here."

The party had to wait a long time before the soldier returned. When he finally came back, Dorothy asked, "Have you seen Oz?"

"Oh, no," replied the soldier. "I have never seen him. But I just spoke to him as he sat behind his screen and gave him your message. Oz said he will see you if you want, but each one of you must enter his presence alone, and he will admit only one each day. Therefore, since you will have to remain in the palace for several days, I will have someone take you to rooms where you may rest in comfort after your journey." ◆

"Thank you," replied Dorothy. "That is very kind of Oz."

The soldier now blew on a green whistle, and at once a young girl, dressed in a pretty green silk gown, entered the room. She had lovely green hair and green eyes, and she bowed low before Dorothy as she said, "Follow me."

So Dorothy said goodbye to all her friends except Toto. She took the dog in her arms and followed the green girl through seven hallways and up three flights of stairs until they came to a room at the front of the palace.

It was the sweetest little room in the world, with a soft comfortable bed that had sheets of green silk and a green blanket. There was a tiny fountain in the middle of the room, which shot a spray of green perfume into the air, and the perfume fell back into a beautifully carved green marble basin. Beautiful green flowers stood in the windows, and there was a shelf with a row of little green books. When Dorothy had time to open these books she found them full of strange green pictures that made her laugh.

The closet had many green dresses, made of silk and satin and velvet, and all of them fit Dorothy exactly.

"Make yourself at home," said the green girl. "And if you want anything, ring the bell. Oz will send for you tomorrow morning."

Then the girl left Dorothy alone and went back to the others. She led each one to a different room in a pleasant part of the palace. Of course, this politeness was wasted on the Scarecrow; for when he found himself alone in his room, he stood in one spot, right next to the door. He had no need to lie down, and he could not close his eyes. So he stood up all night staring at a little spider weaving its web in a corner of the room. The spider didn't act as if it were in one of the most wonderful rooms in the world.

The Tin Woodman lay down on his bed, for he remembered what he had done when he was made of flesh. But since he was unable to sleep, he spent the night moving his legs and arms up and down to make sure that they were in good working order. The Lion would have preferred a bed of dried leaves in the

forest and did not like being shut up in a room. But he had too much sense to let this worry him, so he sprang on the bed and rolled himself up like a cat and fell asleep in a minute.

The next morning after breakfast, the green girl came to get Dorothy, whom she helped dress in a pretty green satin gown. Then Dorothy put on a green silk apron and tied a green ribbon around Toto's neck, and the little party started for the throne room of the Great Oz.

First they came to a great hall in which many ladies and gentlemen were standing around, all dressed in fancy clothes. These people had nothing to do but talk to each other, but they always came to wait outside the throne room every morning, even though they were never permitted to see Oz. As Dorothy entered, they looked at her curiously, and one of them whispered, "Are you really going to look upon the face of Oz the Terrible?"

"Of course," answered Dorothy, "if he will see me."

"Oh, he will see you," said the soldier who had taken her message to the Wizard, "although he does not like to have people ask to see him. Indeed, at first he was angry and said I should send you back where you came from. Then he asked me what you looked like, and when I mentioned your silver shoes, he was very much interested. At last I told him about the mark on your forehead, and he decided he would admit you to his presence."

Just then a bell rang, and the green girl said to Dorothy, "That is the signal. You must go into the throne room alone."

# C COMPREHENSION

Write the answers.

1. Why was the Guardian of the Gates so surprised when he heard the travelers' request?
2. Why do you think people in the Emerald City had to wear green spectacles?
3. What do you think the Emerald City would look like without spectacles?
4. When the Scarecrow stays in his room, the story says, "This politeness was wasted on the Scarecrow." What does that mean?
5. What do you think Oz will look like when Dorothy finally sees him?

# D WRITING

If you could make a city, what would it be like? Write a paragraph that explains your answer. Be sure your paragraph answers the following questions:

- What would the buildings look like?
- What kinds of stores and parks would the city have?
- How would people get from one part of the city to another?

# A WORD LISTS

| 1<br>*Hard Words* | 2<br>*Word Endings* | 3<br>*Word Practice* | 4<br>*New Vocabulary* |
|---|---|---|---|
| 1. rhinoceros | 1. enormous | 1. giant | 1. enormous |
| 2. singe | 2. tremendous | 2. disappointed | 2. meek |
| 3. grindstone | 3. anxious | 3. dreadfully | 3. weep |
| | 4. gorgeous | 4. expect | 4. willingly |
| | | | 5. tremendous |
| | | | 6. grant |
| | | | 7. terror |
| | | | 8. request |
| | | | 9. singed |

# B READING

## Chapter 16
# The Wizard and Dorothy

Dorothy opened the door to the throne room and walked boldly through. She found herself in a wonderful place. It was a big round room with a high arched roof. The walls, ceiling, and floor were covered with large emeralds set closely together. In the center of the roof was a great light, as bright as the sun, which made the emeralds sparkle in a wonderful way.

But what interested Dorothy most was the big throne of green marble that stood in the middle of the room. It was shaped like a chair and sparkled with gems, as did everything else. ✿

In the center of the chair was an enormous head, floating by itself, without a body, arms, or legs. There was no hair on the floating head, but it had eyes and a nose and a mouth and was much bigger than the head of the biggest giant.

As Dorothy gazed at the head in

wonder and fear, the eyes turned slowly and looked at her sharply and steadily. Then the mouth moved, and Dorothy heard a voice say, "I am Oz, the Great and Terrible. Who are you, and why do you want to see me?"

Oz's voice was not as awful as Dorothy had expected, so she took courage and answered, "I am Dorothy, the Small and Meek. I have come to you for help."

The eyes looked at her thoughtfully for a full minute. Then Oz said, "Where did you get the silver shoes?"

"I got them from the Wicked Witch of the East when my house fell on her and killed her," she replied.

"Where did you get the mark on your forehead?" Oz continued.

"That is where the Good Witch of the North kissed me when she said goodbye and sent me to you," said the girl.

Again the eyes looked at her sharply, and they saw that she was telling the truth. Then Oz asked, "What do you want me to do?"

"Send me back to Kansas, where Aunt Em and Uncle Henry are," she answered earnestly. "I don't like your country, although it is beautiful. And I am sure Aunt Em is dreadfully worried by my being away so long."

The eyes blinked three times. Then they turned up to the ceiling and down to the floor and rolled around so strangely that they seemed to see every part of the room. And at last they looked at Dorothy again.

"Why should I do this for you?" asked Oz.

"Because you are strong and I am weak; because you are a great wizard and

I am only a small child."

"But you were strong enough to kill the Wicked Witch of the East," said Oz.

"That just happened," answered Dorothy. "I could not help it."

"Well," said Oz, "I will give you my answer. You have no right to expect me to send you back to Kansas unless you do something for me. In this country, people must pay for everything they get. If you want me to use my magic power to send you home again, you must do something for me first. Help me and I will help you."

"What must I do?" asked the girl.

"Kill the Wicked Witch of the West," answered Oz. ♦

"But I cannot!" exclaimed Dorothy, greatly surprised.

"You killed the Witch of the East, and you wear the silver shoes, which have a magic charm. There is now only one Wicked Witch left in all this land, and when you can tell me that she is dead, I will send you back to Kansas—but not before."

The girl was so disappointed that she began to weep. The eyes blinked again and looked at her anxiously, as if the great Oz felt that she could help him if she wanted to.

"I never killed anything willingly," she said. "And even if I wanted to, how could I kill the Wicked Witch? If you, who are great and terrible, cannot kill her yourself, how do you expect me to do it?"

"I do not know," said Oz. "But that is my answer, and until the Wicked Witch dies, you will not see your uncle and aunt again. Remember that the Witch is wicked—tremendously wicked—and must be killed. Now go and do not ask to see me again until you have done your task."

## C COMPREHENSION

Write the answers.

1. Do you think that Oz is really a floating head? Explain your answer.
2. Why do you think Oz was so interested in the silver shoes and the witch's kiss?
3. What did Oz mean when he told Dorothy, "Help me and I will help you"?
4. Do you think that Dorothy is the kind of person who would kill somebody? Explain your answer.

## D WRITING

Write a paragraph that describes the throne room. Be sure your paragraph answers the following questions:
- What shape is the room?
- What is the room made of?
- What is in the room?

## A WORD LISTS

**1**
*Hard Words*
1. daisies
2. telescope
3. castle

**2**
*Word Practice*
1. singe
2. single
3. sorrowfully
4. rhinoceros
5. singed
6. cackle
7. cackling

**3**
*Vocabulary Review*
1. tremendous
2. meek
3. enormous
4. terror
5. singed
6. request
7. grant

**4**
*New Vocabulary*
1. slightest
2. kingdom
3. grindstone
4. pure
5. advance

## B READING

# Chapter 17
# The Wizard's Commands

Dorothy was very sad when she left the throne room. She went back to where the Lion and the Scarecrow and the Tin Woodman were waiting to hear what Oz had said to her.

"There is no hope for me," Dorothy said sadly. "Oz will not send me home until I have killed the Wicked Witch of the West, and I cannot do that."

Her friends were sorry, but they could do nothing to help her. So she went to her own room and lay down on the bed and went to sleep. ✿

The next morning the soldier with the green whiskers came to the Scarecrow and said, "Come with me, for Oz has sent for you."

So the Scarecrow followed him and went into the great throne room, where he saw a most lovely lady sitting on the emerald throne. She was dressed in green silk and wore a crown of jewels

upon her flowing green hair. Gorgeously colored wings were attached to her shoulders. The wings were so light that they fluttered if the slightest breath of air reached them.

The Scarecrow made a clumsy bow before this beautiful creature. She looked upon him sweetly and said, "I am Oz, the Great and Terrible. Who are you, and why do you seek me?"

The Scarecrow, who had expected to see the great head Dorothy had told him about, was amazed that Oz was now a woman.

"I am only a Scarecrow, stuffed with straw. Therefore, I have no brains, and I come to you hoping that you will put brains in my head instead of straw so that I may become as much a man as any other in your kingdom."

"Why should I do this for you?" asked Oz.

"Because you are wise and powerful, and no one else can help me," answered the Scarecrow.

"In this country, people must pay for everything they get," said Oz. "If you will kill the Wicked Witch of the West for me, I will give you a great many brains—and such good brains that you will be the wisest man in all the Land of Oz."

"I thought you asked Dorothy to kill the witch," said the Scarecrow in surprise.

"So I did. I don't care who kills her. But until she is dead, I will not grant your wish. Now go, and do not ask to see me again until you have earned the brains you so greatly desire."

The Scarecrow went sorrowfully back

to his friends and told them what Oz had said. Dorothy was surprised to find that the great Wizard was not a head, as she had seen him, but a lovely lady.

"All the same," said the Scarecrow, "she needs a heart as much as the Tin Woodman."

On the next morning, the soldier with green whiskers came to the Tin Woodman and said, "Oz has sent for you. Follow me."

So the Tin Woodman followed the soldier and came to the great throne room. He did not know whether Oz would be a lovely lady or a head, but he hoped Oz would be the lovely lady.

The Tin Woodman said to himself, "If it is the head, I am sure I will not be given a heart, for a head has no heart of its own and therefore cannot feel for me. But if it is the lovely lady, I will beg hard for a heart, for all ladies are supposed to be kindhearted."

But when the Tin Woodman entered the great throne room, he saw neither the head nor the lady, for Oz had taken the shape of a terrible beast. It was nearly as big as an elephant, and the green throne seemed barely strong enough to hold its weight.

The beast had a head like a rhinoceros, except that its face had five eyes. There were five long arms growing out of its body, and it also had five long, slim legs. Thick hair covered every part of it, and it was the most dreadful looking monster that the Tin Woodman had ever seen. It was fortunate that the Tin Woodman had no heart, for it would have beat loud and fast from terror. But because he had no heart, the Tin Woodman was not at all afraid. ◆

"I am Oz, the Great and Terrible," said the beast in a roaring voice. "Who are you, and why do you seek me?"

"I am a Woodman and made of tin. Therefore, I have no heart and cannot love. I want you to give me a heart so that I may be like other men."

"Why should I do this?" demanded the beast.

"Because I ask it and because you alone can grant my request," answered the Tin Woodman.

Oz gave a low growl at this but said, "If you really want a heart, you must earn it."

"How?" asked the Tin Woodman.

"Help Dorothy kill the Wicked Witch of the West," replied the beast. "When the Witch is dead, come to me, and I will then give you the biggest and kindest and most loving heart in all the Land of Oz."

So the Tin Woodman was forced to return sorrowfully to his friends and tell them of the terrible beast he had seen. They were all amazed by how many forms the great Wizard could take, and the Lion said, "If he is a beast when I go to see him, I will roar my loudest and frighten him so much that he will grant all I ask. And if he is the lovely lady, I will pretend to spring at her and make her do what I want. And if he is the great head, I will roll him all around the room until he promises to give us what we desire. So be happy, my friends, for everything will go well."

The next morning the soldier with the green whiskers led the Lion to the great throne room.

The Lion at once passed through the door and, glancing around, saw to his surprise that a ball of fire was in front of

the throne. The ball was so fierce and glowing that the Lion could scarcely bear to look at it. The Lion's first thought was that Oz had accidentally caught on fire and was burning up. But when the Lion tried to go nearer, the heat was so great that it singed his whiskers, and he crept back to a spot near the door.

Then a low, quiet voice came from the ball of fire and said, "I am Oz, the Great and Terrible. Who are you, and why do you seek me?"

The Lion answered, "I am a cowardly Lion, afraid of everything. I come to you to beg that you give me courage so that I may become the King of Beasts."

"Why should I give you courage?" demanded Oz.

"Because, of all the Wizards, you are the greatest and because you alone have the power to grant my request," answered the Lion.

The ball of fire burned fiercely for a time, and then the voice said, "Help Dorothy kill the Wicked Witch of the West, and then I will give you courage. But as long as the Witch lives, you must remain a coward."

The Lion was angry at this speech but could say nothing in reply. While he stood silently gazing at the ball of fire, it became so unbearably hot that he turned around and rushed from the room. He was glad to find his friends waiting for him, and he told them about his terrible meeting with the Wizard.

"What shall we do now?" asked Dorothy sadly.

"There is only one thing we can do," answered the Lion, "and that is to go to the Land of the West, seek out the Wicked Witch, and destroy her."

"But suppose we cannot?" said the girl.

"Then I will never have courage," declared the Lion.

"And I will never have brains," added the Scarecrow.

"And I will never have a heart," said the Tin Woodman.

"And I will never see Aunt Em and Uncle Henry," said Dorothy.

Dorothy looked at her friends and said, "I suppose we must try it. But I am sure I do not want to kill anybody, even to see Aunt Em again."

"I will go with you," said the Lion. "But I'm too much of a coward to kill the Witch."

"I will go, too," declared the Scarecrow. "But I won't be much help to you because I am a fool without any brains."

"I haven't the heart to harm even a witch," remarked the Tin Woodman. "But if you go, I certainly must go with you."

Therefore, they decided to start their journey to the Land of the West the next morning. The Tin Woodman sharpened his axe on a green grindstone and had all his joints properly oiled. The Scarecrow stuffed himself with fresh straw, and Dorothy put new paint on his eyes so that he could see better. The green girl, who was very kind to them, filled Dorothy's basket with good things to eat and fastened a little green bell around Toto's neck with a green ribbon.

Dorothy, Toto, and the Lion went to bed quite early and slept soundly.

They were awakened by the crowing of a green rooster that lived in the backyard of the palace and by the cackling of a green hen that had laid a green egg. The travelers were ready to start on their journey to the west.

## C COMPREHENSION

Write the answers.
1. Why do you think Oz wants the travelers to kill the Wicked Witch?
2. After the Scarecrow saw the lovely lady, he said, "She needs a heart as much as the Tin Woodman." What did he mean by that?
3. What do you think the real Wizard of Oz looks like? Explain your answer.
4. Why do you think Oz appeared in a different form to each traveler?
5. Why did the travelers decide to try to kill the Wicked Witch?

## D WRITING

The Wizard takes different forms. Write a paragraph that describes what he might look like if you saw him. Be sure the paragraph answers the following questions:
• What does his body look like?
• What does his voice sound like?

# 23

## A WORD LISTS

### 1
*Hard Words*
1. seize
2. seized
3. desperate
4. desperately

### 2
*Word Practice*
1. buttercups
2. daisy
3. daisies
4. hill
5. hillier
6. fierce

### 3
*Word Practice*
1. chatter
2. invisible
3. struggle
4. strange
5. chattering

### 4
*New Vocabulary*
1. untilled
2. castle
3. spear
4. seize
5. fate
6. tempt
7. fine

### 5
*New Vocabulary*
1. chattering
2. battered
3. bundle
4. courtyard
5. desperately
6. cunning

# Chapter 18
# The Search for the Wicked Witch

The soldier with the green whiskers led Dorothy and her friends through the streets of the Emerald City until they reached the room where the Guardian of the Gates lived. The Guardian unlocked their spectacles and put them back in his green box, and then he politely opened the gate for the travelers.

"Which road leads to the Wicked Witch of the West?" asked Dorothy.

"There is no road," answered the Guardian of the Gates. "No one ever wishes to go that way."

"How, then, can we find her?" inquired the girl. ✿

"That will be easy," replied the man. "When she knows you are in the country of the Winkies, she will find you and make you all her slaves."

"Perhaps not," said the Scarecrow, "for we hope to destroy her."

"Oh, that is different," said the Guardian of the Gates. "No one has ever destroyed her before, so I naturally thought she would make slaves of you. But take care, for she is wicked and fierce and may try to destroy you first. Keep going west, where the sun sets, and you cannot fail to find her."

They thanked him and said goodbye and turned toward the west, walking over fields of soft grass dotted here and there with daisies and buttercups. Dorothy still wore the pretty silk dress she had put on in the palace; but now, to her surprise, she found that it was no longer green, but pure white. The ribbon around Toto's neck had also lost its green color and was as white as Dorothy's dress.

The Emerald City was soon far behind them. As they advanced, the ground became rougher and hillier, for there were no farms or houses in this country of the West, and the ground was untilled.

In the afternoon, the sun shone hot in their faces, for there were no trees to offer them shade. The sun made Dorothy and Toto and the Lion very tired, and before night, they lay down on the grass and fell asleep, with the Tin Woodman and the Scarecrow keeping watch.

Now the Wicked Witch of the West had only one eye, but it was as powerful as a telescope and could see everywhere. As she sat in the door of her yellow castle, she happened to see Dorothy lying asleep, with her friends all around her. They were a long way away, but the Wicked Witch was angry to find them in her country. So she called a dozen of her slaves, who were the Winkies, and gave them sharp yellow spears and told them to go to the strangers and destroy them.

The Winkies were not a brave people, but they had to do as they were told, so they marched away until they came near Dorothy. Then the Lion gave a great roar and sprang toward them, and the poor Winkies were so frightened that they ran back to the castle as fast as they could.

When the Winkies returned to the Wicked Witch, she sent them back to their work. Then she sat down to think. She could not understand why her plan to destroy these strangers had failed. But she was a powerful Witch, as well as a wicked one, and she soon decided what to do next. ♦

Now, the Wicked Witch had a golden cap in her cupboard. The cap was studded with diamonds and rubies, and it had a special power. Whoever owned the cap could call upon the Winged Monkeys, who would obey any order they were given. But no one could command these strange creatures more than three times.

The Wicked Witch had already used the cap twice. The first time was when she had made the Winkies her slaves and become the ruler of their country. The Winged Monkeys had helped her do this. The second time was when she had fought against the great Oz and driven him out of the Land of the West. The monkeys had also helped her do this.

The Witch could use the golden cap only one more time, but she knew that it was the only way to destroy Dorothy and her friends. So she took the golden cap from her cupboard and placed it on her head. Then she stood on her left foot and said slowly, "Ep-pe, pep-pe, bep-pe!"

Next she stood on her right foot and said, "Hil-lo, hol-lo, hel-lo!"

After that she stood on both feet and cried in a loud voice, "Ziz-zy, zuz-zy, zik!"

Now the charm began to work. The sky was darkened, and a low rumbling sound came through the air. The Witch heard the flapping of many wings, then a great chattering and laughing. When the sun came out of the dark sky, the Wicked Witch was surrounded by a crowd of monkeys. Each monkey had a pair of large and powerful wings on his shoulders.

One monkey, much bigger than the others, seemed to be the leader. He flew close to the Witch and said, "You have called us for the third and last time. What do you command?"

"Go to the strangers who are within my land and destroy them all except the lion," said the Wicked Witch. "Bring the beast to me, for I have a mind to harness him like a horse and make him work."

"Your commands shall be obeyed," said the leader. And then, with a great deal of chattering and noise, the Winged Monkeys flew away to the place where Dorothy and her friends were walking.

Some of the monkeys seized the Tin Woodman and carried him through the air until they were over a plain that was thickly covered with sharp rocks. Here they dropped the poor Tin Woodman, who fell a great distance to the rocks. He became so battered and dented that he could neither move nor groan.

Other monkeys caught the Scarecrow, and pulled all the straw out of his clothes and head with their long fingers. They made his hat and boots and clothes into a small bundle and threw the bundle into the top branches of a tall tree.

The remaining monkeys threw pieces

of thick rope around the Lion and wound the rope around his body and head and legs until he was unable to bite or scratch or struggle in any way. Then they lifted him up and flew away with him to the Witch's castle, where he was placed in a small yard with a high iron fence around it so that he could not escape.

But they did not harm Dorothy at all. She stood, with Toto in her arms, watching the sad fate of her comrades and thinking it would soon be her turn. The leader of the Winged Monkeys flew up to her with his long, hairy arms stretched out and his ugly face grinning terribly. But when he saw the mark of the Good Witch's kiss on Dorothy's forehead, he stopped short and told the other monkeys not to touch her.

"We dare not harm this girl," he said to them, "for the mark on her forehead shows that she is protected by the Power of Good, and that is greater than the Power of Evil. All we can do is carry her to the castle of the Wicked Witch and leave her there."

So, carefully and gently, they lifted Dorothy in their arms and carried her swiftly through the air until they came to the yellow castle, where they set her down on the front doorstep. Then the leader said to the Witch, "We have obeyed you as far as we were able. The Tin Woodman and the Scarecrow are destroyed, and the Lion is tied up in your yard. We dare not harm the girl, nor the dog she carries in her arms. Your power over us is now ended."

Then all the Winged Monkeys, with much laughing and chattering and noise, flew into the air and were soon out of sight.

The Wicked Witch was both surprised and worried when she saw the mark on Dorothy's forehead, for she knew very well that she dare not hurt the girl in any way. She looked down at Dorothy's feet, and when she saw the silver shoes, she began to tremble with fear, for she knew what a powerful charm the shoes had.

At first the Witch was tempted to run away from Dorothy, but she happened to look into the girl's eyes and realized that the girl did not know of the wonderful power of the silver shoes. So the Witch laughed to herself and thought, "I can still make her my slave, for she does not know how to use her power."

Then she said to Dorothy, severely, "Come with me. And see that you obey me, for if you do not, I will make an end of you, as I did of the Tin Woodman and the Scarecrow."

Dorothy followed the Witch through many of the beautiful rooms in her castle until they came to the kitchen, where the Witch ordered her to clean the pots and kettles and sweep the floor and feed the fire with wood. The girl went to work meekly, with her mind made up to work as hard as she could, for she was glad the Wicked Witch had decided not to kill her.

## C COMPREHENSION

Write the answers.
1. Do you think the inside of the Emerald City was really green? Explain your answer.
2. Do you think the Tin Woodman is really dead? Explain your answer.
3. What do you think will happen to the Scarecrow?
4. The silver shoes have a powerful charm. What do you think that charm is?
5. At the end of the chapter, why did Dorothy decide to work as hard as she could?

## D WRITING

Write a paragraph that describes the commands you would give the Winged Monkeys. Be sure your paragraph answers the following questions:
- What would your three commands be?
- Why would you give each command?
- What would you do when you had used up all your commands?

# A WORD LISTS

| 1 | 2 | 3 | 4 |
|---|---|---|---|
| *Word Endings* | *Word Practice* | *Vocabulary Review* | *New Vocabulary* |
| 1. anxious | 1. holiday | 1. cunning | 1. cruelty |
| 2. gorgeous | 2. despair | 2. desperately | 2. feast |
| 3. enormous | 3. desperate | 3. fate | 3. tenderly |
| 4. tremendous | 4. despairing | 4. seize | 4. mend |
|  | 5. straightened | 5. tempt |  |
|  | 6. invisible |  |  |
|  | 7. bathe |  |  |
|  | 8. bathing |  |  |

# B READING

## Chapter 19
# The Rescue

Now, the Wicked Witch desperately wanted to have Dorothy's silver shoes. She had used up all the power of the golden cap; but if she could only get hold of the silver shoes, they would give her more power than before. She watched Dorothy carefully to see if she ever took off her shoes. But Dorothy was so proud of her pretty shoes that she never took them off except at night and when she took her bath.

The Witch was too afraid of the dark to go into Dorothy's room at night to take the shoes. ✿ And the Witch's fear of water was greater than her fear of the dark, so she never came near when Dorothy was bathing. Indeed, the old Witch never touched water, nor ever let water touch her in any way.

But the Witch was very cunning, and she finally thought of a trick that would give her what she wanted. She placed an iron bar in the middle of the kitchen floor, and then, using her magic arts, she made the bar invisible to human eyes. When Dorothy walked across the floor,

she stumbled over the invisible bar and fell down. She was not hurt, but as she fell, one of the silver shoes came off. Before she could reach the shoe, the Witch seized it and put it on her own skinny foot.

The wicked woman was greatly pleased with the success of her trick. As long as she had one of the shoes, she owned half the power of their charm, and Dorothy could not use the magic against her, even if she had known how to do so.

The girl, seeing that she had lost one of her pretty shoes, grew angry and said to the Witch, "Give me back my shoe!"

"I will not," replied the Witch, "for it is now my shoe and not yours."

"You are a wicked creature!" said Dorothy. "You have no right to take my shoe from me."

"I will keep it, just the same," said the Witch, laughing at her, "and someday I will get the other one from you, too."

This made Dorothy so angry that she picked up the bucket of water that stood near and threw it over the Witch, soaking her from head to foot.

Instantly, the wicked woman gave a loud cry of fear, and then, as Dorothy looked at her in wonder, the Witch began to shrink and fall away.

"See what you have done!" the Witch screamed. "In a minute I will melt away."

"I'm very sorry," said Dorothy, who was truly frightened to see the Witch actually melting away before her eyes.

"Didn't you know that water would be the end of me?" asked the Witch in a wailing, despairing voice.

"Of course not," answered Dorothy. "How could I?"

"Well, in a few minutes I will be all melted, and you will have the castle to yourself. I have been wicked in my day, but I never thought a girl like you would ever be able to melt me and end my wicked deeds. Look out—here I go!"

With these words, the Witch fell down in a brown, melted, shapeless mass that began to spread over the kitchen floor. Seeing that the Witch had really melted away to nothing, Dorothy got another bucket of water and threw it over the mess. Then she swept it all out the door. She picked up the silver shoe, which was all that was left of the old woman, cleaned and dried it with a cloth, and put it on her foot again. Then free at last, she ran out to the courtyard to tell the Lion that the Wicked Witch had died and that they were no longer prisoners in a strange land. ♦

The cowardly Lion was very pleased to hear that the Wicked Witch had been melted by a bucket of water, and Dorothy at once unlocked the gate of his yard and set him free. They went into the castle, where Dorothy called all the Winkies together and told them that they were no longer slaves.

There was great rejoicing among the yellow Winkies, for the Wicked Witch had made them work hard and had always treated them with great cruelty. The Winkies decided to make that day a holiday and began feasting and dancing.

"If only our friends, the Scarecrow and the Tin Woodman, were with us," said the Lion, "I would be quite happy."

"Don't you think we could rescue them?" asked the girl anxiously.

"We can try," answered the Lion.

So they called the yellow Winkies and asked for help to rescue their friends. The Winkies said that they would be delighted to do everything they could for Dorothy, who had set them free from bondage. Dorothy chose the Winkies who looked as if they knew the most, and they all started away.

They traveled that day and part of the next until they came to the rocky plain where the Tin Woodman lay, all battered and bent. His axe was near him, but the blade was rusted and the handle was broken.

The Winkies lifted him tenderly in their arms and carried him back to the yellow castle. Dorothy shed many tears at the sad fate of her old friend, and the Lion looked sober and sorry. When they reached the castle, Dorothy said to the Winkies, "Do you have any tinsmiths?"

"Oh, yes, we have some very good tinsmiths," they told her.

"Then bring them to me," she said. And when the tinsmiths came, bringing with them all their tools in baskets, Dorothy asked, "Can you straighten out those dents in the Tin Woodman and bend him back into shape again and put him back together?"

The tinsmiths looked the Tin Woodman over carefully and then answered that they thought they could mend him so he would be as good as ever. They set to work in one of the big yellow rooms of the castle and worked for three days and four nights, hammering and twisting and bending and polishing and pounding at the legs and body and head of the Tin Woodman. At last he was straightened out into his old form, and his joints worked as well as ever. To be sure, there were several patches on him, but the tinsmiths did a good job, and the Tin Woodman did not mind the patches at all.

When, at last, he walked into Dorothy's room and thanked her for rescuing him, he was so pleased that he wept tears of joy, and Dorothy had to wipe every tear carefully from his face with her apron so his joints would not be rusted. At the same time, her own tears fell thick and fast at the joy of meeting her old friend again, and these tears did not need to be wiped away. As for the Lion, he wiped his eyes so often with the tip of his tail that it became quite wet, and he had to go out into the courtyard and hold his tail in the sun until it dried.

"If we only had the Scarecrow with us again," said the Tin Woodman when Dorothy had finished telling him everything that had happened, "I would be quite happy."

"We must try to find him," said the girl.

So she called the Winkies to help her, and they walked all that day and part of the next until they came to the tall tree where the Winged Monkeys had tossed the Scarecrow's clothes.

It was a very tall tree, and the trunk was so smooth that no one could climb it. The Tin Woodman said at once, "I'll chop it down, and then we can get the Scarecrow's clothes."

Now, while the tinsmiths had been mending the Tin Woodman, another Winkie, who was a goldsmith, had made an axe handle of solid gold and fitted it on the Tin Woodman's axe in place of the old broken handle. Other Winkies had polished the blade until all the rust was removed, and it glistened like silver.

As soon as he had spoken, the Tin

Woodman began to chop. In a short time, the tree fell over with a crash, and the Scarecrow's clothes fell out of the branches and dropped to the ground.

Dorothy picked them up and had the Winkies carry them back to the castle, where they were stuffed with nice, clean straw—and behold, here was the Scarecrow as good as ever, thanking them over and over again for saving him.

## C COMPREHENSION

Write the answers.
1. Do you think it's strange that the Witch was afraid of the dark? Explain your answer.
2. Why do you think the Witch was so afraid of water?
3. Why did Dorothy throw the water over the Witch?
4. How were the tinsmiths able to bring the Tin Woodman back to life?
5. Do you think the Scarecrow will be different now that he is stuffed with new straw? Explain your answer.

## D WRITING

Why do you think the water melted the Witch? Write a paragraph that explains your answer. Be sure your paragraph answers the following questions:
• What kind of person was the Witch?
• What do you think the Witch was made of?
• Why was the water more powerful than the Witch?

## A WORD LISTS

| 1 | 2 | 3 |
|---|---|---|
| *Hard Words* | *Word Endings* | *New Vocabulary* |
| 1. reunited | 1. promptly | 1. reunited |
| 2. tongue | 2. fortunately | 2. exclaim |
| 3. mischief | 3. solemnly | 3. pattering |
| | 4. presently | 4. mischief |
| | | 5. lining |

## B READING

# Chapter 20
# The Journey Back

Now that they were reunited, Dorothy and her friends spent a few happy days at the Witch's castle, where they found everything they needed to make themselves comfortable. But one day the girl thought of Aunt Em and said, "We must go back to Oz and claim his promise."

Then Dorothy went to the Witch's cupboard to fill her basket with food for the journey, and there she saw the golden cap. She tried it on her own head and found that it fit her exactly. She did not know anything about the charm of the cap, but she saw that it was pretty, so she made up her mind to wear it and carry her sunbonnet in the basket. ✿

Then they all started for the Emerald City. The Winkies gave them three cheers and many good wishes to carry with them.

Now, you will remember there was no road—not even a pathway—between the castle of the Wicked Witch and the Emerald City. When the four travelers had gone in search of the Witch, she had seen them coming and sent the Winged Monkeys for them. But it was much harder to find their way back through the big fields of buttercups and bright daisies. They knew, of course, that they had to go straight east, toward the rising sun, and they started off in the right way.

But then at noon, when the sun was over their heads, they did not know which was east and which was west, and they soon became lost in the great fields. They kept on walking, however, and at night the moon came out and shone brightly. So they lay down among the sweet-smelling flowers and slept soundly until morning—all but the Scarecrow and the Tin Woodman.

The next morning the sun was behind a cloud, but they started on as if they were quite sure which way they were going.

"If we walk far enough," said Dorothy, "we will soon come to some place, I am sure."

But day by day passed away, and they still saw nothing before them but the yellow fields.

Then Dorothy became discouraged. She sat down on the grass and looked at her companions, and they sat down and looked at her. Toto found that for the first time in his life he was too tired to chase a butterfly that flew past his head. So he put out his tongue and panted and looked at Dorothy as if to ask her what they should do next.

Dorothy and her friends sat in the fields for a long time. Then she said, "Why don't we call the field mice? They could probably tell us the way to the Emerald City."

"Why, of course they could," cried the Scarecrow. "Why didn't we think of that before?" ♦

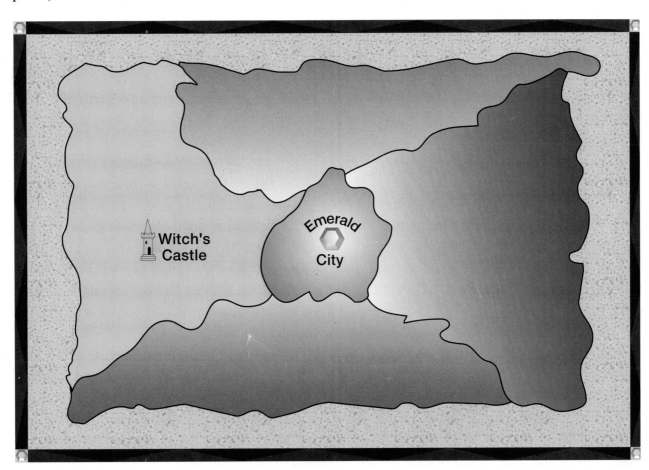

Dorothy blew the little whistle she had always carried around her neck since the Queen of the Mice had given it to her. In a few minutes, they heard the pattering of tiny feet, and many of the small gray mice came running up to her. The Queen was among them, and she asked in her squeaky little voice, "What can I do for my friends?"

"We have lost our way," said Dorothy. "Can you tell us where the Emerald City is?"

"Certainly," answered the Queen. "It is a great way off, for it has been behind you all this time." Then she noticed Dorothy's golden cap and said, "Why don't you use the charm of the cap and call the Winged Monkeys? They will carry you to the Emerald City in less than an hour."

"I don't know how to use the charm," answered Dorothy in surprise. "How do I make it work?"

"The directions for using the charm are written inside the golden cap," replied the Queen of the Mice. "But if you are going to call the Winged Monkeys, we must run away, for they are full of mischief and think it is great fun to chase us."

"Won't the Winged Monkeys hurt me?" asked the girl anxiously.

"Oh, no, they must obey the wearer of the cap. Goodbye!" And the Queen scampered out of sight, with all the mice hurrying after her.

Dorothy looked inside the golden cap and saw some words written on the lining. These, she thought, must be the charm, so she read the directions carefully and put the cap on her head.

"Ep-pe, pep-pe, bep-pe!" she said, standing on her left foot.

"Hil-lo, hol-lo, hel-lo!" she went on, standing this time on her right foot.

"Ziz-zy, zuz-zy, zik!" she said at last, standing on both feet.

Suddenly, the travelers heard a great chattering and flapping of wings as the band of Winged Monkeys flew up to them. The King bowed low before Dorothy and asked, "What is your command?"

"We want to go to the Emerald City," said the girl, "and we have lost our way."

"We will carry you," replied the King, and no sooner had he spoken than two of the monkeys caught Dorothy in their arms and flew away with her. Other monkeys took the Scarecrow and the Tin Woodman and the Lion, and one little monkey seized Toto and flew after the others, although the dog tried hard to bite him.

The Scarecrow and the Tin Woodman were rather frightened at first, for they remembered how badly the Winged Monkeys had treated them before. But they soon saw that the monkeys were not going to hurt them, so they rode through the air quite cheerfully and had a fine time looking at the pretty gardens and woods far below.

Dorothy was carried by two of the biggest monkeys, and one of them was the King Monkey. They had made a chair out of their hands and were careful not to hurt her.

Less than an hour later, Dorothy looked down and saw the shining green walls of the Emerald City below them. She was amazed by how rapidly the monkeys had flown, but she was glad the journey was over.

The monkeys set the travelers down carefully in front of the gate of the city. Then the King bowed low to Dorothy before flying swiftly away, followed by all his band.

"That was a good ride," said the girl.

"Yes, and a quick way out of our troubles," replied the Lion. "How lucky it was that you took the wonderful cap!"

The four travelers walked up to the great gate of the Emerald City and rang the bell. After several rings, the gate was opened by the same Guardian of the Gates they had met before.

"What! Are you back again?" he asked in surprise. "I thought you had gone to visit the Wicked Witch of the West."

"We did visit her," said the Scarecrow.

"And she let you go again?" asked the man in wonder.

"She could not help it, for she is melted," explained the Scarecrow.

"Melted! Well, that is good news, indeed," said the man. "Who melted her?"

"It was Dorothy," said the Lion solemnly.

"Good gracious!" exclaimed the man, and he bowed very low before her.

Then he led them into his little room and locked spectacles on their eyes, just as he had done before. Next they passed on through the gate into the Emerald City. When the people heard from the Guardian of the Gates that Dorothy and the others had melted the Wicked Witch of the West, they all gathered around the travelers and followed them in a great crowd to the palace of Oz.

The soldier with the green whiskers was still on guard before the door, but he let them in at once, and they were again met by the beautiful green girl, who showed each of them to their old rooms. She told them they could rest there until the Great Oz was ready to receive them.

The soldier sent a message to Oz that Dorothy and the other travelers had come back again, after destroying the Wicked Witch. But Oz made no reply.

Dorothy and the others thought the great wizard would send for them at once, but he did not. They had no word from him the next day nor the next nor the next. The waiting was tiresome, and at last they became angry with Oz for treating them so poorly after they had killed the Witch for him. So the Scarecrow asked the green girl to take another message to Oz, saying that if Oz did not let them in to see him at once, they would call the Winged Monkeys.

When Oz received this message, he was so frightened that he sent word for them to come to the throne room at nine o'clock the next morning. He had once met the Winged Monkeys in the Land of the West, and he did not want to meet them again.

The travelers spent a sleepless night, each thinking of the gift Oz had promised. Dorothy fell asleep only once, and then she dreamed she was in Kansas, where Aunt Em was telling her how glad she was to have her home again.

---

# C COMPREHENSION

Write the answers.
1. Why did the travelers get lost on their way back to the Emerald City?
2. Why had the Queen of the Mice promised always to help the travelers?
3. Why were the Scarecrow and the Tin Woodman frightened of the Winged Monkeys at first?
4. Why was the Guardian of the Gates so surprised to see the travelers?
5. Why do you think Oz is treating the travelers so poorly?

# D WRITING

Why do you think the Winged Monkeys have to obey the owner of the golden cap? Make up a story that explains why the monkeys have to obey the cap's owner. Make sure your story answers the following questions:
• Where did the Winged Monkeys come from?
• Who made the golden cap?
• Why did the monkeys have to obey the owner of the cap?
• When will the monkeys be free?

# A WORD LISTS

| 1 | 2 |
|---|---|
| *Word Endings* | *New Vocabulary* |
| 1. solemnly | 1. promptly |
| 2. presently | 2. bald |
| 3. promptly | 3. overheard |
| | 4. humbug |

# B READING

## Chapter 21
# Another Meeting With Oz

Promptly at nine o'clock the next morning, the green-whiskered soldier came to the travelers. Four minutes later they all went into the throne room of the Great Oz.

Of course, each one of the travelers expected to see the Wizard in the shape he had taken before, and all were greatly surprised when they looked around and saw no one at all in the room. They kept close to the door and closer to one another, for the stillness of the empty room was more dreadful than any of the forms they had seen Oz take. ✿

Presently they heard a voice that seemed to come from somewhere near the top of the great dome. The voice said solemnly, "I am Oz, the Great and Terrible. Why do you want to see me?"

They looked again in every part of the room, and then, seeing no one, Dorothy asked, "Where are you?"

"I am everywhere," answered the voice, "but to your eyes I am invisible. I will now seat myself upon the throne so that you may speak with me." The voice seemed to move toward the throne, so Dorothy and the others walked toward the throne and stood in a row. But Oz was still invisible.

Dorothy said, "We have come to claim your promise, great Oz."

"What promise?" asked Oz.

"You promised to send me back to Kansas when the Wicked Witch was destroyed," said the girl.

"And you promised to give me brains," said the Scarecrow.

"And you promised to give me a heart," said the Tin Woodman.

"And you promised to give me courage," said the cowardly Lion.

"Is the Wicked Witch really destroyed?" asked the voice. Dorothy noticed that it trembled a little.

"Yes," Dorothy answered. "I melted her with a bucket of water."

"Dear me," said the voice. "Well, come to me tomorrow, for I must have time to think it over."

"You've had plenty of time already," said the Tin Woodman angrily.

"We won't wait a day longer," said the Scarecrow.

"You must keep your promises to us!" exclaimed Dorothy.

The Lion thought he might as well frighten the Wizard, so he gave a large, loud roar, which was so fierce and dreadful that Toto jumped away from him in alarm and tipped over a screen that stood in a corner of the throne room.

The travelers looked at the screen as it fell with a crash, and the next moment all of them were filled with wonder. They saw a little old man with a bald head and a wrinkled face. He was standing in the spot the screen had hidden, and he seemed to be as surprised as they were.

The Tin Woodman raised his axe and

rushed toward the little man, crying out, "Who are you?"

"I am Oz, the Great and Terrible," said the little man in a trembling voice. "Don't strike me—please don't! I'll do anything you want me to."

Everybody looked at him in surprise. ♦

"I thought Oz was a great head," said Dorothy.

"And I thought Oz was a lovely lady," said the Scarecrow.

"And I thought Oz was a terrible beast," said the Tin Woodman.

"And I thought Oz was a ball of fire," exclaimed the Lion.

"No, you are all wrong," said the little man meekly. "I have been making believe."

"Making believe!" cried Dorothy. "Aren't you a great wizard?"

"Hush, my dear," he said. "Don't speak so loudly, or you will be overheard— and I will be ruined. I'm supposed to be a great wizard."

"And aren't you?" Dorothy asked.

"Not a bit, my dear, I'm just a common man."

"You're more than that," said the Scarecrow in a sad tone. "You're a humbug."

"Exactly so!" declared the little man. "I am a humbug."

"But this is terrible," said the Tin Woodman. "How will I ever get my heart?"

"Or I my courage?" asked the Lion.

"Or I my brains?" wailed the Scarecrow.

"But, my dear friends," said Oz, "think of me and the terrible trouble I'm in at being found out."

"Doesn't anyone else know you're a humbug?" asked Dorothy.

"No one knows it but you—and myself," replied Oz. "I have fooled everyone so long that I thought I would never be found out. It was a great mistake ever to let you into the throne room. Usually I will not even see the people I rule over, and so they believe that I am something terrible."

"But I don't understand," said Dorothy. "How was it that you appeared to me as a great head?"

"That was one of my tricks," answered Oz. "Step this way, please, and I will tell you all about it."

## C STORY DETAILS

Write the answers.
1. Why didn't the travelers see Oz when they first entered the throne room?
2. Why did the travelers stand in front of the throne?
3. How did the Lion try to frighten Oz?
4. Who was hiding behind the screen?
5. What did the real Oz look like?

## D VOCABULARY

For each item, write a sentence that uses the word.
1. terror
2. advanced
3. admit
4. desperately
5. cruelty
6. tenderly

# E COMPREHENSION

Write the answers.

1. When the travelers entered the throne room, the book says, "The stillness of the empty room was more dreadful than any of the forms they had seen Oz take." What does that sentence mean?
2. How do you think Oz made his voice move around the room?
3. Why do you think Oz pretended to forget his promises to the travelers?
4. Why was Oz afraid of being overheard when he spoke with the travelers?
5. Why did Oz hardly ever see the people he ruled over?

# F WRITING

Write a story that explains how you think the little old man became the Wizard of Oz. Be sure your story answers the following questions:

- Where did the man come from?
- What skills did the man have?
- How did he fool the people of the Emerald City into thinking he was a wizard?

# A WORD LISTS

**1**
*Hard Words*
1. experience
2. knowledge
3. imitate
4. ventriloquist

**2**
*Word Endings*
1. imagination
2. hesitation
3. explanation
4. imitation

**3**
*New Vocabulary*
1. ventriloquist
2. imitate
3. confidence
4. consider
5. gradually
6. high spirits
7. knowledge
8. experience

# B READING

## Chapter 22
# The Wizard's Story

Oz led Dorothy and the others to a small room in the rear of the throne room. He pointed to a corner of the small room, and there was the great head. It was made out of paper, and it had a carefully painted face.

"I hung this from the ceiling by a wire," said Oz. "I stood behind the screen and pulled a thread to make the eyes move and the mouth open."

"But how about the voice?" Dorothy inquired.

"Oh, I am a ventriloquist," said the little man. "I can throw the sound of my voice wherever I want. You thought my voice was coming out of the head. Here are the other things I used to trick you." ✿

Then he showed the Scarecrow the dress and the mask he had worn when he seemed to be the lovely lady. And the Tin Woodman saw that his terrible beast was nothing but a lot of animal skins sewn together. As for the ball of fire, the false wizard had also hung that from the ceiling. It was really a ball of cotton, but when oil was poured on it, the ball had burned fiercely.

"Really," said the Scarecrow, "you ought to be ashamed of yourself for being such a humbug."

"I am—I certainly am," answered the little man sorrowfully. "But it was the only thing I could do. Sit down, please— there are plenty of chairs—and I will tell you my story."

Dorothy and the others sat down and listened while the Wizard told the following tale:

*I was born near Kansas. When I grew up, I became a ventriloquist, and I was very well trained at that by a great master. I could imitate any kind of bird or beast.*

*After a time, I tired of ventriloquism and became a balloonist for a circus. I went up in my balloon on circus day and called down to people. Then I got them to go to the circus.*

*Well, one day I went up in a balloon and the ropes got twisted so that I couldn't come down again. The balloon went way up above the clouds. It went so far up that a current of air struck it and carried it many, many miles away. For a day and a night, I traveled through the air. On the morning of the second day, I awoke and found the balloon floating over a strange and beautiful country.*

*The balloon came down gradually, and I was not hurt a bit. But I found myself among strange people, who, when they saw me come from the clouds, thought I was a great wizard. Of course, I let them think I was a wizard because they were afraid of me, and they promised to do anything I wanted.*

*Just to amuse myself and to keep the people busy, I ordered them to build this city and my palace; and they did it all willingly and well. Then I thought, because the country was so green and beautiful, that I would call the city the Emerald City; and to make the name fit better, I put*

*green spectacles on all the people so that everything they saw was green.*

*The Emerald City is no greener than any other city. But when you wear green spectacles, everything you see looks green to you. It was built a great many years ago, for I was a young man when the balloon brought me here, and I am a very old man now. But my people have worn green glasses on their eyes so long that most of them think it really is an Emerald City.*

*And it certainly is a beautiful place, full of jewels and precious metals and every good thing that is needed to make people happy. I have been good to the people, and they like me; but ever since this palace was built, I have shut myself up and do not see any of them.* ♦

*One of my greatest fears was the witches, for I soon found out that they were really able to do powerful things. There were four of them in this country, and they ruled the people who live in the North and South and East and West. Fortunately, the Witches of the North and South were good, and I knew they would do me no harm.*

*But the Witches of the East and West were terribly wicked. I knew that if they ever figured out that I was less powerful than they were, they would destroy me. As it was, I lived in deadly fear of them for many years, so you can imagine how pleased I was when I heard that Dorothy's house had fallen on the Wicked Witch of the East. When you came to me, I was willing to promise anything if you would only do away with the other witch. But now that you have melted her, I am ashamed to say that I cannot keep my promises.*

"I think you are a very bad man," said Dorothy after Oz had finished his story.

"Oh, no, my dear. I'm really a very good man; but I'm a very bad wizard, I must admit."

"Can't you give me brains?" asked the Scarecrow.

"You don't need them. You are learning something every day. A baby has brains, but it doesn't know much. Experience is the only thing that brings knowledge, and the longer you are alive the more experience you are sure to get," replied Oz.

"That may all be true," said the Scarecrow, "but I shall be very unhappy unless you give me brains."

The false wizard looked at him carefully.

"Well," he said with a sigh, "I'm not much of a magician, but if you will come to me tomorrow morning, I will stuff your head with brains. I cannot tell you how to use them, however; you must find that out for yourself."

"Oh, thank you, thank you!" cried the Scarecrow. "I'll find a way to use them, never fear!"

"But how about my courage?" asked the Lion anxiously.

"You have plenty of courage, I am sure," answered Oz. "All you need is confidence in yourself. Every living thing is afraid when it faces danger; but if you have confidence, you can face danger even when you are afraid. You have plenty of that kind of courage."

"Perhaps I do, but I'm scared just the same," said the Lion. "I will really be very unhappy unless you give me the sort of courage that will make me less afraid."

"Very well. I will give you that sort

of courage tomorrow," replied Oz.

"How about my heart?" asked the Tin Woodman.

"Why, as for that," answered Oz, "I think you are wrong to want a heart. It makes most people unhappy. If you only knew it, you are lucky not to have a heart."

"I don't agree," said the Tin Woodman. "I will bear all the unhappiness without a grumble."

"Very well," answered Oz meekly. "Come to me tomorrow and I will give you a heart. I have played wizard for so many years that I may as well continue the part a little longer."

"And now," said Dorothy, "how am I going to get back to Kansas?"

"We will have to think about that," replied the little man. "Give me two or three days to consider the matter, and I'll try to find a way to carry you over the desert. In the meantime, you will all be treated as my guests. While you live in the palace, my people will wait upon you and obey your slightest wish. There is only one thing I ask in return for my help—you must keep my secret and tell no one I am a humbug."

They agreed to say nothing of what they had learned and went back to their rooms in high spirits. Even Dorothy had hope that "The Great and Terrible Humbug," as she called him, would find a way to send her back to Kansas. And if he did, she was willing to forgive him for everything he had done.

## C COMPREHENSION

Write the answers.
1. Why do you think Oz wanted his people to see nothing but green?
2. Oz said that "Experience is the only thing that brings knowledge." Give an example that shows how experience brings knowledge.
3. Oz also said, "If you have confidence, you can face danger even when you are afraid." Give an example of how confidence can help you face danger.
4. What did Oz mean when he said that having a heart makes most people unhappy?
5. How do you think Oz could carry Dorothy over the desert?

## D WRITING

When Oz finished his story, Dorothy said that he was a very bad man. Do you agree with Dorothy? Write a paragraph that explains your answer. Make sure your paragraph answers the following questions:
• What bad things had Oz done?
• What good things had Oz done?
• What kind of man do you think Oz was?
• What could Oz do to make Dorothy change her opinion?

# A WORD LISTS

| 1 | 2 | 3 | 4 |
|---|---|---|---|
| *Hard Words* | *Word Endings* | *Vocabulary Review* | *New Vocabulary* |
| 1. uneasily | 1. congratulation | 1. imitate | 1. uneasy |
| 2. bulged | 2. hesitation | 2. confidence | 2. congratulate |
| 3. congratulate | 3. imitation | 3. consider | 3. contents |
| 4. deceive | 4. explanation | | 4. deceive |
| 5. liquid | 5. imagination | | 5. shears |
| | | | 6. sawdust |
| | | | 7. replaced |

# B READING

## Chapter 23
# Brains, Heart, and Courage

The next morning, the Scarecrow said to his friends, "Congratulate me. I am going to Oz to get my brains at last. When I return, I will be like other men."

"I have always liked you as you are," said Dorothy.

"It is kind of you to like a scarecrow," he replied. "But surely you will think more of me when you hear the splendid thoughts my new brains are going to turn out."

Then he said goodbye to them in a cheerful voice and went to the throne room, where he knocked on the door.

"Come in," said Oz. ✿

The Scarecrow went in and found the little man sitting by the window, thinking hard.

"I have come for my brains," remarked the Scarecrow, a little uneasily.

"Oh, yes. Sit down in that chair, please," replied Oz. "You must excuse me for taking your head off, but I will have to do it in order to put your brains in their proper place."

"That's all right," said the

Scarecrow. "You are quite welcome to take my head off as long as it will be a better one when you put it on again."

So the Wizard unfastened the Scarecrow's head and emptied out the straw. Then he entered the back room and got hundreds of pins and needles. After shaking them together thoroughly, he filled the top of the Scarecrow's head with the mixture and stuffed the rest of the space with straw to hold the pins and needles in place.

When Oz had fastened the Scarecrow's head onto his body, the Wizard said to him, "I have filled your head with pins and needles. Now you have all the brains you need."

"I don't understand," replied the Scarecrow thoughtfully. "How can I have brains if I have nothing but straw, pins, and needles in my head?"

The Wizard replied, "People who have brains are very sharp. Anybody looking at the pins and needles sticking out of your head will know at once that you are very sharp."

The Wizard patted the Scarecrow on the back and continued, "From now on, you will be a great man, for I have given you new brains."

The Scarecrow was both pleased and proud to have new brains, and after thanking Oz warmly, he went back to his friends.

Dorothy looked at him curiously. His head bulged out at the top with brains.

"How do you feel?" she asked.

"I feel wise indeed," he answered earnestly. "When I get used to my brains, I will know everything."

Then the Tin Woodman said, "Well, I must go to Oz and get my heart." He walked to the throne room and knocked on the door.

"Come in," called Oz, and the Tin Woodman entered.

The Tin Woodman stood before Oz and said, "I have come for my heart."

"Very well," answered the little man. "But I will have to cut a hole in your chest so I can put your heart in the right place. I hope it won't hurt you."

"Oh, no," answered the Tin Woodman. "I won't feel it at all."

So Oz brought a pair of shears and cut a small, square hole in the left side of the Tin Woodman's chest. Then, Oz went to his cupboard and took out a pretty heart that was made entirely of silk and stuffed with sawdust.

"Isn't it a beauty?" he asked.

"It is, indeed!" replied the Tin Woodman, who was greatly pleased. "But is it a kind heart?"

"Oh, very!" answered Oz. He put the heart into the Tin Woodman's chest and then replaced the square of tin.

"There," said Oz. "Now you have a heart that any man would be proud of. I'm sorry I had to put a patch on your chest, but it really couldn't be helped."

"Never mind the patch," exclaimed the happy Tin Woodman. "I am very grateful to you, and I will never forget your kindness."

"Don't mention it," replied Oz.

Then the Tin Woodman went back to his friends, who were very happy for him. ♦

The Lion now walked to the throne room and knocked on the door.

"Come in," said Oz.

"I have come for my courage," announced the Lion, entering the room.

"Very well," answered the little man, "I will get it for you."

He went to his cupboard, reached up to a high shelf, and took down a large green bottle. He poured the contents of the bottle into a beautifully carved dish. Then he placed the dish in front of the cowardly Lion, who sniffed at it as if he did not like it.

"What is it?" asked the Lion.

"Courage," replied the Wizard.

"Do I have to drink it?" asked the Lion.

"Of course," said Oz. "You know that courage is something inside you. If you don't drink it, you will not have courage inside you."

"But," said the Lion slowly, as he looked at the large dish of liquid. "Do I have to drink all of it?"

Oz replied, "You want to be full of courage, don't you?"

"Yes," said the Lion.

"Then you must drink it all. That is the only way you will be full of courage."

The Lion hesitated no longer and drank until the dish was empty.

"How do you feel now?" asked Oz.

"Full of courage," replied the Lion, who went joyfully back to his friends to tell them about his good fortune.

When Oz was alone, he smiled at his success in giving the Scarecrow and the Tin Woodman and the Lion exactly what they wanted. He said, "It was easy to make the Scarecrow and the Lion and the Tin Woodman happy because they imagined I could do anything. But it will take a lot more imagination to carry Dorothy back to Kansas, and I don't know how it can be done."

For three days, Dorothy heard nothing from Oz. These were sad days for the girl, although her friends were all quite happy and comfortable. The Scarecrow told them that there were wonderful thoughts in his head, but he would not say what they were because he knew no one could understand them but himself. When the Tin Woodman walked around, he felt his heart rattling in his chest, and he told Dorothy that it was a kinder and more tender heart than the one he had owned when he was made of flesh. The Lion declared he was afraid of nothing on earth and would gladly face an army of men or a dozen of the fierce Kalidahs.

Thus, each of the friends was satisfied except Dorothy, who wanted more than ever to get back to Kansas.

On the fourth day, Oz sent for Dorothy. When she entered the throne room, he said pleasantly, "Sit down, my dear. I think I have found the way to get you out of this country."

"And back to Kansas?" Dorothy asked eagerly.

"Well, I'm not sure about Kansas," said Oz, "for I haven't the faintest idea of how to get there. But the first thing to do is to cross the desert, and then it should be easy to find your way home."

"How can I cross the desert?" Dorothy inquired.

"Well, I'll tell you what I think," said the little man. "You see, I came to this country in a balloon. You also came through the air, carried by a cyclone. So I believe the best way to get across the desert will be through the air. Now, it is quite beyond my powers to make a cyclone. But I've been thinking the matter over, and I believe I can make a balloon."

"How are you going to build a balloon?" asked Dorothy.

"As you know," said Oz, "a balloon is a large bag that floats when it is filled with gas. The balloon I had was made of silk, which was coated with glue to keep the gas from leaking out. I destroyed my old balloon, but I have plenty of silk in the palace, so it will be no trouble to make a new one. Unfortunately, in this whole country there is no gas to fill the balloon with to make it float."

"If it won't float," remarked Dorothy, "it will be of no use to me."

"True," answered Oz. "But there is another way to make the balloon float, which is to fill it with hot air. Hot air isn't as good as gas, for if the air were to get cold, the balloon would come down in the desert, and we would be lost."

"We!" exclaimed Dorothy. "Are you going with me?"

"Yes, of course," replied Oz. "I am tired of being such a humbug. If I were to leave this palace, my people would soon discover that I am not a wizard, and then they would be angry with me for having deceived them. So I have to stay shut up in these rooms all day, and it gets tiresome. I'd much rather go back to Kansas and be in a circus again."

"I will be glad to have your company," said Dorothy.

"Thank you," Oz answered. "Now if you will help me sew the silk together, we will begin to work on our balloon."

---

# C COMPREHENSION

Write the answers.
1. Do you think the Scarecrow will change now that he has brains? Explain your answer.
2. Do you think the Tin Woodman will change now that he has a heart? Explain your answer.
3. Do you think the Lion will change now that he has courage? Explain your answer.
4. How could Oz get hot air into his balloon?
5. Do you think Dorothy and Oz can get back to Kansas in a balloon? Explain your answer.

# D WRITING

Pretend that the Wizard of Oz has agreed to grant you a wish. Write a paragraph that describes your wish and how Oz grants it. Make sure your paragraph answers the following questions:
- What is your wish?
- What does Oz do to answer your wish?
- How well does Oz's answer work for you?

## A  WORD LISTS

| 1 | 2 | 3 |
|---|---|---|
| *Word Practice* | *Vocabulary Review* | *New Vocabulary* |
| 1. towel | 1. uneasy | 1. tug |
| 2. vibrate | 2. contents | 2. farewell |
| 3. underneath | 3. deceive | 3. extend |
| 4. collar | 4. gradually | 4. dose |
| 5. precious | | 5. utter |
| 6. ventriloquism | | 6. hush |
| 7. thorough | | |
| 8. through | | |

## B  READING

# Chapter 24
# The Witch of the South

Oz and Dorothy began working on the balloon right away. First Oz got some silk and cut it into strips. Then Dorothy took the strips and sewed them together with needle and thread. She began with a strip of light green silk, then a strip of dark green, and then a strip of emerald green—for Oz wanted to make the balloon in different shades of his favorite color.

It took three days to sew all the strips together, but when Dorothy was finished, they had a big bag of green silk more than twenty feet long. ✿ Oz painted the inside of the bag with a coat of thin glue to make it airtight, and then he announced that the balloon was ready.

"But we must have a basket to ride in," Oz said. So he sent the soldier with the green whiskers for a big clothes basket, which he fastened to the bottom of the balloon with many ropes.

When it was all ready, Oz sent word to his people that he was going to make a visit to his great brother wizard who lived in the clouds. The news spread rapidly throughout the city, and everyone came to see him leave.

Oz ordered the balloon carried out in front of the palace, and the people gazed at it with much curiosity. The Tin Woodman chopped a big pile of wood and made a fire. Oz held the bottom of the balloon over the fire so that the hot air that rose from the fire would be caught in the bag. The balloon swelled and rose into the air, until finally the basket started to leave the ground.

Then Oz got into the basket and said to all the people in a loud voice, "I am now going away to make a visit. While I am gone, the Scarecrow will rule over you. I command you to obey him as you would me."

By this time, the balloon was tugging hard at the rope that held it to the ground. The air in the balloon was hot, and the heat made the inside air so much lighter than the outside air that the balloon started to rise.

"Come, Dorothy!" cried the Wizard. "Hurry up, or the balloon will fly away."

"I can't find Toto anywhere," replied Dorothy, who did not want to leave her little dog behind. Toto had run into the crowd to bark at a kitten, and Dorothy found him at last. She picked him up and ran toward the balloon.

Dorothy was within a few steps of the balloon, and Oz was holding out his hands to help her into the basket, when the ropes suddenly snapped, and the balloon rose into the air without her.

"Come back!" Dorothy screamed. "I want to go, too!"

"I can't come back, my dear," called Oz from the basket. "Goodbye!"

"Goodbye!" shouted everyone, and all eyes were turned upward to where the Wizard was riding in the basket, rising every moment farther and farther into the sky.

And that was the last any of them ever saw of Oz, the wonderful Wizard. He may have reached Kansas safely and be there now. But the people remembered him lovingly and said to one another, "Oz was always our friend. When he was here, he built this beautiful Emerald City for us, and now he has left the wise Scarecrow to rule over us." ♦

But Dorothy was sad after the Wizard left without her. The Tin Woodman came to her and said, "I feel sad also, for the Wizard was the man who gave me my lovely heart. I would like to cry a little because Oz is gone. Will you kindly wipe away my tears so that I will not rust?"

"With pleasure," she answered and brought a towel at once. Then the Tin Woodman wept for several minutes, and Dorothy watched the tears and wiped them away with the towel. When he had finished, he thanked her kindly and oiled himself thoroughly.

The Scarecrow was now the ruler of the Emerald City, and although he was not a wizard, the people were proud of him. They said, "There is not another city in all the world that is ruled by a stuffed man." And so far as they knew, they were quite right.

The morning after Oz left in the balloon, the four travelers met in the throne room and talked matters over. The Scarecrow sat on the big throne, and the others stood before him.

"We are not so unlucky," said the new ruler. "This palace and the Emerald

City belong to us, and we can do whatever we want. Why, just a short time ago I was on a pole in a farmer's cornfield, and now I am the ruler of this beautiful city, so I am quite satisfied with my life."

The Lion said, "As for me, I am content to know that I am as brave as any beast that ever lived, if not braver."

The Tin Woodman said, "And as for me, I feel that my new heart is the kindest in the land."

"If Dorothy would be content to live in the Emerald City," said the Scarecrow, "we would all be happy together."

"But I don't want to live here," cried Dorothy. "I want to go to Kansas and live with Aunt Em and Uncle Henry."

"Well, then, what can we do?" inquired the Tin Woodman.

The Scarecrow decided to think, and he thought so hard that the pins and needles in his head began to vibrate. The others hushed while the Scarecrow thought. Finally the Scarecrow said, "Let us call in the soldier with the green whiskers and ask his advice."

So the soldier was called to the throne room. He entered timidly, for while Oz was ruler, the soldier had been allowed to come no farther than the door.

The Scarecrow said to him, "This girl wants to cross the desert. How can she do so?"

"I do not know," answered the soldier. "Nobody has ever crossed the desert, other than Oz himself."

"Is there no one who can help me?" asked Dorothy earnestly.

"Glinda might," he suggested.

"Who is Glinda?" inquired the Scarecrow.

"The Witch of the South. She is the most powerful of all the witches, and she rules over the Quadlings. Glinda's castle stands on the edge of the desert, so she may know a way to cross it."

"Glinda is a good witch, isn't she?" asked Dorothy.

"The Quadlings think she is good," said the soldier, "and she is kind to everyone. I have heard that Glinda is a beautiful woman who knows how to keep young in spite of the many years she has lived."

"How can I get to her castle?" asked Dorothy.

"The road to the south is straight," the soldier answered, "but it is said to be dangerous to travelers. There are wild beasts in the woods and odd-looking men who can extend their arms and legs. For this reason, none of the Quadlings ever come to the Emerald City." The soldier then left them.

The Scarecrow said, "It seems, in spite of dangers, that the best thing Dorothy can do is to travel to the Land of the South and ask Glinda to help her. For, of course, if Dorothy stays here, she will never get back to Kansas."

The Tin Woodman remarked to the Scarecrow, "You must have been thinking again."

"I have been," said the Scarecrow.

"I will go with Dorothy," declared the Lion, "for I am tired of your city and long for the woods and the country again. I need a dose of fresh air. Besides, Dorothy will need someone to protect her."

"That is true," agreed the Tin Woodman. "My axe may be of service to her, so I will also go with her to the Land of the South."

"When should we start?" asked the Scarecrow.

"Are you going?" they asked in surprise.

"Certainly. If it wasn't for Dorothy, I would never have gotten brains. She lifted me from the pole in the cornfield and brought me to the Emerald City. So my good luck is all due to her, and I will never leave her until she starts back to Kansas."

"Thank you," said Dorothy gratefully. "You are all very kind to me. I would like to start as soon as possible."

The Scarecrow said, "Why not call the Winged Monkeys and ask them to carry us to the Land of the South?"

"I never thought of that!" said Dorothy joyfully. "It's just the thing. I'll go at once for the golden cap."

She brought the cap into the throne room and uttered the magic words. Soon the band of Winged Monkeys flew in through the open window and stood beside her.

"This is the second time you have called us," said the King Monkey, bowing before Dorothy. "What do you want?"

"I want you to fly us to the Land of the South."

"It shall be done," said the king, and at once, the Winged Monkeys took the four travelers and Toto in their arms and flew away with them. After a long journey, they set the group down in the beautiful country of the Quadlings.

"Farewell, and thank you very much," said Dorothy. The Monkeys rose into the air and were out of sight in a moment.

---

## C COMPREHENSION

Write the answers.
1. How did Dorothy help Oz make the balloon?
2. Why did the balloon rise when Oz held it over the fire?
3. Why was the Scarecrow so happy with his life now?
4. Why might Glinda be able to help Dorothy?
5. Why did the travelers ask the Winged Monkeys to carry them to the Land of the South?

## D WRITING

Write a story that tells what happened to Oz after he left the Emerald City. Be sure your story answers the following questions:
- What happened to him during the balloon ride?
- Where did the balloon land?
- What happened to him after the balloon landed?

## A WORD LISTS

| 1<br>*Hard Words* | 2<br>*Word Practice* | 3<br>*New Vocabulary* |
|---|---|---|
| 1. ease | 1. overhear | 1. disgusting |
| 2. chorus | 2. singe | 2. chorus |
| 3. echo | 3. grant | 3. whisk |
| | 4. crackling | |
| | 5. giant | |
| | 6. cackling | |
| | 7. timid | |
| | 8. timidly | |

## B READING

# Chapter 25
# The Silver Shoes

The Land of the Quadlings seemed rich and happy. There was field upon field of grain, with well-paved roads running between them. The fences and houses and bridges were all painted bright red, just as they had been painted yellow in the Land of the Winkies and blue in the Land of the Munchkins. The Quadlings were short and good-natured. They were dressed all in red, which looked bright against the green grass and the yellow grain.

Dorothy and the others walked up to a farmhouse and knocked on the door, which was opened by the farmer's wife. ✿ When Dorothy asked for something to eat, the woman gave the girl and the Lion a good dinner, with many fruits and nuts, and a bowl of milk for Toto.

"How far is it to Glinda's castle?" asked Dorothy.

"It is not a great way," answered the farmer's wife. "Take the road to the south and you will soon reach it."

They thanked the good woman and started walking by the fields and across the pretty red bridges until they saw a beautiful red castle before them. Three young girls, dressed in handsome red uniforms trimmed with gold braid, were in front of the gates. As Dorothy approached, one of them said to her, "Why have you come to the South Country?"

"To see the Good Witch who rules here," Dorothy answered. "Will you take me to her?"

"I will ask Glinda if she will see you," said the girl.

Dorothy and the others told her who they were, and the girl went into the castle. After a few moments, she came back to say that the travelers could see Glinda at once.

Before they went to see Glinda, however, they were taken to a room of the castle, where Dorothy washed her face and combed her hair. The Lion shook the dust out of his mane. The Scarecrow patted himself into his best shape. The Tin Woodman polished his tin.

Then Dorothy and the others followed the girl soldier into a big room where the Witch Glinda sat on a throne of rubies. Glinda looked both beautiful and young to them. Her hair was a rich red and flowed over her shoulders. Her dress was pure white, and her eyes were blue.

Glinda looked at Dorothy in a kindly way and asked, "What can I do for you?"

So Dorothy told the Witch her story. She told how the cyclone had brought her to the Land of Oz and how she had found her companions and of the wonderful adventures they had had.

"My greatest wish now," she added, "is to get back to Kansas, for Aunt Em will surely think something dreadful has happened to me, and that will make her and my uncle very sad."

Glinda leaned forward and kissed Dorothy.

"Bless your heart," Glinda said. "If I tell you of a way to get back to Kansas, will you give me the golden cap?"

"Certainly!" exclaimed Dorothy. "I have it with me now, and when you have it, you can command the Winged Monkeys three times."

Glinda smiled and said, "I know just what to do with those three commands."

So Dorothy gave the golden cap to the Witch. Then Glinda said to the Scarecrow, "What will you do when Dorothy has left us?"

"I will return to the Emerald City," the Scarecrow replied, "for Oz has made me its ruler, and the people like me. The only thing that worries me is how to return there, for the road to Oz is very dangerous."

"I will command the Winged Monkeys to carry you to the gates of the Emerald City," said Glinda.

Turning to the Tin Woodman, Glinda asked, "What will become of you when Dorothy leaves this country?"

He leaned on his axe and thought a moment. Then he said, "I became a Tin Woodman because I loved a Munchkin maiden. I would like to go back to the Land of the East and marry her." ♦

Glinda said to the Tin Woodman, "My second command to the Winged Monkeys will be to carry you safely to the Land of the East so that you may find your maiden."

Then the Witch looked at the big, shaggy Lion and asked, "When Dorothy has returned to her own home, what will become of you?"

The Lion answered, "There is a grand old forest where I used to live and be the king. If I could only get back to that forest, I would be very happy there."

Glinda said, "My third command to the Winged Monkeys will be to carry you to your forest. Then, since I will have used up the powers of the golden cap, I will give it to the King of the Monkeys so that he and his band may be free at last."

The Scarecrow and the Tin Woodman and the Lion thanked the good Witch Glinda earnestly for her kindness. Dorothy exclaimed, "You are certainly as good as you are beautiful! But you have not yet told me how to get back to Kansas."

"Your silver shoes will carry you over the desert," replied Glinda. "If you had known their power, you could have gone back to your Aunt Em the very first day you came to this country."

"But then I would not have had my wonderful brains!" cried the Scarecrow. "I might have passed my whole life in the farmer's cornfield."

"And I would not have had my lovely heart," said the Tin Woodman. "I might have stood and rusted in the forest until the end of the world."

"And I would have been a coward forever," declared the Lion. "And no beast in all the forest would have had a good word to say to me."

"This is all true," said Dorothy. "But now that each of my friends has what he wanted most, I think I would like to go back to Kansas."

"The silver shoes," said the good Witch, "have wonderful powers. One of the most curious things about them is that they can carry you to any place in the world in the wink of an eye. All you have to do is to knock the heels together three times and command the shoes to carry you wherever you want to go."

"If that is so," said Dorothy, "I will ask them to carry me back to Kansas at once."

She threw her arms around the Lion's neck and kissed him, patting his big head tenderly. Next she kissed the Tin Woodman, who was weeping in a way that was very dangerous to his joints. Then she hugged the soft, stuffed body of the Scarecrow in her arms. Dorothy felt very sad at the thought of leaving her good friends.

At last Dorothy picked up Toto and said one final goodbye to her companions. Then she clapped the heels of her shoes together three times, saying, "Take me home to Aunt Em and Uncle Henry!"

Instantly she was whirling through the air, so swiftly that all she could feel was the wind whistling past her ears. The next moment, she noticed that she was rolling on the ground. She sat up and looked around her.

"Oh, my!" she cried. She was sitting on the broad Kansas prairie, and just in front of her was the new farmhouse Uncle Henry had built after the cyclone carried away the old one. Uncle Henry was milking the cows in the barnyard. Toto instantly jumped out of Dorothy's arms and ran toward the barn, whisking his tail from side to side.

Dorothy stood up and found she was in her stocking feet, for the silver shoes had fallen off in her flight through the air and were lost forever in the desert.

Aunt Em had just come out of the house to water the cabbages. She looked up and saw Dorothy running toward her.

"My darling child!" she cried, hugging Dorothy. "Where in the world did you come from?"

"From the Land of Oz," said Dorothy gravely. "And here is Toto, too. And oh, Aunt Em! I'm so glad to be home again!"

---

# C COMPREHENSION

Write the answers.
1. Why did the Scarecrow want to return to the Emerald City?
2. Why did the Tin Woodman want to return to the Land of the East?
3. Why did the Lion want to return to the forest?
4. What was the power of the silver shoes?
5. How did Dorothy feel about leaving the Land of Oz?

# D WRITING

Pretend you are Dorothy. Write a paragraph that explains two or three important things you learned from your visit to the Land of Oz. Be sure your paragraph answers the following questions:
- What is one important thing you learned?
- Where and how did you learn that thing?
- How will you use that thing back in Kansas?
- What is another important thing you learned?

# Unit 2

# The World of Animals

Ducks, horses, cats, dogs, snakes, goldfish, goats, frogs . . . the list of animals goes on and on. They live all over the world—in the mountains, the oceans, the forests, and the plains.

In this unit, you will read short stories, poems, and articles about many different animals. They look different, they sound different, and they act in different ways. At the same time, they are all alike. They all move, they all breathe, and they all need to eat. Most important, they are all alive.

The Ugly Duckling

A Horse to Remember

The Cat That Walked by Himself

Buck

Adventure on the Rocky Ridge

# 31

## A HYPHENS

Sometimes, words that appear at the end of a printed line are too long to fit on that line, so only the first part of the word appears on the line. That part is followed by a hyphen, which is a mark that looks like this: - .

The rest of the word appears at the beginning of the next line. The following passage includes words that run from the end of one line to the beginning of the next line.

That morning Dorothy kissed the pretty green girl goodbye. Then the four travelers walked through the Emerald City toward the gate. When the guard saw them approaching, he knew that they were planning to go on a new adventure. As he unlocked their green spectacles, he congratulated the Scarecrow, who was now the ruler of the city. The guard smiled and gladly shook the Scarecrow's hand.

## B READING

# Open Range
## *by Kathryn and Byron Jackson*

Prairie goes to the mountain,
    Mountain goes to the sky.
The sky sweeps across to the distant hills
And here, in the middle,
    Am I.

Hills crowd down to the river,
    River runs by the tree.
Tree throws its shadow on sunburnt grass
And here, in the shadow,
    Is me.

Shadows creep up the mountain,
    Mountain goes black on the sky,
The sky bursts out with a million stars
And here, by the campfire,
    Am I.

# A WORD LISTS

| 1 | 2 | 3 |
|---|---|---|
| *Word Practice* | *Vocabulary Review* | *New Vocabulary* |
| 1. snarling | 1. extend | 1. reeds |
| 2. worry | 2. chorus | 2. ease |
| 3. braid | 3. hush | 3. echo |
| 4. worries | 4. utter | 4. bruise |
| 5. fierce | 5. disgusting | |
| 6. duckling | | |
| 7. valley | | |
| 8. blossom | | |
| 9. swan | | |

# B HYPHENS

1. Name this mark: -
2. Read the hyphenated words in the passage below.

The sun was bright as the friends slowly turned toward the Land of the Quadlings. They were all cheerful and chatted happily. Dorothy was almost certain she would get home, and the Woodman smiled at her. The Lion was wagging his tail back and forth. He was joyful to be outside again. Toto was chasing butterflies, jumping, and barking merrily all the time.

# The Ugly Duckling
### *by Hans Christian Andersen*
## Chapter 1

It was summer, and the valley was beautiful. The wheat was yellow, the oats were green, and the hay was golden. A river flowed through the valley, next to riverbanks that were covered with tall reeds.

It was under those reeds that a mother duck had built herself a warm nest and was now sitting all day on six eggs. Five of them were white, but the sixth, which was larger than the others, was an ugly gray color. The duck was puzzled about the egg and couldn't understand why it was so different from the rest. She often wondered if another bird had slipped the egg in while she was swimming in the river. But ducks are neither clever nor good at counting. So this duck did not worry herself about the egg but just made sure that it was as warm as the rest.

Because this set of eggs was the first one the duck had ever laid, she was very pleased and proud, even though she was tired of sitting in her nest. However, she knew that if she left her eggs, the ducklings inside them might die. So she stayed in her nest, getting off the eggs several times a day only to see if the shells were cracking.

The mother duck had looked at the eggs at least a hundred and fifty times when to her joy she saw tiny cracks on two of them. She quickly drew the eggs closer to each other. Then she sat on them for the rest of the day.

The next morning, she noticed cracks in all the white eggs, and by midday, two little heads were poking from the shells. She broke the shells with her bill so that the little ducklings could get out of them. Then she sat steadily for a whole night upon the others. Before the sun arose, the five white eggs were empty, and five pairs of eyes were gazing out upon the green world.

The mother duck felt delighted to have some other ducks to talk to until the last egg hatched. But day after day went by, and the big egg showed no signs of cracking. The duck grew more and more impatient.

"This egg is a real problem," the duck grumbled to her neighbor one day. "Why, I could have hatched ten eggs in the time that this one has taken."

"Let me look at it," said the neighbor. "Ah, I thought so; it is a turkey's egg. Once, when I was young, I was tricked into sitting on a nest of turkey eggs, and when they were hatched, the birds were so stupid that I could not even teach them how to swim." ♦

"Well, I will give this big egg another chance," sighed the mother duck, "but if the duckling does not come out of its shell in another twenty-four hours, I will just leave it alone and teach the rest of my ducklings how to swim properly and how to find their own food. I really can't be expected to do two things at once." And with a fluff of her feathers, she pushed the egg into the middle of the nest.

All through the next day she sat on the big egg, even giving up her morning bath for fear that a blast of cold air might strike the egg. In the evening, when she looked at the egg, she thought she saw a tiny crack in the upper part of the shell. She was so filled with hope that she could hardly sleep all night. When the sun rose, she felt something stirring under her. Yes, there it was at last, and as she moved, a big awkward bird tumbled headfirst onto the ground.

The duckling was quite ugly. The mother looked with surprise at his long clumsy neck and the dull brown feathers that covered his back. He did not look at all like the little yellow ducklings who were playing in the nest.

The old neighbor came over the next day to look at the new duckling. "No, it is not a young turkey," she said to the mother. "It is skinny and brown, but there is something rather beautiful about it, and it holds its head up well."

"It is very kind of you to say so," answered the mother. "Of course, when you see the duckling by itself, it seems all right. But when I compare it with the others, I can see how different it is. However, I cannot expect all my children to be beautiful."

Later that day, the mother and her ducklings went down to a clearing by the river. Some full-grown ducks were swimming in the river, and others were waddling around and quacking in chorus. ★

One large duck quacked much louder than the rest, and when he saw the ugly duckling, he said, in a voice that seemed to echo, "I have never seen anything as ugly as that great tall duckling. He is a disgrace. I shall go and chase him away." And he ran up to the brown duckling and bit his neck, making a small bruise.

The ugly duckling gave out a loud quack because this was the first time he had felt any pain. His mother turned around quickly.

"Leave him alone," she said fiercely to the loud duck. "What has he done to you?"

"Nothing," answered the duck. "He is just so disgusting that I can't stand him!"

Although the ugly duckling did not understand the meaning of the loud duck's words, he felt he was being blamed for something. He became even more uncomfortable when the loud duck said, "It certainly is a great shame that he is so different from the rest of us. Too bad he can't be hatched over again."

The poor little fellow dropped his head and did not know what to do, but he was comforted when his mother answered, "He may not be quite as handsome as the others, but he swims with ease, and he is very strong. I am sure he will make his way in the world as well as anybody."

"I doubt it," said the loud duck as he waddled off.

Life was very hard for the duckling after that day. He was snapped at by the big ducks when they thought his mother was not looking. Even his brothers and sisters mocked him. Yet they would not have noticed how different he was if they hadn't heard the loud duck's complaints.

The ugly duckling became sadder and sadder. At last he could bear it no longer and decided to run away. So one night when the other ducks were asleep, he slipped quietly out of the nest and made his way through the reeds.

---

## D COMPREHENSION

Write the answers.
1. Where do you think the big egg came from? Explain your answer.
2. Why did the mother duck almost give up on the big egg?
3. The mother duck said, "When you see the duckling by itself, it seems all right." Explain what she meant.
4. What was the main reason that the loud duck disliked the ugly duckling?
5. Why did the duckling decide to run away?

## E WRITING

The other ducks dislike the ugly duckling just because he is different. Do you think that people might also dislike someone just because he or she is different?
• Write a paragraph that explains your answer.

## 33

## A WORD LISTS

**1**
*Word Practice*
1. blow
2. scratch
3. strangle
4. bowl
5. stretch
6. struggle

**2**
*New Vocabulary*
1. reflection
2. moss

## B HYPHENS

1. Name this mark: -
2. Read the hyphenated words in the passage below.

In the morning, they traveled until they reached a forest. There was no way of going around it. It seemed to extend to the right and left farther than they could see. However, the Woodman and the Scarecrow left the group and soon discovered a way to enter the forest.

# The Ugly Duckling
## Chapter 2

The ugly duckling walked for a long time that night. At last he reached a wide plain, full of soft, mossy places where the reeds grew. Here he rested, but he was too tired and too frightened to fall asleep. The reeds began to move when the sun rose, and the duckling saw that he had accidentally ventured into a group of wild geese.

"It does not matter to us what you look like," said the wild geese after they had looked him over. "You are welcome to stay here."

So for two whole days the duckling lay quietly among the reeds, eating what food he could find and drinking the marsh water until he felt strong again. He wanted to stay where he was forever because he was so comfortable and happy away from the other ducks with nobody to bite him and tell him how ugly he was.

He was thinking about how contented he was when two young geese saw him. They were having their evening splash among the reeds, looking for their supper.

"We are tired of this place," they said. "Tomorrow we will fly to another place, where the lakes are larger and the food is better. Will you come with us?"

"Is it nicer than this place?" asked the duckling doubtfully. The words were hardly out of his mouth when two shots rang out, and the two geese were stretched dead before him.

At the sound of the gun, the rest of the wild geese flew into the air. For a few minutes, the firing continued. While the shooting was going on, the ugly duckling, who could not fly, waddled along through the shallow water. He had gone just a few feet when he noticed a dog standing on the bank gazing at him, with a long, red tongue hanging out of its mouth. The duckling grew cold with terror and tried to hide his head beneath his little wings. But the dog sniffed at him and trotted away.

"I am so ugly that dogs won't eat me," the duckling said to himself. Then he hid in some tall reeds and curled up in the soft grass until the shots died away in the distance. ♦

The duckling stayed in the reeds for several months. For a while, he was quite happy and content, but winter was approaching. Snow began to fall, and everything became wet and uncomfortable.

One day in late fall, the sun was setting like a great scarlet globe, and the river, to the duckling's amazement, was getting hard and slippery. The duckling heard a sound of whirring wings. High up in the air a flock of swans flew by. They were as white as the snow that had fallen during the night, and their long necks with yellow bills were stretched toward the south. They were going to a land that was warm in the winter. Oh, if only the duckling could have gone with them! But that was not possible, of course. Besides, what sort of companion would an ugly duckling like him be to those beautiful swans?

Every morning grew colder and colder, and the duckling had to work hard to keep himself warm. Soon, he was never warm.

After one bitterly cold night, he discovered that he could not move his legs and that his feathers were frozen to his body. The duckling's life might have ended that day, but a man walked through the reeds and saw what had happened. He picked up the duckling and tucked him under his sheepskin coat, where the bird's frozen feathers began to thaw a little.

Instead of going on to his work, the man turned back and took the duckling to his children, who gave the bird something to eat. Then they put him in a box by the fire before they went to school. When the children returned from school, the duckling was much more comfortable than he had been in a long time. They were kind children and wanted to play with him, but the duckling had never played in his life. He thought the children were trying to tease him, so he ran straight out the door and hid himself in the snow among the bushes at the back of the house.

He never could remember exactly how he spent the rest of the winter. He only knew that he was very cold and that he never had enough to eat. But eventually things grew better. The earth became softer, and the sun felt hotter. The birds sang, and the flowers once more appeared in the grass. When the duckling stood up, he felt different than he had ever felt before. His body seemed larger and his wings stronger. Something pink looked at him from the side of a hill. He thought he would fly toward it and see what it was. He spread his wings, and in a moment, he was flying. ★

Oh, how glorious it felt to be rushing through the air, wheeling first one way and then the other! He had never thought that flying could be like that! The duckling was almost sorry when he drew near the pink thing and found that it was only a small apple tree covered with pink blossoms. The apple tree was beside a cottage. Behind the cottage, a garden ran down to the banks of a river.

The duckling fluttered slowly to the ground and paused for a few minutes near the river. As he was gazing around, a group of swans walked slowly by. The duckling remembered the swans he had seen so many months ago. He watched them with great interest. One by one, they stepped into the river and floated quietly upon the water as if they were a part of it.

"I will follow them," said the duckling to himself. "As ugly as I am, I would rather be killed by the swans than suffer all I have suffered from the cold and from the ducks who have treated me so poorly." And he flew quickly down to the water and swam after them as fast as he could.

It did not take him long to reach the

swans, for they had stopped to rest in a green pool shaded by a tree. As soon as they saw him coming, some of the younger swans swam out to meet him with cries of welcome. The duckling hardly understood these cries. He approached the swans gladly, yet he was trembling.

The duckling turned to one of the older birds and said, "If I am to die, I would rather have you kill me. I don't know why I was ever hatched, for I am too ugly to live." And as he spoke, he bowed his head and looked down into the water.

Reflected in the still pool he saw many white shapes with long necks and golden bills. He looked for his dull brown body and his awkward skinny neck. But no such body was there. Instead, he saw a beautiful white swan beneath him. With great amazement, he spread his wings and looked at his reflection in the water.

Just then, some children ran up to the river, and they threw bread into the water. "Look at that pretty new swan," one of them said. "He is the most beautiful of them all."

And when the duckling had seen his true self at last, he felt that all his suffering had been worth it. Otherwise, he would never have known what it was like to be really happy.

# D COMPREHENSION

Write the answers.
1. Why would the duckling have been happy to stay with the wild geese?
2. How did the duckling feel when he saw the swans flying south before the winter set in?
3. Even before he saw his reflection, the duckling noticed that he had changed. In what ways had he changed?
4. How else could the duckling have discovered that he was really a swan?
5. At the end of the story, why did the duckling feel that all his suffering had been worth it?

# E WRITING

Write a short story that is like "The Ugly Duckling," except make the main character a boy or a girl. Explain how the boy or girl feels about being ugly. Then explain what happens in the end.

# A WORD LISTS

**1**

*Hard Words*
1. England
2. London
3. Derick
4. ridiculous

**2**

*Word Practice*
1. sway
2. disbelief
3. inexpensive
4. swayed

**3**

*New Vocabulary*
1. alert
2. nag
3. pasture
4. develops
5. plod
6. Thoroughbred
7. nudge

Scotland

UNITED KINGDOM

Northern Ireland

Ireland

England

Wales

London

Briggs Farm

# A Horse to Remember
## *by Luisa Miller*
## Chapter 1

Nobody knows exactly how Nellie developed her bad habit, but she developed it. And nothing that Mr. Briggs or Tara did seemed to break her of the habit. The Briggs family lived in England on a small farm about fifty miles from London.

The farm was too small to keep **Mr.** Briggs and his family busy all the time, so Mr. Briggs had a full-time job on the railroad, and Mrs. Briggs worked for the telephone company. They took care of the small farm in their spare time. Tara, their eleven-year-old daughter, also helped them.

Because the farm was so small, the Briggs family didn't own a tractor. Instead, they used horses to plow the fields in the spring. That's why they had Nellie. They had bought Nellie when she was three years old. She wasn't a very good-looking horse. She was a large gray horse with tiny black spots. Her legs were heavy and her back was swayed.

When Nellie was only three, she already looked like a ten-year-old horse. But the Briggses thought she would be well-suited to their needs. Nellie was gentle. She loved to have somebody ride her. She was a good worker, and in most situations, she obeyed well.

During the planting season, Mr. Briggs or Tara would harness Nellie to the plow

with their other horse, Derick. He was a large brown horse who looked handsome when he stood alone in the fields or rested in the small barn next to the house. He looked at least twice as handsome when he was hitched to the plow with Nellie. Derick looked straight and tall and alert, but Nellie looked like an old swaybacked nag.

Although Nellie behaved well in most situations, she had her bad habit. That habit was jumping fences.

The first time the Briggses found out about this habit was during a thunderstorm that occurred one summer night. Nellie was four years old at the time. Tara was looking out the kitchen window at the bending trees and the driving rain. From time to time, a brilliant flash of lightning would streak through the sky and make things appear to be as bright as day. Following each flash would come a terrible crash of thunder.

It was during one of these flashes that Tara noticed Nellie standing right outside the house. She was eating flowers from the flower garden next to the kitchen door. Tara called to her mother, "Nellie got out of the pasture."

"You must have left the gate open," her mother replied.

Tara put on her raincoat, went outside,

and led Nellie back to the small pasture that surrounded the barn. But when Tara approached the gate, she noticed that it was firmly bolted. She led Nellie through the pasture, then walked around the entire pasture, checking the fence to make sure it had not blown down.

The fence was in perfect condition. It was over four feet high, and it was made of strong wire mesh. When Tara went inside, she reported to her mother the condition of the gate and the fence. Then she added, "I don't know how she got out, Mom. The only possible way would be to jump over the fence, but . . ."

Tara's voice trailed off. The idea of Nellie jumping a fence was ridiculous.

Mr. and Mrs. Briggs didn't think that Nellie could jump that high either—until a few minutes later, when they saw Nellie once more nibbling on flowers in the garden next to the kitchen door.

Tara's father asked, "Are you sure you checked the entire fence, Tara?"

"Every part of it," Tara replied.

Mr. Briggs shook his head gravely. His expression was one of disbelief. "Perhaps I'd better have a look at it myself," he said and reached for his raincoat. Mrs. Briggs was also curious about Nellie's strange escapes, so she went outside with her husband and Tara.

Mr. Briggs led Nellie back through the pasture, bolted the gate carefully, and walked around the entire pasture, shining a flashlight on every part of the fence. It was in perfect condition. He shook his head and said, "If this isn't the strangest thing . . ."

Before Mr. Briggs could finish his

statement, a brilliant bolt of lightning brightened the sky. The bolt was followed by another and another. To the wonder of the Briggs family, they saw how Nellie had escaped from the pasture. There she was, in a moment of dazzling bright light, looking as if she was frozen in midair, easily jumping over the top of the fence.

"I don't believe it!" Mr. Briggs exclaimed. Tara said nothing. She was still staring into the darkness at the spot where Nellie had been caught in the light. Two things amazed Tara. The first was that Nellie—plodding, swaybacked Nellie—could jump like that. Tara had never seen any horse jump so high, not even the mayor's horse, which was a handsome Thoroughbred that looked shimmering red-brown when he stood in the sunlight.

The other thing that amazed Tara was that when she saw Nellie frozen in the air, Nellie didn't look like an old plow horse. She looked very graceful, with her front legs tucked up under her head and her back legs extended. She looked beautiful. ♦

Mr. Briggs didn't seem to appreciate Nellie's beauty. He said, "We've got a serious problem, I'm afraid." He called Nellie and led her back through the pasture, then into the barn, where he put her in a stall and attached a rope to her so she couldn't get out.

"I think the thunder frightens her," he explained. "Whenever it looks like rain, we're going to have to tie her up in the barn."

The plan worked for a while, until one stormy day when Nellie figured out how to bite through the rope. The side door of the barn didn't close well. A few moments after biting through the rope, Nellie nudged the door open, trotted into the pasture, jumped the fence, and went straight to the flower garden.

At first, Nellie jumped the fence only during thunderstorms. But within two months of her first escape, she began jumping fences whenever she was alone for more than a few minutes. One time she jumped the pasture fence and the fence next to the road. She then jumped four fences on the neighboring farm and three fences on the next farm, finally stopping to eat in Mr. Fanning's vegetable garden. ★

After Tara rode Nellie back, put her in the barn, and tied her up, Tara's father said sternly, "I know you like Nellie. So do I, and so does your mother. But Nellie is becoming far too much of a problem. Unless we can figure out some inexpensive way of keeping her inside, we're going to have to get rid of her."

"Couldn't we make the fence higher?" Tara asked.

"It would be very expensive," her father explained. "The top wire of the fence is attached to the fence posts, but the posts don't go up more than a few inches beyond the top wire. So we'd have to put in new posts all the way around the pasture. I can't afford to do that."

Tara came up with other suggestions, but her father didn't approve of them. Then Mr. Briggs concluded, "Well, I hope we can come up with a solution. If we can't, Nellie must go."

# C COMPREHENSION

Write the answers.
1. How was Nellie's body different from the bodies of good-looking horses?
2. The story says, "The idea of Nellie jumping a four-foot fence was ridiculous." Why was it ridiculous?
3. When Tara saw Nellie jumping, she was amazed by two things. What were those things?
4. What was Mr. Briggs's opinion of Nellie? How was it different from Tara's opinion?
5. In what ways is Nellie like the ugly duckling?

# D WRITING

How do you think Tara could solve the problem with Nellie?
- Write a paragraph that describes your solution and explains how it would work.

# 35

## A WORD LISTS

| 1<br>Hard Words | 2<br>Word Family | 3<br>Vocabulary Review | 4<br>New Vocabulary |
|---|---|---|---|
| 1. encyclopedia | 1. mound | 1. nudge | 1. resist the impulse |
| 2. steeplechase | 2. loudly | 2. alert | 2. barrier and obstacle |
| 3. obstacles | 3. ground | 3. develop | 3. cock your head |
| 4. exhaustion | 4. mounted | | 4. blurt out |
| 5. endurance | 5. sound | | 5. stall |
| | 6. grouch | | 6. stray |
| | | | 7. exhausted |
| | | | 8. endurance |

## B READING

# A Horse to Remember
## Chapter 2

Tara's father had told her that the Briggs family might have to get rid of Nellie. As Tara prepared for bed that night, she felt discouraged. She kept thinking about possible ideas for keeping Nellie inside the pasture, but all the ideas cost money. Nellie couldn't stay tied up in her stall all day, but if Nellie was left alone in the pasture . . .

Tara got into bed and tried to sleep, but Nellie kept popping into her mind. And every time she thought about Nellie, Tara remembered the instant she first saw her leaping the fence.

Tara punched her pillow, rolled over angrily, and told herself that she had to come up with a solution to the problem. Suddenly, she sat upright in bed with a smile. An idea came to her with such force that she wondered why she hadn't thought of it before. "No horse can jump like that," she said aloud. "She's probably the greatest jumping horse in the world."

Tara had to resist the impulse to jump out of bed and tell her parents of the plan that was forming in her mind. But she controlled herself, thinking, "I'll get all the facts first, and then I'll tell them about it."

The morning after Tara got her marvelous idea, she woke up very early, when the sky was still dark, with just a hint of light along the horizon to the east. Tara was up early because she wanted to find out about jumping horses. Her family didn't own a computer, but they did have a few horse books on their living room shelves. Tara skimmed through those books, but they didn't have indexes, so it was hard to find what she was looking for.

Next she tried the old set of encyclopedias on the bottom shelf. First she looked in the index and found the entry for steeplechases. Then she turned to the article in the encyclopedia that told about steeplechases.

A steeplechase is a horse race, but horses in a steeplechase do not simply run around a mile-long track. They run farther, and they jump barriers and obstacles. Some barriers are wide ditches filled with water. Others include fences, hedges, and shelves. The shelves are the most dangerous. A horse must leap from a mound and land on ground that is three or four feet lower than the mound.

From the encyclopedia article, Tara learned that younger horses are not permitted to compete in steeplechases because the bones in their legs are still growing. If they broke a leg bone, they might never be able to run again.

As Tara read more about steeplechases, she began to have serious doubts about whether her idea was as good as she thought. Part of the encyclopedia article told about the Grand National Steeplechase Championship that was held each year. The

Water barrier

Fence

Hedge

Shelf

article said that sometimes as many as fifty horses enter the competition, but usually no more than a few are able to finish. Some horses fall from exhaustion. Some fail to make one of the thirty jumps in the four-and-a-half-mile course. Some throw their riders and continue without them.

The article did provide Tara with some good news. Horses that run in steeplechases do not have to be Thoroughbreds. Usually, the only requirement is that a horse must be at least four years old. According to the article, "The horses that win this event are usually large horses with tremendous endurance." The article also pointed out that Thoroughbreds are sometimes entered in steeplechases, but the most successful horses are only part Thoroughbred. The other part may be Arabian. ◆

Tara looked out the window after reading the description. The eastern sky was now bright, and the roosters in the barn were beginning to crow loudly. She was just about ready to forget the idea of training Nellie to be a jumping horse, when Mrs. Briggs padded down the stairs in her bare feet. "What are you reading so early in the morning?" she asked.

As Tara explained, her mother smiled and cocked her head. "I've never seen a horse that could jump like Nellie, but I'm sure there are lots of them. Some very rich people do nothing but raise horses for steeplechases. It wouldn't surprise me if a lot of them could outjump our old Nellie."

"She's not that old," Tara objected. "She's only four years old."

"I know," her mother said thoughtfully. Then she snapped her fingers and said, "Why don't you talk to Mr. Jones, the blacksmith? He used to make shoes for steeplechase horses when he lived in Liverpool.

I'm sure he could tell you a lot about the chances that Nellie might have as a jumping horse."

• • •

Tara had never talked much with Mr. Jones because he seemed to be a grouchy person who always complained about things. But after she had finished her chores, she rode Nellie down the road to the village. She knew that Mr. Jones was making horseshoes in his blacksmith's shop because she could hear the ringing of his hammer on red-hot metal from several blocks away.

When Tara arrived at the large open door of the blacksmith's shop, she stayed on Nellie's back and waited for Mr. Jones to look up. Then Tara blurted out, "I want to know what I'd have to do to make Nellie a jumping horse and if she's good enough to compete in steeplechases." ★

Mr. Jones had been hammering on a red-hot horseshoe that he held with a long pair of tongs. He dipped the shoe into a bucket of water and waited until the sizzling sound stopped. Then he took an old rag from his pocket and wiped the sweat from his face. He studied Nellie for a few moments, then smiled. "Why would you want to make her a jumping horse?" he asked at last.

Before Tara could answer, Mr. Jones continued, "She's a plow horse, not the kind of horse that is used in steeplechases."

"But she can jump like no horse I've ever seen," Tara said.

"Oh, can she now?" Mr. Jones asked in a doubting tone. He wiped his hands on the old rag and said, "I'll tell you what I'll do. If you can show me that she can jump, I'll help you train her. But I'm not going to be responsible for any injuries."

Mr. Jones began looking around for a pole that he could use as a jumping barrier. He talked to himself as he searched through his workshop. "I'll have to make it about four feet high," he said.

Tara said, "Your fence out back is about that high. Why don't we just have Nellie jump that fence?"

"No," Mr. Jones replied firmly. "I'm having no part of that poor old nag getting torn up on my fence."

"Here," Tara said, getting down from Nellie's back. "She won't get hurt. Let me show you." Before Mr. Jones could object, Tara climbed over the fence and ran into the field beyond. Then she turned and called, "Come on, Nellie."

The horse looked up quickly and trotted toward the fence. Just as Mr. Jones started to say, "But she can't . . . ," Nellie cleared the fence with a foot to spare.

Tara smiled and patted Nellie on the nose, but Mr. Jones didn't smile. He stood there with his mouth hanging open and his dirty rag in his hand. His eyes were wide. "I don't believe it," he said.

# C COMPREHENSION

Write the answers.

1. Why do you think Tara wanted to get all the facts before she told her parents about her plan for Nellie?
2. Explain at least two ways that steeplechases are different from regular horse races.
3. After Tara read about steeplechases, she began to have doubts about her idea. Why do you think she had doubts?
4. What was Mr. Jones's attitude toward Nellie when he first saw her?
5. Why did his attitude change at the end of the chapter?

# D WRITING

Do you think Nellie would be a good steeplechase horse?

• Write a paragraph that explains your answer. Give examples to support your opinion.

# A WORD LISTS

| 1 | 2 | 3 | 4 |
|---|---|---|---|
| *Hard Words* | *Word Practice* | *Vocabulary Review* | *New Vocabulary* |
| 1. anvil | 1. demonstrate | 1. blurt out | 1. brace yourself |
| 2. Arabian | 2. select | 2. resist the impulse | 2. abruptly |
| 3. abruptly | 3. encyclopedia | 3. barrier and obstacle | 3. gallop |
| 4. county | 4. customer | 4. endurance | 4. dilapidated |
| 5. dilapidated | 5. mayor | 5. exhausted | 5. marvel |
| | 6. competition | | 6. spectators |
| | 7. thirty | | 7. mock |

# B READING

# A Horse to Remember
## Chapter 3

"A deal is a deal," Mr. Jones said after Tara demonstrated two more times that Nellie could clear the fence with ease. "I told you I would help you train her if she could jump. And train her I will."

"You don't really have to," Tara said. "I . . ."

Mr. Jones interrupted. "I'll also have to train a rider, you know. And I suppose that rider will be you."

"I'd love to be her rider," Tara said. "But you don't have to . . ."

"It's not a chore, Tara," the old man said. "When I worked with steeplechase horses, I always dreamed of having one of my own. I never did, of course, but I dreamed. And now I have a chance to do something more interesting than standing over an anvil, hammering out horseshoes, and fixing wheels."

"If you could train Nellie and me, I'd be very grateful," Tara said.

Mr. Jones grunted and then pointed at the horse. "You know, that horse is not what she seems to be when you first look at her. Her swayback makes you think she's a broken-down nag. But when you take a good look, she's as strong as an ox. Her legs

are good—maybe a little heavy, but good. And her color makes me think she may be part Arabian."

Later that day, Tara told her parents that Mr. Jones would help her work with Nellie each day. The rest of the time, Nellie would be tied up in the pasture or in the barn.

During the weeks that followed, Tara and Nellie spent a lot of time with Mr. Jones. Tara discovered that although Mr. Jones talked like a grouch, he was a very fine person.

Mr. Jones laid out a little course in the pasture behind his shop. He made four jumps, and each one was a little less than three feet high. He explained to Tara, "When you can stay on her as she goes over these jumps, we'll make them higher."

The jumps stayed at the same height for three weeks. During those weeks, Tara fell off Nellie and landed on the soft grass of the pasture more than twenty times. At first, she lost her balance when Nellie took off. Nellie seemed to fly upward suddenly. To stay on her, Tara had to lean far forward, with her head right against Nellie's neck. Tara found out about leaning forward the hard way. Four times, she didn't lean forward far enough, and when Nellie took off, Tara fell backward.

After Tara learned about leaning forward for Nellie's takeoff, she learned about bracing herself for the landing. The first time that she didn't fall off on the takeoff, she fell on the landing. She flew right over Nellie's head when Nellie landed, and Nellie almost stepped on her.

By the third day of practice, however, Tara was able to make most of the jumps without falling. But just about the time that Tara thought she had mastered the art of jumping, Nellie would fool her by jumping a little higher than Tara expected or by coming down a little more abruptly.

Several times, Tara had the wind knocked out of her. One time she hurt so much that she couldn't keep the tears from forming in her eyes. As she lay on her back after that fall, seeing spots in front of her eyes, Tara wondered whether she really wanted to become the rider of a jumping horse.

• • •

Before the first month of training had gone by, Mr. Jones raised the poles on the barriers half a foot. Two weeks later, they went up another half foot. Then the training moved from the pasture to a stream south of the village.

The banks of the stream were steep. In most places, the streambed was three or four feet lower than the banks. The stream covered only part of the streambed. The rest of the streambed was dry, flat, sandy land.

Mr. Jones selected a place where there was a wide, flat area below the banks. The streambed here was nearly thirty feet wide. The stream ran slowly next to one of the banks. The other bank was perfect for jumping. The sand below the perfect bank was soft, but not so soft that Nellie would sink into it when she landed.

First, Nellie jumped off the bank without a rider. Then Tara mounted her and got ready for jumping her first shelf. "Remember," Mr. Jones told her, "you'll have to lean way, way back when you land, or you'll go flying right over her head." ♦

Tara's heart was beating so loudly that she could hear it in her ears. "Come on, Nellie," she said and nudged her heels into the horse's belly. Nellie broke into a gentle run, took off at the edge of the bank, and sailed

gracefully to the sand below. Tara stayed on. "Good horse!" Tara shouted, and she felt very proud. When Nellie jumped, Tara felt like part of her. She seemed to know exactly where Nellie would land and how it would feel.

Mr. Jones was smiling. Then his expression quickly became serious. "Now try it with a fast run," he said.

Tara got off and led Nellie back up the bank. Then she got on again, rode Nellie about a hundred feet from the bank, and turned around. A few seconds later, she bent forward, gave Nellie a sharp nudge with her heels, and shouted, "Go, Nellie, go!"

Within two steps, Nellie was at a full gallop, going much faster than Tara had intended. She leaned forward, grabbed a handful of Nellie's mane with her right hand, and hung on. Nellie took one great leap from the bank, sailed over the entire streambed, and landed on the other bank.

Somehow, Tara managed to stay on until Nellie abruptly stopped after landing. Nellie stopped right in front of a row of thick bushes, and Tara went sailing into them.

As Tara walked away from the bushes, brushing herself off, Mr. Jones came toward her in a waddling run. "Tara, are you all right?" he asked. ★

Tara nodded her head. In an angry tone, Mr. Jones shook his finger at Nellie and hollered, "You! You are the most amazing horse I have ever seen in my life. You are the greatest jumping horse that ever

lived!" Then Mr. Jones's face broke into a broad, wrinkled smile. "Amazing!" he shouted. "Amazing!"

When Nellie, Tara, and Mr. Jones returned to the blacksmith shop, an angry customer met them. It was the mayor. Mr. Jones had promised to have the mayor's tractor wheel repaired that day. "I'm sorry," Mr. Jones said flatly. "But I won't get it done until next week. I'm busy training Nellie here to be a steeplechase champion."

The mayor laughed and said, "You've been working around hot fires too much, Elmer, if you think you'll ever make anything out of that nag."

"Is that so?" Mr. Jones said as he approached the mayor. "Well, I've just about decided to have Tara enter Nellie in the county steeplechase next month."

"Are you quite serious?" the mayor demanded. "There will be some fine horses in that race. In fact, I'm entering one of my own. You couldn't possibly think that poor old Nellie could stand a chance in that competition."

"Tell you what I'll do," Mr. Jones said. "If Nellie does not win, I'll fix your tractor wheel for free."

The mayor laughed and shook his head. "If you're fool enough to repair the wheel for nothing, I'm not going to argue with you."

Mr. Jones turned to Tara and stared at her with a stern expression. Suddenly, he winked.

# C COMPREHENSION

Write the answers.
1. What reasons did Mr. Jones have for helping Tara train Nellie?
2. At the beginning of the training, the jumps were less than three feet high. What did Tara have to show before Mr. Jones raised the jumps?
3. During training, Tara wondered if she really wanted to become a rider of a jumping horse. Why did she feel that way?
4. Why did Mr. Jones think that Nellie was the greatest jumping horse ever?
5. At the end of the chapter, Mr. Jones made a deal with the mayor. Do you think that was a good deal for Mr. Jones? Why or why not?

# D WRITING

Pretend you are riding Nellie when she jumps all the way across the stream.
• Write a paragraph that describes what happens and how you feel.

# 37

## A WORD LISTS

**1**

*Hard Words*
1. official
2. circular
3. triangular
4, Rudy
5. reins
6. numb

**2**

*Word Practice*
1. decorate
2. Arabian
3. fiftieth
4. hooves

**3**

*Vocabulary Review*
1. brace yourself
2. mock
3. abruptly
4. gallop
5. dilapidated
6. marvel
7. spectators

**4**

*New Vocabulary*
1. mount a horse
2. officials
3. shabby
4. numb

## B READING

# A Horse to Remember
## Chapter 4

The county racetrack was about twenty miles from the Briggs farm. Mr. Jones pulled Nellie's horse trailer with his dilapidated truck. He drove as Tara sat next to him. Tara's mother and father followed in their car, along with two boys from Tara's school. A third vehicle followed the Briggs car. It was packed with seven neighbors. All of them had seen Nellie jump, and they had marveled over her ability.

Before they left, one of the neighbors shouted, "You'll hear some cheers for old Nellie even if she doesn't win."

Mr. Jones responded coldly, "She'll win."

The steeplechase at the county racetrack was a colorful affair. Just before the contest was to begin, Tara became so nervous that she didn't think she'd be able to ride. She was confused, and her mind seemed to go numb. Officials for the race examined the horse, asked Tara questions, and had Mr. Jones and Tara's father fill out some forms. Then one official said, "Well, she's a strong horse. She might even finish the race."

Tara didn't answer the official. She smiled politely, feeling embarrassed. She was wearing a shiny green shirt and a pair of riding boots that were too big for her. She wore a helmet and motorcycle goggles that she had found in Mr. Jones's shop. Her outfit looked shabby compared to the ones the other riders wore.

Nellie looked even shabbier compared to the other horses. Some of them were so beautiful that they gave Tara chills. One great horse was as white as snow. Another was as black as night. That horse was probably the most beautiful. When it moved, it glistened, and every muscle in its fine body seemed to ripple with power.

Tara tried to keep Nellie away from the other horses that were prancing about. From time to time, one of the riders would look over at Nellie and smile.

Before leaving the farm, Tara had decorated Nellie's neck with ribbons of green silk. When she put the ribbons on, she thought that Nellie looked pretty. But now she thought Nellie looked silly. "We'll show them," she said softly to her horse, but she knew that Nellie must have looked strange in the company of these other horses.

There were about a thousand spectators, most of them gathered near the finish line. As handlers led the horses to the starting line, an announcement came over the loudspeakers. "Ladies and gentlemen," the announcer said, "welcome to the county steeplechase. As you know, this is a one-mile circular course with five jumps. The horses go around the course three times."

The announcer continued, "For a horse to finish, it must be successful in clearing all fifteen jumps and must still have a rider

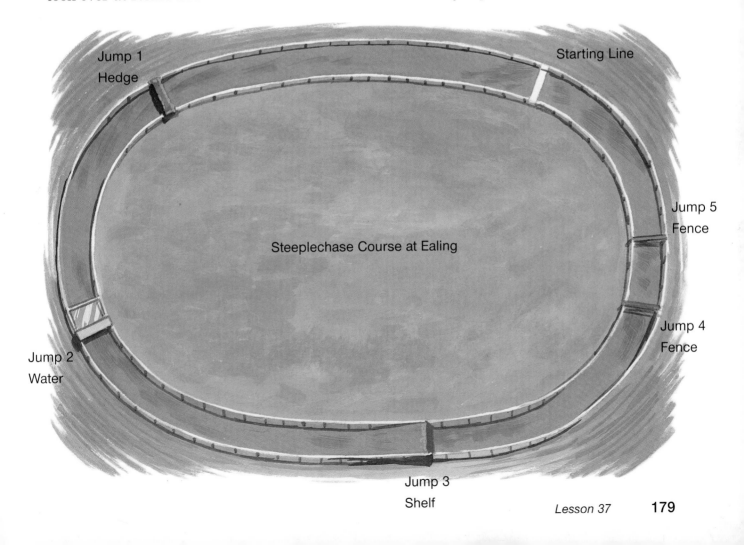

Jump 1
Hedge

Starting Line

Jump 5
Fence

Steeplechase Course at Ealing

Jump 4
Fence

Jump 2
Water

Jump 3
Shelf

at the end of the course. A rider who falls may remount and continue running the course. The hardest parts of the course are the two fence jumps. Both fences are slightly more than five feet high, and they are spaced close together. The horse must clear the first and within a few strides get ready for the second. In a few moments, the race will begin."

A handler led Nellie to the starting line and stood next to the horse. Tara judged that there were more than twenty-five horses in this race. She put on her motorcycle goggles and looked at the other horses. She could see the mayor's horse with the mayor's oldest son on its back. The mayor's son shouted to Tara, "You'll need those goggles. Rudy here is going to throw a lot of mud in your face." He patted Rudy on the neck.

Tara was still trying to organize her thoughts when a terribly loud gun sounded. ♦

Nellie jumped and threw Tara. The other horses pounded across the soft ground, throwing chunks of grass and dirt into the air. Fortunately, Tara managed to hold on to the reins when she fell. Nellie wanted to run after the other horses, but Tara shouted, "Stop, Nellie! Stop!"

Nellie pulled Tara along the ground for a few steps; then she stopped calmly, waiting for Tara to mount her. Some of the spectators shouted mock encouragement to Tara. "You can still win!" one of them yelled, and a few people broke into loud laughter.

By the time Tara told Nellie, "Go Nellie! Run fast!" the other horses were so far ahead that Tara could no longer hear the pounding of their hooves. She bent forward and let Nellie run, but not as fast as Nellie wanted to run. Tara remembered what Mr. Jones had told her. "It's a long, tiring race, and a good horse will run until it drops dead. So you hold her in. Don't let her go at full speed."

Tara followed Mr. Jones's directions, but it seemed hopeless. The first jump was the hedge jump. One horse had fallen trying to go over this jump, and the rider was walking slowly back toward the starting line.

The other horses were already approaching the third jump when Nellie was clearing the first jump. For an instant, Tara's attention was drawn to the crowd near the first jump. Almost in one voice, they said "Ooooo" as Nellie cleared it. Now Tara could hear the people near the first jump applauding Nellie's performance.

At the second jump there was more applause. Two more horses were out of the race—one of them standing next to the jump, holding one of its front hooves off the ground. "I hope he's all right," Tara said to herself.

Then she heard part of an announcement over the loudspeakers. She couldn't hear it very well above the sound of squeaking leather, pounding hooves, and heavy breathing. From what she could hear, she gathered that the announcer was talking about Nellie. ★

Here's what Tara heard: ". . . call your attention to . . . She's worth watching . . . a long way behind, but possibly the best jumper in . . ."

The two fence jumps were at the end of the circle, jumps four and five. The crowd cheered wildly as Nellie sailed over these jumps. Three other horses hadn't cleared them.

Tara's mind was starting to clear now, and she was becoming more confident. As she started around the course the second time, she figured that there were only about ten horses left in the race. She was already catching some of them, including the mayor's horse and the brilliant white horse. But far ahead of these horses was the black horse. It was at least three jumps ahead of Nellie. She hadn't gained on that horse at all.

During the second round of the course, Nellie caught up to the mayor's horse at the second jump. Tara could see that the mayor's horse was tiring and straining, but Nellie was still running easily.

The second jump was a water jump about ten feet across. Nellie and the mayor's horse took off for the jump at exactly the same time. Nellie cleared the jump with at least five feet to spare. The mayor's horse got off a poor jump, landed with its front hooves in the water, stumbled, and fell forward, tossing the mayor's son from the saddle. Tara looked back. The mayor's son was sitting in the water. The horse was standing up.

Tara heard the loudspeakers. "Her name is Nellie," the announcer was saying, "and she jumps as if she has rockets in her feet."

Loud shouts of "Come on, Nellie!" came from the crowd.

Tara finished the second round of the course and started the third round. Nellie was starting to breathe very hard now, and Tara could feel her tug a little with each stride. She was tiring. But still the black horse was three jumps ahead of her.

## C COMPREHENSION

Write the answers.

1. Before the race began, Tara whispered to Nellie, "We'll show them." What did Tara mean?
2. Before the race began, what did the mayor's son think of Nellie? How do you know?
3. Do you think the mayor's son's opinion of Nellie changed during the race? Why or why not?
4. Why did the spectators say "Ooooo" when Nellie cleared the first jump?
5. Do you think that Nellie will win the race? Why or why not?

## D WRITING

Pretend you are riding a handsome horse next to Nellie.

• Write a paragraph that explains how your opinion of Nellie changes during the race.

## A WORD LISTS

| 1 | 2 | 3 |
|---|---|---|
| *Hard Words* | *Word Practice* | *New Vocabulary* |
| 1. concentrate | 1. familiar | 1. push a horse too hard |
| 2. photographer | 2. camera | 2. let a horse out |
| 3. idiot | 3. statue | 3. hold a horse in |
| 4. Kelvin | 4. Nighthawk | 4. caution |
| 5. caution | | 5. magnificent |
| 6. Liverpool | | 6. turf |
| | | 7. pound |

## B READING

# A Horse to Remember
## Chapter 5

Tara didn't want to push Nellie too hard, but she wanted her to win. Oh, how she wanted her to win! As Tara cleared the first jump on the third round, she heard a familiar voice above the cheering crowd. "Let her out Tara!" said the voice. "Let her out!" It was Mr. Jones's voice.

"Okay," Tara thought, and she bent forward. "A little faster, Nellie," she said. She nudged Nellie with her heels, and the horse responded by running a little faster.

Tara cleared the second jump and then looked ahead. She had now passed all the horses except one—the black horse—which was approaching the fourth jump. Nellie was gaining on the black horse, but all the black horse had to do to finish the race was to clear jumps four and five and then run to the finish line. Tara didn't think Nellie could make up the distance.

But Tara decided to try. She put her head right against Nellie's neck, out of the wind. She was concentrating on the third jump when she heard a loud roar from the crowd. After completing the jump, she looked toward the finish line. The black horse was approaching the finish line, but without a rider. The rider had fallen off at the fifth jump, and the brave horse had continued alone to the finish line.

Now the crowd was cheering wildly. Tara looked behind to see if any horses were gaining on Nellie. None were even near, so Tara held Nellie in a little bit. Nellie cleared the last two jumps with two easy leaps. The crowd roared with delight as Nellie—swaybacked Nellie—ran easily across the finish line.

Photographers pointed cameras at Tara and Nellie. Flash bulbs went off. Hundreds of people crowded around the tired horse. A wrinkled, smiling face pushed through the crowd. "I knew she could do it," Mr. Jones hollered, giving Nellie a big hug. Then he grabbed the reins, shouted at the crowd to move back, and began to walk the horse.

Tara jumped down, gave Nellie a big hug, and started walking next to Mr. Jones. Tara couldn't stop smiling, no matter how hard she tried and how many times she told herself she must look like a grinning idiot. She smiled and smiled and smiled.

Tara smiled all the way home. In her lap, she held the large first-prize trophy. It was silver, topped with a statue of a handsome horse leaping over a jump. Tara thought the horse on the trophy looked much more handsome than Nellie, but that didn't matter. Nellie was the greatest horse in the world.

Tara stopped smiling when Mr. Jones's truck pulled up in front of the blacksmith shop. A long, black, expensive-looking car was parked in front of the shop, and a tall man in a dark suit was standing next to the car. As Tara and Mr. Jones got out of the

truck, the man approached them. "I'm Kelvin Longly," he said in a pleasant voice. "I own Nighthawk, the black horse that would have beaten Nellie if he hadn't thrown his rider."

"That's a beautiful horse," Tara said. "I'm sorry for you that he didn't win."

Mr. Longly said, "I'll come right to the point. If you hadn't fallen at the starting line, you might have beaten Nighthawk. I don't like that kind of doubt. I bought Nighthawk because he was a winner. That's what I want, a winner. Because your horse may be the real winner, I want to buy her."

"I'm sorry," Tara said. "We couldn't sell her."

By now, the cars that had followed Mr. Jones's truck from the racetrack were parked, and everybody who had been riding in them was standing behind Tara and Mr. Jones. Tara's father said, "How much are you prepared to pay for Nellie?"

Tara was shocked, and she looked at her father. "But, Dad, . . ." she started to say.

"Tara," her father interrupted. "Let's hear what Mr. Longly has to say." ♦

Mr. Longly looked at Tara's father and said, "I paid fifty thousand pounds for Nighthawk, and I'm willing to pay the same amount for Nellie."

Tara's father earned less than twenty thousand pounds a year working for the railroad. The farm brought in another ten thousand pounds a year, but no more. So you can understand why Mrs. Briggs gasped when Mr. Longly made his offer for Nellie. She said, "Fifty thousand pounds is more money than we'll earn in . . ."

Mr. Briggs interrupted. "Well," he said. Then he faced Mr. Longly, and Tara noticed her father's hands were trembling.

"Well," Mr. Briggs repeated. "I think we have to talk this over with Tara. Would it be all right if I gave you a call later?"

"Certainly," Mr. Longly said. He handed Tara's father a card with his phone number on it. "Call me any time," he said pleasantly. Then he said farewell and got into the back seat of his car. Tara heard him tell the driver to go to Longly Place in London.

Tara was no longer smiling. She was stunned. As soon as the black car pulled away, she turned to her father and said, "But, Dad, you can't sell Nellie. She's the best . . ."

Mr. Briggs interrupted quietly. "Tara," he said, "we'll talk about it at home."

Mr. Jones pointed at Nellie and said, "I think Tara's right. That horse may be the best jumping horse that has ever lived."

"I respect your opinion," Mr. Briggs said, "but I'm not sure that we should try to keep anything as valuable as Nellie. If she's worth fifty thousand pounds, she should have an owner who can afford horses that are worth that much. I'm just a poor farmer."

"Oh, Dad, you can't . . ."

"Tara, we'll talk about it at home." ★

The thought of losing Nellie hurt so much that it almost broke Tara's heart. She ached with far more pain than she had experienced when she had fallen from Nellie's back. She couldn't believe her father would even think of selling Nellie.

Tara drove to the farm with Mr. Jones, who was silent during the trip. She just stared straight ahead as the old truck bounced down the road. Once Tara said, "He can't do that. It's not fair."

Without taking his eyes from the road, Mr. Jones said, "He's your father. You listen to what he says."

"I'll try," Tara said, almost choking. "I'll try."

When Mr. Jones pulled up in back of the house, he said, "You take care of Nellie. I'm going to say a few things to your father."

Tara led Nellie from the trailer, unbolted the gate, and stopped. She could hear Mr. Jones speaking loudly inside the house.

"If you knew anything about horses," Mr. Jones said, "you would know that your Nellie is worth much more than fifty thousand pounds. People pay that much for a steeplechase horse that has a chance of winning. Nellie has a lot more than a chance. She *will* win. I've seen horses sell for one hundred thousand pounds that couldn't stay within three jumps of Nellie. If you want to sell her, give her a chance to show what she can do. Then you can name your own price."

Tara could hear other voices, but she couldn't hear what they were saying. Slowly, she led Nellie into her stall. She gave Nellie a big hug and said, "You're the most beautiful horse in the world."

When she looked up, her father and Mr. Jones were standing at the barn door, smiling. Tara's father said, "Well, I guess we're going to have to keep old Nellie for a while."

Tara started smiling again.

---

# C COMPREHENSION

Write the answers.
1. Do you think Mr. Longly is rich? Explain your answer.
2. Why did Mr. Longly want to buy Nellie?
3. What reasons did Mr. Briggs have for selling Nellie?
4. How did Tara feel about selling Nellie?
5. What reasons did Mr. Jones give for keeping Nellie?

# D WRITING

Do you think the Briggses should sell Nellie?
- Write a paragraph that explains your answer. Give reasons for selling Nellie and reasons for keeping her.

# A WORD LISTS

### 1
*Word Family*
1. hedge
2. sledge
3. nudge
4. ledge

### 2
*Word Practice*
1. incredible
2. photographer
3. concentrate
4. microphone
5. photograph

### 3
*Word Practice*
1. urge
2. eighteenth
3. twenty
4. twentieth

### 4
*Vocabulary Review*
1. turf
2. caution
3. magnificent

### 5
*New Vocabulary*
1. lagging behind
2. prance
3. dangling
4. straining
5. frantically

# B READING

# A Horse to Remember
## Chapter 6

The Grand National Steeplechase is run on one of the most demanding steeplechase courses in the world. The course is shaped like a triangle. It has sixteen jumps. The distance around the triangular course is a little over two miles, and the horses must go around the course twice. The first time around, the horses must go over all sixteen jumps. The second time around, the horses go over only fourteen jumps. Altogether, the horses must run about four and a half miles and make thirty jumps.

Only those horses with incredible endurance can finish this demanding event, but a lot of horses try each year. They come from all over the world—from the United

States, France, Australia, Japan, and many other countries. Many horses that enter the competition are worth a lot of money. These horses are big and strong and have a great deal of endurance.

The Grand National takes place near the large city of Liverpool, which is about two hundred miles north of London.

• • •

By the time Nellie, Tara, Mr. Jones, and more than twenty neighbors from Tara's village made the long trip to Liverpool, people were no longer laughing at Nellie.

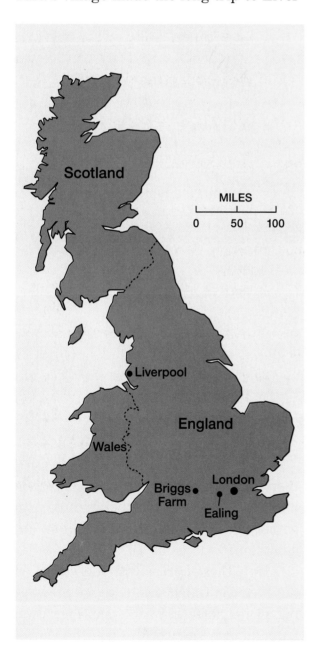

Nellie had entered two steeplechases after winning the county steeplechase. She won first prize in one of those contests. In the other contest, she was the first horse to cross the finish line, but she had thrown Tara on a hedge jump. Tara had tumbled to the ground without holding onto the reins, and Nellie had continued to the finish line without her. But when she had thrown Tara, Nellie was ahead of the other horses and was clearly the best jumping horse in the field.

Shortly before the trip to Liverpool, Mr. Longly had visited the Briggses and made another offer for Nellie. This time, he offered seventy thousand pounds, and he cautioned Tara, "You may be making a great mistake. Nellie is very good on these shorter courses, but Nighthawk has tremendous endurance. The rider was holding him in near the end of the county race when you were gaining on him. I know Nighthawk can run the four and a half miles at Liverpool. I honestly don't think your Nellie will be able to stay with him." ♦

The words Mr. Longly had said kept popping into Tara's mind as she rode to Liverpool in the cab of the truck. Tara had already practiced running a four-mile course with Nellie, and she had done very well; but the course used for the practice was not as difficult as the one at Liverpool. Some of the jumps at Liverpool were over five feet high, and there were many jumps.

This time, Tara was ready for the starting gun. She wore a smart green jacket and riding boots that fit. Nellie wore handsome green ribbons and the number 31. At the starting line, more than fifty horses lined up side by side. ★

On one side of Nellie was a handsome Arabian horse that was almost white, with just a hint of gray spots on its legs. On the other side was Nighthawk. Even in this field of magnificent horses, Nighthawk was still the most beautiful. He pranced and kicked at the turf with his front hooves as he shook his head and snorted.

Tara lowered the goggles that were attached to her new helmet, patted Nellie on the neck, and listened to the announcements. The announcer introduced each horse, told where it was from, and gave some information about it. When the announcer said, "And number thirty-one . . ." a tremendous roar went up from the crowd. The announcer told about Nellie's record in jumping contests and then said, "Nellie is one of the horses you should keep your eye on during this competition." The announcer then continued, "Another great horse you should watch is Nighthawk."

At last the announcer stopped. The thousands of people who had gathered to watch the competition became silent, the riders got ready and . . . the race began.

## C COMPREHENSION

Write the answers.
1. What qualities must a horse have to win the Grand National?
2. How had Nellie proved that she might be able to win the Grand National?
3. Why did Mr. Longly visit the Briggs family again?
4. Why do you think Mr. Longly said that Nellie had less endurance than Nighthawk?
5. Which horse do you think will win the race? Why?

## D WRITING

Pretend you are Tara at the beginning of the Grand National.
- Write a paragraph that describes what you are thinking. Tell about your hopes and fears.

## A WORD LISTS

### 1
*Hard Words*
1. advantage
2. domestic
3. relatives

### 2
*Word Family*
1. continued
2. developed
3. returned
4. domesticated

### 3
*Word Practice*
1. alligators
2. couple
3. receives

### 4
*Vocabulary Review*
1. lagging behind
2. frantically
3. straining
4. dangling

### 5
*New Vocabulary*
1. domestic animals
2. relatives

## B READING

# A Horse to Remember
## Chapter 7

As the horses started the race, they snorted and grunted. Some of the riders shouted as they urged their horses to go fast. In the distance was a deafening roar from the crowd. Tara was aware of all these things, but her mind was concentrating on Nellie. She put Nellie into a slow, easy run and noticed the way she was moving. Tara checked to make sure that she was sitting forward in the saddle and moving easily with Nellie.

Some of the other horses shot away from the starting line. When Tara looked at them pulling far ahead of Nellie, she felt anxious, but she remembered what Mr. Jones had told her. "The idea is not to be the winner when you reach the first jump or even the fifth jump. The idea is to be the winner at the finish line. Hold Nellie in until there are only three or four jumps left in the race. Then let her out if you have to."

Tara looked around to see which horses were near Nellie. About three-fourths of the horses were ahead of her. A few were lagging behind. But right next to Nellie was the magnificent Nighthawk, matching Nellie stride for stride. The two horses were running almost as if they were one horse. They approached the first jump together, in step. They both cleared the jump at the same instant, traveling almost the same height and landing almost together. "This is incredible," Tara said to herself as a thunderous roar went up from the crowd.

Now the second jump, a great hedge that was at least five feet high. Five riders failed to make this jump. The crowd gasped loudly as one of the horses directly in front of Nellie charged up to the hedge and then stopped abruptly, tossing its rider over the hedge. For a moment, Nellie got off stride with Nighthawk. She had to turn a little to the right to avoid the horse standing in front of the hedge. But Nellie and Nighthawk once more pleased the crowd by jumping over the hedge together and landing at almost the same instant. "Two incredible horses," the announcer said. "If they continue this way, we'll have two winners."

Now came a high fence jump followed by a difficult shelf. Nighthawk and Nellie cleared the fence and the shelf together, but Tara wasn't prepared for the jolt of the landing from the shelf jump. She fell forward and grabbed onto Nellie's neck. She was out of the saddle, with one leg dangling near Nellie's front shoulder. Somehow, she managed to get back into the saddle. As she scolded herself for being careless, she heard

a large cheer from the crowd.

By the time Nellie and Nighthawk had gone around the course one time, only about a dozen horses were left in the race. Horses and riders were scattered on the ground near every jump. Some horses had been seriously injured. Tara tried not to think about Nellie getting injured. She told herself, "Nellie will win if I can stay on her." But as Nighthawk and Nellie started on their second time around the course, Tara thought about what Mr. Longly had said.

Tara glanced over at Nighthawk. His mouth was open, and he tossed his head from time to time. But he was running with ease. Only three horses were ahead of Tara now, the white Arabian and two brown horses. They seemed to be straining. Nighthawk and Nellie, still running stride for stride, caught the Arabian horse at the eighteenth jump. They passed the other two horses before the twentieth jump. "There are only ten more jumps to go," Tara said to herself. But a moment after having that thought, Tara noticed that Nighthawk was moving ahead.

Tara's first impulse was to stay with Nighthawk. But then she remembered what Mr. Jones had told her. Tara held Nellie at an easy run and watched nervously as Nighthawk pulled away, by ten feet, by twenty feet, now by thirty feet. When Nellie had cleared the twenty-sixth jump, Nighthawk was at least fifty feet ahead. ♦

"Go, Nellie!" Tara shouted as she nudged the horse. "Go!" Nellie bounded forward with such speed that Tara was amazed. The horse was covered with sweat and breathing hard. But she ran with the kind of power you would expect from a horse that was just starting a race.

The crowd screamed and cheered. The

announcer shouted, "She's not out of this race yet. Look at her go."

Nellie caught up to Nighthawk two steps before the twenty-seventh jump. The horses jumped together again, but this time they didn't land together. Nellie landed at least five feet ahead of Nighthawk, and that was as close as Nighthawk ever came to Nellie for the rest of the race. Nellie moved away from Nighthawk so fast that Tara could hardly believe what was happening.

Nellie cleared the rest of the jumps with ease and reached the finish line at least three hundred feet ahead of Nighthawk.

Above the frantic crowd and the thunderous applause, Tara could hear the announcer ". . . a new track record . . . the greatest steeplechase horse that has ever run on this course . . ."

There were pictures, questions from reporters, and prizes for winning the race. Tara made a brief victory speech. As a re-

porter held a microphone in front of her face and people with television cameras crowded close, she said, "I knew she could do it if I could stay on her. She's incredible."

The trip home was a very pleasant one. Imagine winning the Grand National Steeplechase Championship with a horse that everybody called an old nag! Tara polished the first-prize trophy with the sleeve of her jacket as she rode in the cab of the truck. ★

After arriving at the farm, Tara took care of Nellie and gave her a special dinner and an extra special brushing. Then Tara, Mr. Jones, Tara's parents, and all the neighbors gathered at the Briggs farmhouse for a celebration dinner.

During dinner, the phone kept ringing.

Reporters wanted to talk to Tara. Other people called to congratulate her. Mr. Longly called and made a new offer of two hundred thousand pounds, but Mr. Briggs turned him down. After the seventh call, Mr. Briggs took the phone off the hook so callers wouldn't disturb the celebration.

After dinner, Mr. Briggs announced, "I was worried about having enough money to keep Nellie, but now we have enough money to keep her forever."

Mr. Jones shook his finger and said, "You have enough money to keep ten horses forever." Everybody laughed.

• • •

Nellie's story continued. She ran the Grand National Steeplechase two more times, and she won each time. She became the most photographed, most talked about steeplechase horse that ever lived.

When Nellie was nine years old, she gave birth to a magnificent male colt. The colt's father was a famous black horse. After Nellie was ten years old, she retired from racing, but she had two more colts.

Nellie lived until Tara was a grown woman with a family of her own.

The day Nellie died was a very sad day, but Tara has fond memories and something else to remind her of Nellie—one of Nellie's colts.

## C COMPREHENSION

Write the answers.
1. What did Mr. Jones mean when he said, "The idea is to be the winner at the finish line"?
2. Why didn't Tara try to catch up with Nighthawk when he first pulled away?
3. Why did Tara let Nellie out at the twenty-sixth jump?
4. Why were the Briggses able to keep Nellie for the rest of her life?
5. If you had a horse, would you want to race in the Grand National? Why or why not?

## D WRITING

In the story, Tara made a brief victory speech.
• Write that speech. Have Tara describe how she feels and tell who she wants to thank.

## A WORD LISTS

**1**
*Hard Words*
1. prey
2. generation

**2**
*Place Names*
1. China
2. Africa
3. Asia
4. Egypt
5. India

**3**
*Word Family*
1. domestic
2. domesticate
3. domesticated
4. domestication

**4**
*Word Practice*
1. house cat
2. half
3. respect
4. jerky
5. keen
6. eyesight
7. warmth

**5**
*New Vocabulary*
1. advantages
2. prey
3. generation
4. keen

# The Domestication of Animals
## Chapter 1

All animals can be divided into two groups: wild animals and domestic animals.

Wild animals do not live with people. Instead, they live in forests, jungles, rivers, oceans, and other wild places. Bears, tigers, snakes, eagles, alligators, and sharks are wild animals.

Domestic animals live with people. They live in people's houses or on people's farms. Dogs, horses, cows, chickens, and goats are domestic animals.

More than twenty thousand years ago, all animals were wild. But some of those animals were relatives of animals that are now domesticated. There were wild dogs that looked like wolves. There were wild goats that climbed mountains, wild horses that ran across the prairies, even wild chickens and wild sheep.

### Domestication of Dogs

The first animal to become domesticated was probably the dog. The dog became domesticated thousands of years ago, when many people still lived in caves. The cave people had to hunt to stay alive, but they were not very good hunters. They could not run as fast as the wild animals, and they were not as strong as many of these animals.

We don't know exactly how the cave people domesticated dogs. Possibly, the wild dogs came near the cave during the cold winter months. They might have smelled the food cooking inside. They might have felt the warmth of the fire. They might have been hungry.

The people inside the cave might have tried to get rid of the wild dogs by throwing heavy bones at them. The dogs might have fought over the bones and then returned to the mouth of the cave, howling and waiting for more bones.

Puppies may have been the first wild dogs to come inside the caves and live with people. The puppies were wild, but a young wild animal is easier to tame than an older one. If a puppy receives food and warmth from people, the puppy will learn to love people, just as a wild puppy learns to love the dogs that it lives with in a pack. ♦

### Dogs and Hunting

Cave people may have learned to hunt with their dogs by accident. A couple of puppies may have followed the cave people as they went hunting. As the puppies grew older, the cave people may have discovered that the dogs could do things that people couldn't do. The dogs could track other animals by following the scent of those animals. The dogs could warn the cave people of danger before the people could see or hear the danger. If a dangerous animal was

near, the dog's fur would stand up, and the dog would growl.

When the tame dogs grew up, they had puppies. These tame puppies lived with the cave people. The tame puppies responded to the cave people in the same way that wild puppies respond to the leaders of a pack of wild dogs. Wild puppies learn to obey the leader dogs; tame puppies learn to obey people.

When the dogs were fully tamed by the cave people, they became domestic animals.

## Domestication of Other Animals

For thousands of years, cave people hunted with their dogs. This plan worked well, but hunting had problems. The main problem was that people had to follow the wild animals they hunted. When deer and other wild animals moved from one place to another, people had to follow them or starve. Wild animals moved around a lot, which meant that people were on the move all the time, going from one place to another.

Then people started to work out better plans. Some of them domesticated animals other than dogs, such as wild goats and wild sheep. The people took these animals with them as they hunted. If hunting was not good, they would kill one of these animals and eat it.

### Domestication and Farming

Other people developed a different plan. Instead of following wild animals from place to place, they stayed in one place and raised domestic animals and plants. These people were the first farmers.

Farming had a big advantage over hunting. When a hunter kills a wild goat, the only food the hunter gets is the meat of the goat. But when a farmer raises goats, the farmer gets goat milk for many years. When the goat is old, the farmer can still kill the goat for its meat.

When people became farmers, they no longer had to move from place to place to find food. Instead, they used domesticated plants and animals to get most of the food they needed.

## C COMPREHENSION

Write the answers.
1. What are the main differences between wild animals and domestic animals?
2. How does a puppy learn to love people?
3. Why did the cave people have to keep moving from place to place?
4. Why didn't the farmers have to move from place to place?
5. Which would you rather be—a farmer or a hunter? Explain your answer.

## D WRITING

What do you think would have happened if people had never domesticated animals?

- Write a paragraph that explains your answer. Tell how life would be different for people without domesticated animals. Tell how life would be different for animals. Give some examples.

## 42

A **WORD LISTS**

| 1<br>*Hard Words* | 2<br>*Animal Names* | 3<br>*Word Endings* | 4<br>*Vocabulary Review* |
|---|---|---|---|
| 1. popular<br>2. talons | 1. falcon<br>2. hawk<br>3. camel<br>4. mongoose<br>5. cheetah<br>6. llama<br>7. cobra | 1. generation<br>2. domestication<br>3. Egyptian | 1. advantages<br>2. relatives<br>3. generation<br>4. prey |

**B** **READING**

# The Domestication of Animals
## Chapter 2

When people started to farm, they continued to use dogs for hunting. They also began domesticating other animals for different uses. Over time, people developed three main uses for domestic animals:

- Helping people hunt.
- Giving people food and other products.
- Carrying things.

### Animals That Hunt

The house cat was first domesticated as a hunting animal. The domestication of the cat took place in Egypt more than three thousand years ago. By that time, people had been using dogs as hunting animals for many years. But the Egyptians had a hunting problem that dogs could not solve.

The Egyptians raised grain, which they stored in large buildings. Mice and rats would get into the storage buildings and feast on the grain. Dogs couldn't help the Egyptians much because dogs are not very good at catching mice and rats. Instead, cats solved the problem because they can easily catch mice and rats.

By placing cats in their storage buildings, the Egyptians protected their grain. They were so grateful to cats that they made large statues of the animals, and they treated them with great respect. Over time, cats began living in people's houses, just as they do today.

Other people trained larger members of the cat family, such as cheetahs. These cats are as big as large dogs, and they can run fast—up to sixty miles per hour. Because of their speed, they became popular with hunters in India.

People also trained many other hunting animals, including ferrets and mongooses. A ferret is half the size of a cat, but it can catch rats and rabbits. A ferret can move some parts of its body so quickly that people can't see the movement. If a ferret turns its head from side to side, you don't see the movement. You simply see the head looking one way, and then, an instant later, you see the head looking the other way.

In India, the mongoose was domesticated to kill cobras, which are poisonous snakes that can kill people with just one bite. The mongoose is smaller than a cat, but it is extremely powerful. Its fast, jerky movements permit it to kill cobras with ease. When a mongoose fights a cobra, the cobra rears up and leans back. Then the mongoose bites the cobra's head, cracking the snake's skull with its powerful bite.

People all over the world have domesticated falcons and other types of hawks for hunting. These birds of prey have strong claws, called talons. They also have keen eyesight and good speed. They can catch other birds in the air or rabbits on the ground.

## Animals That Give Food

Animals such as sheep, cattle, and chickens are very important to people because they give meat and other food. Sheep and cattle give milk, chickens give eggs, and they all give meat.

But people use food-giving animals for many things besides meat, milk, and eggs. The thick skin from cows and pigs is used to make leather. Sheep fur is used to make wool. Goose feathers are used to fill jackets and blankets. ♦

## Animals That Carry Things

Many different animals have been used to carry things. The camel was one of the first carrying animals to be domesticated. People all over Asia and North Africa loved the camel because it could be trained to carry large loads for long distances.

Donkeys and horses were also trained to carry loads. In South America, the llama was widely used for carrying. The llama is good at climbing mountains and walking in places without roads. In Africa and India, some people were able to domesticate elephants. These huge animals can carry tremendous loads and can easily lift an entire tree.

Since the invention of the train, the car and the airplane, people don't depend on carrying animals as much as they did in the old days.

## Animal Breeding

After they learned how to domesticate animals, people discovered a process for changing animals to make them more useful. This process is called animal breeding.

Let's say a person who hunts has several male and female dogs. One of the male dogs is much better at hunting than any other male because it has a keen sense of smell. One of the female dogs is also better at hunting than the other females. ★

If these two good hunting dogs have

puppies, some of their puppies will be better hunters than any of the other dogs in the pack. If the person keeps breeding only the best hunting dogs, some of their puppies will be even better hunters. After several generations, the last-bred dogs will be much better at hunting than the dogs the person used to start the breeding process.

Chickens, horses, and goats changed in the same way dogs changed. When farmers kept only the chickens that laid the biggest eggs, the chickens' eggs grew larger and larger from generation to generation. At first, the eggs were no bigger than ping-pong balls. But after many years, the eggs were almost as big as tennis balls.

The same thing happened with horses. Farmers kept only the biggest and most powerful horses, so the horses changed from generation to generation. After hundreds of years, the newest horses were much bigger than the horses the earlier farmers had.

Before people discovered how to breed domestic animals, there were only a few types of each animal. Now there are many types. Along with hunting dogs, for example, there are herding dogs, sled dogs, and guard dogs. People developed all these different types of dogs through breeding.

## C COMPREHENSION

Write the answers.
1. Why were Egyptians so grateful to cats?
2. Which of the food-giving animals do you think is most useful to people? Explain your answer.
3. Why don't people today depend on carrying animals as much as they did in the old days?
4. Explain how people could breed sheep with thicker fur.
5. If you were a goat, would you rather be a wild goat or a domesticated one? Explain your answer.

## D WRITING

What is your favorite domesticated animal?
• Write a paragraph that explains your answer. Tell why the animal is your favorite, and show why you like it more than other animals.

# 43

| 1<br>*Hard Words* | 2<br>*Word Endings* | 3<br>*Word Practice* | 4<br>*New Vocabulary* |
|---|---|---|---|
| 1. gnawed | 1. fiction | 1. flavor | 1. gnaw |
| 2. fantasy | 2. selection | 2. comb | 2. bargain |
| 3. bargain | 3. nation | 3. flavored | 3. shall |
|  | 4. domestication | 4. combed | 4. pounce |
|  | 5. imagination |  | 5. accept |

## B STORY BACKGROUND

# Fact and Fiction

Some of the material you read presents facts. The article in the last two lessons, for example, presented facts about the domestication of animals. Because the main purpose of the article is to present facts, it is called a factual article.

Another type of reading material is fiction, such as short stories and novels. Fiction is a story that somebody makes up. *The Wonderful Wizard of Oz* is fiction. "A Horse to Remember" is fiction.

Not all fiction is the same. "A Horse to Remember" is fiction, but the things that happen in the story actually could happen. Farm horses like Nellie have won steeplechases. The Grand National Steeplechase does take place near Liverpool. The prob-

lems that Tara had when she was learning to jump are real problems that anybody could have when learning to jump. So although "A Horse to Remember" is fiction, it is close to fact. Fiction that is close to fact is called realistic fiction.

Some fiction, such as *The Wonderful Wizard of Oz*, is far from fact. The Land of Oz doesn't really exist, and scarecrows can't talk or think. Fiction that is far from fact is called fantasy.

The story that you will start today is a fantasy that tells about the domestication of animals. You already know facts about domestication. When you read the story, compare the things that happen in the story with the facts you know.

# The Cat That Walked by Himself
### by Rudyard Kipling*
### Chapter 1

Once upon a time, all animals were wild. The dog was wild, and the cow was wild, and the horse was wild, and the sheep was wild—as wild as wild could be—and they walked in the wild woods. But the wildest of all the wild animals was the cat. He walked by himself, no matter where he went.

Of course, the man was wild, too. He was very wild. He didn't even begin to be tame until he married the woman. She told him that she did not like his wild ways.

She picked out a nice dry cave to live in, and she lit a nice fire at the back of the cave, and she spread clean sand on the floor, and she said, "Wipe your feet when you come in, dear, so we can keep our house neat and clean."

That night, the man and the woman ate wild sheep that had been roasted on the fire and flavored with wild onion and wild pepper. The man was very happy, and he went to sleep in front of the fire; but the woman sat up and looked at the fire.

*Adapted for young readers

Out in the wild woods all the wild animals gathered together where they could see the light of the fire a long way off, and they wondered what it meant.

Then the wild horse stamped with his wild foot and said, "Oh, my friends and enemies, why have the man and the woman made that great light in that great cave, and what harm will it do us?"

The wild dog lifted up his wild nose and smelled the smell of roast sheep and said, "I will go to the cave and see, for I think something smells good. Cat, come with me."

"No," said the cat. "I am the cat who walks by himself, no matter where I go. So I will not go with you."

"Then we can never be friends," said the wild dog, and he trotted off to the cave. But when the wild dog had gone a little way, the cat said to himself, "It doesn't matter where I go, so I will go and see what happens." The cat followed the wild dog softly, very softly, and hid himself where he could hear everything.

When the wild dog reached the mouth of the cave, he lifted his nose and sniffed the beautiful smell of the roast sheep. The woman heard him and said, "Wild Dog, what do you want?"

The dog said, "What smells so good?"

Then the woman picked up a roasted sheep bone, threw it to the wild dog, and said, "Wild Dog, taste and try."

The wild dog gnawed the bone, and it was more delicious than anything he had ever tasted. When he was finished, he said, "Give me another."

The woman said, "Wild Dog, if you help my man to hunt during the day and guard this cave at night, I will give you as many roasted bones as you need." ♦

"Ah," said the cat, listening. "This is a very wise woman, but she is not as wise as I am."

The wild dog crawled into the cave and laid his head on the woman's lap and said, "Good friend, I will help your man to hunt during the day, and at night I will guard your cave."

"Ah," said the cat, listening. "That is a very foolish dog." And the cat went back through the wild woods, walking by himself and waving his wild tail. But he never told anybody what he had seen and heard.

When the man woke up, he said, "What is Wild Dog doing here?" And the woman said, "His name is not Wild Dog anymore. His new name is First Friend because he will be our friend forever. Take him with you when you go hunting."

That day, the woman cut great green armfuls of fresh grass from a meadow in the wild woods. She dried the grass by the fire.

Out in the wild woods, all the wild animals wondered what had happened to the wild dog, and at last the wild cow stamped her foot and said, "I will go and see why Wild Dog has not returned. Cat, come with me."

"No!" said the cat. "I am the cat who walks by himself, no matter where I go. So I will not go with you." But secretly, he followed the wild cow, very softly, and hid himself where he could hear everything.

When the wild cow reached the mouth of the cave, she lifted her nose and sniffed the beautiful smell of the dried grass. The woman heard the cow and said, "Wild Cow, what do you want?"

The wild cow said, "Where is Wild Dog?" But the cow kept staring at the dried grass.

The woman laughed and said, "Wild Cow, I think you are more interested in grass than you are in Wild Dog."

The wild cow said, "That is true. Give me the grass to eat."

The woman said, "Wild Cow, if you will give me your milk, I will let you eat the wonderful grass three times a day."

"Ah," said the cat as he listened from his hiding place. "This is a clever woman, but she is not as clever as I am."

The wild cow said, "I will give you my milk if you give me the wonderful grass."

"Ah," said the cat. "That is a very foolish cow." And the cat went back through the wild woods, walking by himself and waving his wild tail. But he never told anybody about what he had seen and heard. ★

When the man and the dog came back from hunting, the man said, "What is Wild Cow doing here?"

And the woman said, "Her name is not Wild Cow anymore, but Giver of Good Food. She will give us warm white milk forever, and I will take care of her while you and First Friend go hunting."

On the next day, the woman gathered grass again. Then she sat in front of the cave and made a collar from animal skins.

That night, the wild animals got together again to talk about the wild dog and the wild cow. At last, the wild horse said, "I will go and see why they have not returned. Cat, come with me."

"No," said the cat, "I will not come." But he secretly followed the wild horse, very softly, and hid himself where he could hear everything.

When the wild horse reached the cave, he smelled the dried grass. The woman heard him and said, "Wild Horse, what do you want?"

The wild horse said, "Where are Wild Dog and Wild Cow?" But the horse kept staring at the grass.

The woman laughed and said, "I think you are more interested in grass than in Wild Dog or Wild Cow."

The wild horse said, "That is true. Give me the grass to eat."

The woman said, "If you will wear this collar and be our servant, I will let you eat the grass three times a day."

"Ah," said the cat, as he listened from his hiding place. "This is a very clever woman, but she is not as clever as I am."

The wild horse said, "I will wear the collar and be your servant if you give me the wonderful grass."

"Ah," said the cat, listening. "That is a very foolish horse." And he went back through the wild woods, walking by himself and waving his wild tail. But he never told anybody what he had seen and heard.

When the man and the dog came back from hunting, the man said, "What is Wild Horse doing here?"

And the woman explained, "His name is no longer Wild Horse, but First Servant. He will carry us from place to place forever. You can ride on his back when you go hunting, and he will pull the animals you kill."

That night, the wild animals had another meeting. The wild sheep said, "I'm not going to that cave. No animal that has gone to that place has come back."

The wild chicken, the wild goose, and all the other animals agreed. So no animal went to the cave that night. Instead, they all went back to their homes.

---

# D COMPREHENSION

Write the answers.
1. What are the main differences between fantasy and realistic fiction?
2. How do you know that "The Cat That Walked by Himself" is fantasy?
3. Why was the wild dog attracted to the cave?
4. Why were the wild cow and the wild horse attracted to the cave?
5. Do you think those animals made good bargains with the woman? Explain your answer.

# E WRITING

How do you think "The Cat That Walked by Himself" will end?
- Write an ending for "The Cat That Walked by Himself." Tell what the cat does and what happens to the other animals.

# A WORD LISTS

| 1 | 2 | 3 |
|---|---|---|
| *Hard Words* | *Word Practice* | *New Vocabulary* |
| 1. Yukon | 1. fantasy | 1. eventually |
| 2. Juneau | 2. flavored | 2. scrambled |
| 3. glacier | 3. accept | 3. disgraceful |
| 4. eventually | 4. bargain | 4. lean |
| 5. descend | | 5. vivid |
| 6. treacherous | | 6. descended |
| | | 7. treacherous |

# B NEITHER-NOR SENTENCES

Use the words *neither* and *nor* to change the following sentences.

1. The man was not happy and was not sad.

2. She would not play and would not sleep.

3. The boy would not smile and would not talk.

# The Cat That Walked by Himself
## Chapter 2

The man and the woman were now living with three animals. On the day after the wild animals decided not to send any more animals to the cave, the cat waited to see what the wild animals would do. No animal moved from the wild woods, so the cat walked to the cave by himself. He saw the woman milking the cow, and he saw the light of the fire in the cave, and he smelled the warm white milk.

The cat went up to the woman and said, "Where are Wild Dog, Wild Cow, and Wild Horse?"

The woman laughed and said, "Wild Cat, go back to the wild woods again, for we have all the friends and servants we need."

The cat said, "I am neither a friend nor a servant. I am the cat who walks by himself, and I want to go into your cave."

The woman said, "I saw you hiding near the cave when First Friend came here. If you wanted to come inside, why didn't you come in with First Friend on that first night?"

The cat grew very angry and said, "I want to go inside."

The woman laughed and said, "You are the cat who walks by himself, no matter where you go. You are neither a friend nor a servant. You have said it yourself. So go away and walk by yourself."

Then the cat pretended to be sorry and said, "Can't I ever come into the cave? Can't I ever sit by the warm fire? Can't I ever drink the warm white milk? You are very wise and very beautiful. You should not be cruel, even to a cat."

The woman smiled and said, "I knew I was wise, but I did not know I was beautiful." She gazed at the cat for a few moments. Then she said, "I think you are very cunning, and you are trying to trick me. But I will make a bargain with you. If I ever praise you, you may sit near the mouth of the cave forever."

"And if you praise me twice?" said the cat.

"I never shall," said the woman, "but if I praise you twice, you may sit in the back of the cave by the fire."

"And if you praise me three times?" said the cat.

"I never shall," said the woman, "but if I praise you three times, you may drink the warm white milk anytime you wish."

Then the cat arched his back and said, "I accept your bargain." And he went away through the wild woods, walking by himself and waving his wild tail. ♦

That night when the man and the horse and the dog came home from hunting, the woman did not tell them about the bargain she had made with the cat, because she was afraid they might not like it.

The cat went far away and hid himself in the wild woods. After many days passed, the woman forgot all about him and the bargain she had made. A bat that hung inside the cave knew where the cat was hiding, and every evening the bat would fly to the cat with news of what was happening in the cave.

One evening the bat said, "There is a baby in the cave. He is new and fat, and the woman is very fond of him."

"Ah," said the cat, listening. "And what is the baby fond of?"

"Let's see," the bat said thoughtfully. "He is fond of things that are soft, and he is fond of warm things he can hold in his arms when he goes to sleep. And he is very fond of being played with."

"Ah," said the cat, with a cunning smile. "The time has come for me to move into the cave."

The next morning, the cat walked through the wild woods and hid near the cave until the man and the dog and the horse went hunting. The woman was busy trying to cook that morning, and the baby's crying bothered her. So she carried the baby outside the cave and gave him pebbles to play with. But still the baby cried.

The cat approached the baby, put out his paw, and patted the baby softly on the cheek. The baby cooed and smiled. The cat rubbed against the baby's knees and tickled the baby under his fat chin with his tail. The baby laughed, and the woman heard the baby laugh.

The bat said, "Woman, that baby is happy because a wild animal is entertaining him."

Without going outside of the cave, the woman said, "That wonderful animal is a marvel. That animal has done a great service for me."

Suddenly, the woman noticed the cat sitting quite comfortably inside, near the mouth of the cave. "Woman," said the cat, "you have praised me, and now I can sit in the cave forever. But remember, I am the cat who walks by himself, no matter where I go."

The woman was very angry. She shut her lips tightly, picked up a ball of thread, and began to sew.

Suddenly, the baby cried because the cat was no longer entertaining him. The woman went outside, but she could not hush the baby. The baby struggled and kicked and cried. ★

"Woman," said the cat, "give me a ball of thread, and I will show you how to make your baby laugh as loudly as he is now crying."

"I will do so," said the woman, "but I will not praise you if you do it."

She gave the cat a ball of thread, and the cat ran after it. He patted it with his paws and rolled head over heels and tossed the thread backward over his shoulder and chased it between his legs and pretended to lose it and pounced down upon it again. The baby started to laugh loudly and to scramble after the cat all around the cave. Then the baby grew tired. He put his arms around the soft cat and held it.

"Now," said the cat, "I will sing the baby a song that will put him to sleep for an hour." The cat began to purr, loud and low, until the baby fell fast asleep. The woman smiled as she looked down upon the two of them and said, "That was wonderful. You are a very clever cat."

Suddenly, the cat was sitting quite

comfortably at the back of the cave, close to the fire.

"Woman," said the cat, "you have praised me twice, and now I can sit by the warm fire at the back of the cave forever. But remember, I am the cat who walks by himself, no matter where I go."

Now the woman was very, very angry. She resolved not to praise the cat again.

Hours later, the cave grew so still that a little mouse crept out of a corner and ran across the floor.

"Woman," said the cat, smiling, "I see that a little mouse lives in your cave."

"Oh, no," said the woman.

"Ah," said the cat. "Then you should do something to get rid of it."

The woman said, "Oh, please get rid of it, and I will always be grateful to you."

The cat made one jump and caught the mouse. The woman said, "A hundred thanks. Even First Friend is not quick enough to catch little mice. You are a very skillful animal."

The cat walked over to a bowl and began lapping up the warm white milk. Then he paused and licked his chops. "Woman," he said, "you have praised me three times, and now I can drink the warm white milk any time I wish. But remember—I am still the cat who walks by himself, no matter where I go."

Then the woman laughed and said, "Cat, you are as clever as I am, and I will be glad to keep my bargain with you."

That evening, when the man and the dog came into the cave, the woman told them the story of the bargain.

And the cat just sat by the fire and smiled.

---

# D COMPREHENSION

Write the answers.
1. Why didn't the woman want to let the cat into the cave?
2. Why do you think the cat told the woman that she was wise and beautiful?
3. The woman was afraid the man and the dog might not like the bargain she had made with the cat. Why wouldn't they like the bargain?
4. At the end of the story, what did the cat mean when he said, "I am still the cat that walks by himself"?
5. Which animal do you think made the best bargain with the woman? Explain your answer.

# E WRITING

Write a paragraph that compares "The Cat That Walked by Himself" with the facts that you know about domestication. Tell which parts of the story are based on fact and which parts are fantasy. Also tell why you think the writer made the story a fantasy.

# 45

## A WORD LISTS

| 1 | 2 | 3 | 4 |
|---|---|---|---|
| **Word Endings** | **Word Practice** | **Vocabulary Review** | **New Vocabulary** |
| 1. ugly | 1. volcano | 1. scramble | 1. rustling |
| 2. quietly | 2. volcanic | 2. lean | 2. slosh |
| 3. doubtfully | 3. glacier | 3. eventually | 3. miserable |
| 4. hardly | 4. Juneau | 4. disgraceful | 4. crest |
| 5. bitterly | 5. Yukon | 5. treacherous | |
| 6. exactly | | 6. descend | |
| | | 7. vivid | |

## B NEITHER-NOR SENTENCES

Use the words *neither* and *nor* to change the following sentences.

1. He could not swim, and he could not dive.

2. She was not happy, and she was not sad.

3. They could not walk, and they could not run.

# Journey to Dawson
## Chapter 1

Beginning in lesson 47, you will read an exciting story that takes place in the gold fields of northern Canada.

Before you begin that story, you will learn some facts about the gold fields and the trip that people took to reach those fields. Pretend you are a person going to the gold fields. You are living in the year 1896.

In 1896, gold was discovered in northern Canada near a town called Dawson. You decide to go to Dawson to find your fortune in gold.

All the routes to the gold fields are dangerous. You decide to take a boat down the Yukon River. Before you can go down the Yukon River, you must get to it, which is a difficult and dangerous journey. The river

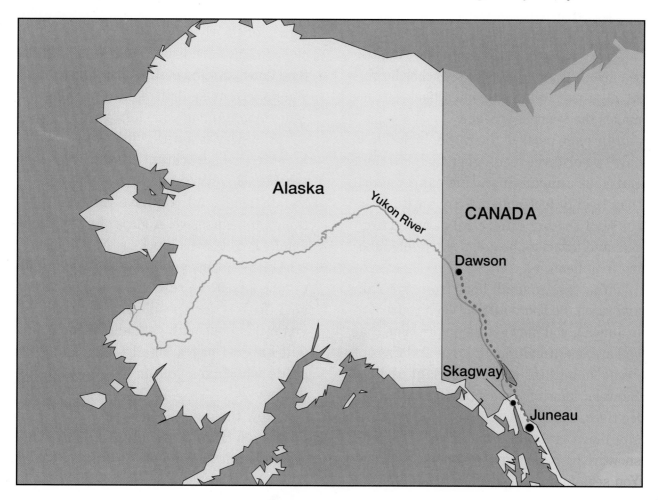

begins in lakes that are high in the mountains. You must climb into the mountains before you can reach those lakes.

The map shows the route you will take to reach Dawson. The route is marked with a colored line. The line on the map starts in Juneau, Alaska. Then the line goes north into the mountains until it reaches Skagway. Then the line goes still farther north, over the mountains, until it comes to one of the magnificent lakes that flows into the Yukon River. From this lake, you travel on the Yukon until you eventually reach the tiny town of Dawson.

The journey from Juneau to Dawson is long and dangerous. But you also experience a dangerous journey trying to reach Juneau on a ship. This journey is treacherous because of the tides.

Each day the sea rises a little and descends a little. This change in the level of the sea is called the tides. At low tide, the sea goes out and makes the beaches larger. At high tide, the sea comes back in and makes the beaches smaller.

In some parts of the world, high tide is only two or three feet higher than low tide. But near Juneau, high tide can be more than twenty feet higher than low tide. Because of the big difference between high tide and low tide, boats have trouble landing in Juneau. ♦

You take a small boat from the ship and reach the shore safely. When you arrive in Juneau, you may get the impression that you are in a wonderland. Rows and rows of great mountains stand like giant castles. Between some of these mountains are great ice floes, called glaciers. The glaciers actually move, as millions of tons of ice and ⸱ in the mountains push down on them.

⸱e one great glacier near Juneau. It moves slowly into a lake, and it looks like a huge tongue with its tip cut off.

As you stand on the rocky shore of this lake and listen, you can hear the glacier moving. It creaks and groans. From time to time, huge chunks of ice fall off the end of the glacier and tumble into the icy lake, making a sound like distant thunder.

When the end of this glacial tongue breaks off, you observe something that is almost unbelievable. The jagged end of the glacier is blue—as blue as the sky. The blue is most vivid just after the end of the glacier falls off. Then the blue begins to fade.

You leave Juneau and continue north on your way to the gold fields. Your next stop will be a little place called Skagway, which is close to the Canadian border. ★

Walking along a path, you leave Juneau and climb into the mountains. On your right, for nearly a hundred miles, is a glacier with hundreds of ice tongues that extend down into the pass. From time to time, you notice smoke drifting from a huge volcanic mountain on your left.

Skagway is a little village, and prices here are disgraceful. Everything that reaches Skagway must be brought in over the difficult trail you have just taken, so things are expensive. A glass of milk, for example, might cost a much as twenty dollars.

In Skagway, you make arrangements to take a boat the rest of the way up to the gold fields. Other people seeking gold will go on this boat with you, and each person will have to pay a small fortune for the guide who takes you on the treacherous journey.

Now the guide leads you and the others as you tramp overland from Skagway through amazing mountain passes. In the middle of this overland route, you cross the border of Alaska and enter Canada. At last you reach the lake. You are ready to start on your boat trip.

It is early morning, and you can see your breath, although it is still summertime. The lake, which is nearly a hundred miles long, is surrounded by mountains with their peaks hidden in the clouds. The only sounds are those of occasional fish splashing in the lake and early morning birds. Some chirp, some cry, and some seem to scream.

## D COMPREHENSION

Write the answers.
1. The story says that you decide to "find your fortune in gold." What does that mean?
2. Explain why the tides near Juneau are dangerous for boats.
3. Why is the trip from Juneau to Skagway difficult?
4. Why are prices high in Skagway?
5. If you were alive in 1896, would you want to make the trip from Juneau to Dawson? Explain your answer.

## E WRITING

Pick a place you know well. Write a paragraph that describes the place. Describe the objects you see, the sounds you hear, and the things you smell.

# 46

## A WORD LISTS

**1**

*New Vocabulary*

1. murmur
2. whittling
3. sneer
4. coil
5. exchanged
6. flickered
7. hurl
8. limp

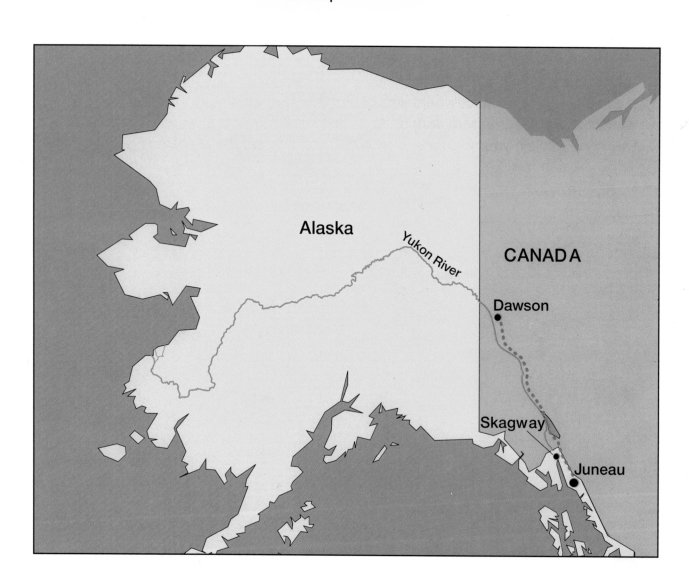

# Journey to Dawson
## Chapter 2

As you and the others seat yourselves in the small riverboat, ripples move out from the boat across the mirror surface of the water. You will never forget this moment. You are the only people for a hundred miles in any direction. You and the others are alone among the tall pines and spruces.

Some of the trees along the shore of the lake are so huge that ten people, standing side by side, could hide behind one of them. The trees reach up so far that, if you stand directly under one and look up, you become dizzy. Everything around you is so grand that your mind is dazzled.

You and the others row the riverboat across the glassy lake. All day and all the next day and all the next day, you row. By now your hands are raw from pulling on the oars. And your nights are now miserable because swarms of mosquitoes and biting insects attack you as soon as the sun sets.

At last, you come to the north end of the lake. Here the river starts, and for the moment, you're delighted. Your delight quickly changes to fright when your boat starts down the river. The lake that you have been on is high in the mountains, but the gold fields are far below in a place called the Yukon Valley. The river that flows north and west to the gold fields is named the Yukon River.

As the river flows from the lake down into the valley, it roars through steep passes that snake between great mountains. In places, the Yukon tumbles and thunders in clouds of spray and dazzling white water. In other places, it becomes wide and shallow. Here you can see the bottom of the river so clearly that there doesn't seem to be any water between the boat and the bottom. Even in places where the water is ten feet deep, the water is so invisible that if you peer over the edge of the boat and look down, you feel as if you are floating ten feet in the air. ♦

When you come to these still places in the river, you observe the things around you. You see fish—thousands of them—in the river. Some are three or four feet long, and they move in great schools. You also look at the trees and the jagged rocks that line the banks of the river.

When you come to places where the river roars down through a narrow pass, you don't think of anything except scrambling through the pass. Above the roaring water you hear the guide shouting directions, "Pull right! Pull right!" His voice is nearly drowned in the thunderous sound of the great river as it hammers and bounces the tiny boat through the snarling, icy water. When the river again slows down, your hands are numb from the cold, and your feet ache from being in the freezing water that sloshes around in the bottom of the boat.

Some passes are so steep that the boat would become nothing but splinters if it tried to go through them. On a still day, you can hear the thundering sound of the rapids more than two miles away. From this distance, the sound is like a far-off wind rustling through the trees. As you get closer, you hear the roar, louder and louder.

If you don't row to the bank and get your boat out of the river at this point, the current will move so fast that you won't be able to stop the boat. You'll get close to the steep banks, but the boat will be moving so quickly that it will nudge the bank a few times and then continue helplessly. It will slide over the glassy crest at the top of the rapids, dive into great waves that are topped with spray, and then scoot down the rapids until it hits a boulder. ★

When you approach one of these terrible rapids, your guide directs you to row to the bank. Everybody gets out, unloads the supplies from the boat, pulls the boat on shore, and turns it over to drain out the water. Then the difficult part starts; you must carry the boat and all the supplies along a rock ledge next to the river.

Sometimes, transporting the boat and supplies for a mile takes all day. It takes so long because you must first haul the boat up hundreds of feet to a ledge above the river. Then you must carry the boat through dense forests and over rough paths made by deer and other animals. Some-times, you carry the boat on the edge of cliffs that are directly above the river. One wrong step, and you could tumble hundreds of feet into the swirling rapids below.

At last the river reaches the Yukon Valley. Now the water moves more steadily, north and west. You must travel about two hundred miles farther to reach Dawson. The days move by slowly, and the nights become longer and colder. The mosquitoes don't bother you as much at night.

You see wild animals—wolves, deer, moose, and millions of birds. On all sides are fantastic mountains, topped with a dazzling white mantle that reaches down to the broad, green valley on either side of the river. The valley is dotted with wild flowers and birds and with an occasional bear standing on its hind legs looking at the strange sight of a boat on the river.

When you reach the tiny town of Dawson, your hands are lean and hard. You feel as if you've left everything you know far, far behind. Even your memories of cities and people are dull. As you stand on the outskirts of this strange little town, you seem to be a part of this northern country. At the same time, you feel like a lonely stranger who doesn't belong here.

The cold air, the crystal waters, and the green meadows do not belong to people, but to the wild things that grow here. The great mountains stand like gigantic guards, keeping people out. But you are here because hidden in those mountains are great riches.

## C COMPREHENSION

Write the answers.
1. The story says that when you are on the lake, "everything around you is so grand that your mind is dazzled." What does that mean?
2. Why do you feel frightened when you start down the river?
3. When you are on the river, why do you sometimes feel as if you're floating on air?
4. When you take the boat on land, why do you need an entire day to move the boat just one mile?
5. When you reach Dawson, why do you feel that you don't belong there?

## D WRITING

The story describes a trip down the Yukon River. Of all the rivers in the world, which one would you like to travel on?

• Write a paragraph that explains your answer. Tell which river you would pick and where it is located. Tell how you would travel on the river and what kinds of things you would see.

## 47

## A WORD LISTS

| 1 | 2 | 3 | 4 |
|---|---|---|---|
| *Word Family* | *Word Practice* | *Vocabulary Review* | *New Vocabulary* |
| 1. overhead | 1. mine | 1. flicker | 1. lingered on |
| 2. hillside | 2. miner | 2. sneer | 2. buds |
| 3. waterfall | 3. baggage | 3. murmur | 3. staggered |
| 4. downstream | 4. cricket | 4. hurl | 4. sap |
| | 5. Thornton | 5. coil | 5. runners |
| | 6. exchanged | 6. miserable | |
| | | 7. reflection | |

## B STORY BACKGROUND

# The Yukon Valley

The story that you will read today takes place near Dawson, in the Yukon Valley. The story begins in early spring, just as the ice is melting. Because the Yukon River is frozen during the winter, miners who venture to the Dawson gold fields can use dog sleds to ride on top of the solid ice.

A dog sled is built to carry heavy loads. It has runners along the bottom that slide over snow and ice. Its sides are high enough to hold baggage.

The sled is pulled by a team of five to thirteen dogs. The best dog, called the "lead dog," is at the front of the team. Sled dogs are big and strong.

The dogs learn to work together, and they learn the commands the driver gives. When the driver wants them to turn right, he says, "Gee!" When he wants them to turn left, he says "Haw!" When he wants them to start running, he says, "Mush on!"

# Buck

### by Jack London*
### Chapter 1

It was beautiful spring weather along the Yukon River. Each day, the sun rose earlier and set later. It was dawn by three in the morning, and twilight lingered on till nine at night. The whole long day was a blaze of sunshine. The ghostly winter silence had given way to the great spring murmur of awakening life.

This murmur arose from all the land and filled it with the joy of living. The murmur came from the things that lived and moved again, things that had been almost dead and had not moved during the long months of winter. The sap was rising in the pines. The trees were bursting out in young buds, and shrubs and vines were putting on

*Adapted for young readers

fresh green leaves. Crickets sang in the nights, and in the days all kinds of creeping, crawling things came out into the sun. Squirrels were chattering, and birds were singing. Overhead, the wild geese flew up from the south in V's that split the air.

From every hillside came the trickle of running water, the music of unseen waterfalls. Everything was thawing, bending, snapping. The Yukon was straining to break loose from the ice that held it motionless. The river flowed under sheets of ice and ate away at the ice from below; the sun ate from above. Cracks formed in the ice on the river's surface, and thin sheets of ice fell into the river.

John Thornton stepped out of his small tent and looked down the Yukon. He could hear the ice cracking, and he wondered how long it would be before the water flowed freely again. Thornton looked to the north and saw the spot where the White River joined the Yukon. He looked to the south and saw a dog sled coming slowly up the frozen river. He looked at the dog sled for a long time, and he did not like what he saw.

A full hour went by before the dogs and their two drivers staggered into Thornton's camp. When they arrived, the dogs dropped down as though they had all been struck dead. One of the drivers sat down on a log to rest. He sat down very slowly and carefully. He looked very stiff. The other man stood next to the sled and did the talking.

Thornton was whittling the last touches on an axe handle he had made from a stout branch. He whittled and listened, gave brief replies and good advice. He knew the kind of driver he was talking to, and as he gave advice, he was certain the man would not follow it. ♦

The man sneered and said, "They told us down at Skagway that the trail on the frozen river wasn't safe and we shouldn't try to take the sled to Dawson. They told us we couldn't make it this far, but here we are."

"And they told you true," Thornton answered. "The bottom's likely to drop out of the trail at any moment. Only fools, with the blind luck of fools, could have made it. I tell you straight, I wouldn't risk my body on that ice for all the gold in Dawson."

"That's because you're not a fool, I suppose," said the man. "All the same, we'll go on to Dawson." He uncoiled his whip and yelled to the lead dog, "Get up there, Buck! Get up there! Mush on!"

Thornton went on whittling. It was a bad idea to get between a fool and his foolish ideas; the world would not change with the loss of these two fools.

But the dog team did not get up at the command. The team had passed into the stage where whipping was required to get it moving. The whip flashed out. Thornton bit his lip.

An old husky was the first to crawl to its feet. A brown dog followed. A white mutt came next, yelping with pain. A fourth dog made painful efforts. Twice he fell over, but on the third attempt he was able to rise.

The lead dog, Buck, made no effort to get up. He lay quietly where he had fallen. He neither whined nor struggled. Several times Thornton started to speak, but he changed his mind. Tears came into his eyes. At last he stood up and walked away.

This was the first time Buck had failed, and his failure drove the foolish man into a rage. He exchanged the whip for a club. Buck still refused to move. Like his mates, he was barely able to get up, but unlike them, he had made up his mind not to get

up. He had a feeling of disaster because he had felt the thin ice under his feet all day. He sensed death, out there ahead on the ice where his master was trying to drive him. He refused to stir. ★

Buck had suffered so greatly that the spark of life within him flickered and went down. It was nearly out. He felt strangely numb. Then, the last feeling of pain left him. He no longer felt anything.

Suddenly, Thornton uttered a cry that was like the cry of an animal. He sprang upon the man who held the club and hurled him backward. The man fell as if struck by a falling tree. The other man looked on, but he was too stiff and cold to get up.

Thornton stood over Buck, struggling to control himself. He was too angry to speak.

"If you strike that dog again, I'll lay into you," he at last managed to say in a choking voice.

"It's my dog," the man replied. "Get out of my way, or I'll fix you. I'm going to Dawson."

Thornton stood between the man and Buck. The man pulled out a hunting knife. But Thornton quickly rapped the man's knuckles with the ax handle, knocking the knife to the ground. He rapped the knuckles again as the man tried to pick up the knife. Then Thornton stooped, picked up the knife himself, and cut Buck's harness with two strokes.

The man had no fight left in him. Besides, Buck was too near death to be of further use in hauling the sled. A few minutes later, the two men started the sled down the river. Buck heard them go and raised his head to watch. The dogs were limping and staggering. One man guided the sled from the side, and the other stumbled along in the rear.

As Buck watched them, Thornton knelt beside him and with rough, kindly hands searched for broken bones. He found nothing more than many bruises and a state of terrible hunger. Dog and man watched the sled crawling along over the ice. Suddenly, they saw its back end drop down. A scream came to their ears as one man fell through the ice. They saw the other man turn and make one step to run back.

Just then, a whole section of ice gave way, and the dogs and the second man disappeared. A yawning hole was all that was to be seen. The bottom had dropped out of the trail.

Thornton and Buck looked at each other.

"You poor beast," said Thornton, and Buck licked his hand.

---

## D COMPREHENSION

Write the answers.
1. The story says, "The Yukon was straining to break loose from the ice that held it motionless." Explain what that sentence means.
2. Why do you think the driver ignored Thornton's advice about the river?
3. At first, why did Thornton walk away when the driver was whipping the dogs?
4. Why did Buck refuse to get up?
5. Why do you think Thornton changed his mind about helping the dogs?

## E WRITING

The story "Buck" begins with a description of springtime along the Yukon River.
• Read that description again, then write a description of springtime in the place where you live. Tell about the things you see, hear, smell, taste, and touch. Tell how those things have changed since the winter.

# A WORD LISTS

| 1 | 2 | 3 | 4 |
|---|---|---|---|
| *Hard Words* | *Word Family* | *Vocabulary Review* | *New Vocabulary* |
| 1. Hans | 1. tumble | 1. lingered on | 1. recover |
| 2. tolerate | 2. grumble | 2. stagger | 2. embrace |
| 3. haunt | 3. muscle | | 3. ideal |
| 4. naked | 4. scramble | | 4. affection |
| | 5. comfortable | | 5. haunt |
| | | | 6. tolerated |
| | | | 7. naked |
| | | | 8. grapple |

# B MAIN IDEA

For each picture, write a main-idea sentence.

Mary

1

Tom

2

Maria

3

# Buck
## Chapter 2

John Thornton had been staying in the tent for two months. He had come down the Yukon with two other men, Pete and Hans. But Thornton had frozen his feet, and his partners had left him there to recover while they went up the river to get logs for a raft. They planned to take the raft to Dawson later that spring. Thornton was still limping slightly at the time he rescued Buck, but with the continued warm weather, the limp went away.

Buck slowly got his strength back. He would lie by the riverbank during the long spring days, watch the running water, and listen to the songs of birds and the hum of nature. Buck's wounds healed, his muscles swelled out, and the flesh came back to cover his bones. Buck now weighed as much as a full-grown man.

Thornton was an ideal master. Other men took care of their dogs in a businesslike way. But Thornton treated Buck as if he were his own child. He always had a kindly greeting and a cheering word. He would sit down for long talks with Buck. At these times, he would take Buck's head between his hands and rest his own head on Buck's. Then he would shake Buck back and forth and talk softly to him. Buck knew no greater joy than Thornton's embrace and the sound of his voice.

Buck had a strange way of showing his love for Thornton. He would often seize Thornton's hand in his mouth and hold it so tightly that teeth marks would show for some time afterward. For the most part, however, Buck kept his love to himself. He went wild with happiness when Thornton touched him or spoke to him, but he did not beg for the man's affection.

Buck would lie for hours at Thornton's feet and look up into his face. He would follow each expression with keen interest. Sometimes, he would lie farther away and watch the outlines of the man and the movements of his body. The strength of Buck's gaze would often make Thornton turn his head. The man would return the gaze without speaking. Thornton's love shone out of his eyes, just as Buck's did.

For a long time after his rescue, Buck never let Thornton out of his sight. From the moment Thornton left the tent to the moment he entered it again, Buck would follow at his heels. The dog remembered that all of his former masters had left him. He was afraid that Thornton would pass out of his life, just as they had. ♦

Even in Buck's dreams, he was haunted by the fear of Thornton leaving. At such times, he would shake off sleep and creep through the chill to the flap of the tent, where he would stand and listen to the sound of his master's breathing.

Buck responded with joy to only one person—Thornton. Other gold rushers might praise or pet Buck, but he was cold toward them, and he would often get up and walk away. When Hans and Pete finally arrived on the raft, Buck refused to notice them until he learned that they were Thornton's friends. After that he tolerated them. They were very much like Thornton, living close to the earth, thinking simply and seeing clearly. They soon understood Buck and his ways.

Buck's love for Thornton seemed to grow and grow. Nothing was too great for Buck to do when Thornton commanded. One day, the men and Buck were sitting on the edge of a cliff that fell away, straight down, to naked rock three hundred feet below. Thornton was sitting near the edge, with Buck at his shoulder. Hans and Pete were nearby.

"Get ready to grab Buck," Thornton said to Hans and Pete. Then Thornton commanded, "Jump, Buck!" and pointed over the cliff. Buck sprang forward. An instant later, the three men grappled with Buck on the edge of the cliff; then they dragged him back to safety. ✳

"I don't want to be the man that lays hands on you while that dog is around," Pete said, nodding his head toward Buck.

The very next day, Buck and the men got on the raft and headed down the Yukon to Dawson. Several days later, all four of them were walking around the muddy streets of the town, when they came upon two men having a fight. Thornton stepped between the men to try to stop them from fighting. Buck lay down in the street, put his head on his paws, and watched his master's every move.

Suddenly, one man struck out, straight

from the shoulder. He hit Thornton and sent him spinning. Thornton fell down.

Those who were looking on heard what was neither bark nor yelp, but something more like a roar. They saw Buck's body rise up in the air as he left the ground. The man threw out his arm and was hurled backward to the street, with Buck on top of him.

The crowd quickly descended on Buck and pulled him off the man. Buck growled furiously and attempted to rush back in. Hans and Pete had to struggle to hold him back. A "miners' meeting" was called on the spot. The miners who saw what had happened decided that the dog was only protecting his master, so Buck was set free. But he was now famous, and from that day, his name spread through every mining camp along the Yukon.

---

## D COMPREHENSION

Write the answers.

1. Why did Thornton have to stay in the tent while Hans and Pete were gone?
2. Why do you think Buck showed his love for Thornton by biting his hand?
3. Why did Buck follow Thornton everywhere?
4. Why did Thornton order Buck to jump off a cliff?
5. At the end of the chapter, why did the miners decide to set Buck free?

## E WRITING

Do you think Thornton did the right thing when he ordered Buck to jump off a cliff?

- Write a paragraph that explains your answer. Tell why Thornton ordered Buck to jump. Describe other ways Thornton could have proved his point. Tell what you think of Thornton.

# 49

## A WORD LISTS

### 1
*Hard Words*
1. guilty
2. Eldorado
3. jutted
4. ashore
5. lunge

### 2
*Word Family*
1. particularly
2. instantly
3. desperately
4. apparently

### 3
*Vocabulary Review*
1. affection
2. grapple
3. tolerate
4. recover
5. embrace
6. haunt
7. ideal

### 4
*New Vocabulary*
1. strangle
2. flushed
3. guilty

### 5
*New Vocabulary*
1. jutted out
2. reared up
3. stretch
4. clutched

## B MAIN IDEA

For each row of pictures, figure out the main idea.

1.

2.

3.

# Buck
## Chapter 3

In the fall of that year, Buck saved John Thornton's life. The three partners were moving a long and narrow boat down a bad stretch of rapids on the Forty Mile Creek. Hans and Pete moved along the bank and guided the boat with a rope. Thornton remained in the boat and pushed it along with a pole. From time to time, Thornton shouted directions to his partners on the bank. Buck ran along the bank beside the men. He was worried and anxious, and he never took his eyes off his master.

They came to a particularly bad spot, where a ledge of rocks jutted out into the river. The boat started to fly downstream in a swift current. Hans and Pete tried to stop the boat by yanking on the rope. But the boat hit the rocks and flipped over. Thornton was flung out. He floated downstream toward the worst part of the rapids—a stretch of wild water in which no swimmer could live.

Buck sprang into the water instantly. At the end of three hundred yards, in the middle of a mad swirl of water, he caught up to Thornton. When he felt the man

grasp his tail, Buck headed for the bank. He swam with all his splendid strength. But the progress to the bank was slow, while the man and the dog traveled downstream with amazing speed. ◆

Thornton and Buck could hear the loud roaring of rapids below them. They could see the rocks that thrust through the water like the teeth of an enormous comb. They could feel the current becoming swifter. Thornton knew it would be impossible to reach the shore. Suddenly, he was hurled into a rock with crushing force. He let go of Buck and clutched the rock's slippery top with both hands. Then he shouted, "Go, Buck!"

Buck could not hold his own, and he was swept farther downstream, struggling desperately, but unable to swim back to Thornton. When he heard Thornton's command repeated, he reared up in the water, threw his head high, then turned toward the shore. He swam powerfully and was dragged ashore by Pete and Hans.

They knew that Thornton could cling to the slippery rock for only a few minutes. They ran as fast as they could up the bank to a point far above where Thornton was hanging on. They attached the rope to Buck's neck and shoulders and threw him into the stream. He struck out boldly, but not far enough into the stream. He came within six feet of Thornton, but then the current carried him past the struggling man.

Hans promptly pulled with the rope, as if Buck were a boat. The dog was jerked under the surface, and he remained under the surface until his body struck against the shore and he was hauled out. He was half drowned, and Hans and Pete threw themselves upon him, pounding the breath into him and the water out of him. He staggered to his feet and fell down.

Just then, the faint sound of Thornton's voice came to them, and although they could not make out the words, they knew that he could not hold on any longer. His master's voice acted on Buck as if it were an electric shock. He sprang to his feet and ran up the bank ahead of the men to the point he had jumped from before.

Again the rope was attached, and again Buck was thrown into the raging stream. But this time he swam far out into the stream. He had made a mistake once, but he would not be guilty of it a second time. Buck swam on until he was directly upstream from Thornton. Then he turned, and with the speed of an express train, he headed down toward his master. Thornton saw him coming. ★

Buck struck him with the whole force of the current behind him. Thornton reached up and grabbed Buck's shaggy neck with both hands. Hans tied the rope around a tree, and Buck and Thornton were jerked under the water. The man and the dog were strangling, choking, sometimes one on top and sometimes the other, dragging over the jagged bottom and smashing against rocks. At last, they came toward the bank.

As soon as they reached the shore, both man and dog passed out. When Thornton came to, he looked for Buck. Hans and Pete were standing over Buck's limp and apparently lifeless body. Thornton was bruised and battered, yet he got up and went carefully over to Buck. He found that the dog was alive, but he had broken ribs.

"That settles it," he announced. "We camp right here." They camped until Buck's ribs mended and he was able to travel again.

• • • •

That winter at Dawson, Buck did something that made him even more famous than he already was. The incident started with a conversation in the Eldorado Hotel.

Some men were bragging about their favorite dogs. These men were claiming that Buck was not the best dog. Thornton spoke loudly in Buck's favor. One man stated that his dog could start a sled with five hundred pounds on it and walk off with it. A second man bragged six hundred, and a third seven hundred.

"That's nothing," said Thornton. "Buck can start a sled with a thousand pounds on it."

A rich miner named Matthewson demanded, "Are you saying he can walk off with it for a hundred yards?"

"Yes, walk off with it for a hundred yards," Thornton said coolly.

"Well," Matthewson said slowly so that all could hear, "I would offer a prize of one thousand dollars to any dog who could pull such a load. But I don't believe that any dog alive could do it." So saying, he slammed down a sack of gold dust the size of a rolling pin.

Nobody spoke. Thornton could feel a flush of warm blood creeping up his face. His tongue had tricked him. He did not know whether Buck could start a sled with a thousand pounds on it. Half a ton! He had great faith in Buck's strength and often thought he was capable of starting such a load. But he had never tested the idea. The eyes of a dozen men fixed upon him, silent and waiting.

# D COMPREHENSION

Write the answers.

1. When Buck first tried to rescue Thornton, why did he move so slowly toward the bank?
2. Explain why Hans and Pete attached a rope to Buck.
3. After the rescue, why did the men decide to camp by the river?
4. In the hotel, Thornton made a claim about Buck that he wasn't sure of. Why do you think he made that claim?
5. Do you think Buck will be able to pull the sled? Explain your answer.

# E WRITING

Do you think Thornton is a good master for Buck?

- Write a paragraph that explains your answer. Tell why some people might think Thornton is a good master; then tell why others might think he's a bad master. Finally, tell what you think.

## A WORD LISTS

|  | 1 | | 2 |
|--|---|--|---|
|  | *Word Family* | | *New Vocabulary* |
|  | 1. admiration | | 1. witness |
|  | 2. condition | | 2. lunge |
|  | 3. conversation | | 3. quiver |
|  | 4. affection | | 4. grate |

## B MAIN IDEA

For each picture or row of pictures, figure out the main idea.

1.

2.

**3.**

Buck

Skit

Rover

**4.**

Phil

---

## C READING

# Buck
### Chapter 4

Matthewson looked at Thornton coldly and said, "I've got a sled standing outside now with twenty fifty-pound sacks of flour on it. That's a thousand pounds."

Thornton did not reply. He did not know what to say. He glanced from face to face like a man who has lost the power of thought. The face of Jim O'Brien, an old-time comrade, caught his eyes.

O'Brien shook his head solemnly and said, "I don't have much faith that the beast can pull such a load."

The men poured out of the Eldorado into the street to see the test. The tables were deserted. Soon, several hundred men in heavy fur coats stood around the sled.

The sled, loaded with a thousand pounds of flour, had been standing for a couple of hours in the intense cold. It was sixty below zero, and the runners had frozen fast to the hard-packed snow.

O'Brien and Matthewson argued about starting the sled. O'Brien suggested that Thornton could knock the runners loose from the ice before Buck began pulling. Matthewson insisted that Buck would have to pull the sled with the runners as they were—in the frozen grip of the snow. Most of the men who had witnessed the argu-

ment decided in Matthewson's favor.

Not one man besides Thornton thought that Buck would succeed. As Thornton looked at the sled, he was heavy with doubt.

"Three thousand," Matthewson suddenly shouted. "Thornton, I'll pay you three thousand dollars if your dog can pull that load!"

Thornton's face showed his doubt, but his fighting spirit was up. That spirit failed to recognize the impossible. The regular team of ten dogs was curled up in the snow in front of the sled. The team was unhitched, and Buck, with his own harness, was put in front of the sled. He sensed the excitement, and he felt that in some way he must do a great thing for John Thornton. ♦

The crowd began to murmur with admiration at Buck's splendid appearance. He was in perfect condition, without an ounce of extra flesh. He weighed one hundred and fifty pounds. His furry coat shone like silk. His muscles showed in tight rolls underneath his skin. The men felt these muscles and said they were as hard as iron.

Suddenly, a tall man said, "Gad, sir! Gad, sir! I offer you eight hundred dollars for him, sir, before the test, sir; eight hundred for that dog just as he stands."

Thornton shook his head no and stepped to Buck's side.

The crowd fell silent. Everybody knew that Buck was a magnificent animal; but the thousand pounds of flour was more than any dog could pull.

Thornton knelt by Buck's side. He took the dog's head in his two hands and rested his cheek on Buck's cheek. He did not playfully shake him or murmur softly. But he whispered something in the dog's ear. Buck whined eagerly.

The crowd was watching curiously. The affair was growing mysterious. It seemed like a magic trick. As Thornton got to his feet, Buck seized Thornton's hand between his jaws, pressing in with his teeth and releasing slowly. It was Buck's answer.

Thornton stepped back. "Now, Buck," he said.

Buck pulled his harness tight, then let it slacken a bit.

"Gee!" Thornton's voice rang out, sharp in the tense silence.

Buck followed the command. He swung to the right, ending the movement in a lunge that jerked the harness and stopped his one hundred and fifty pounds. The load quivered, and a crisp crackling rose from under the runners.

"Haw!" Thornton commanded.

Buck made the same move, this time to the left. The crackling turned into a snapping. The sled turned slightly, and the runners slipped and grated several inches to the side. The sled was broken out. Men were holding their breath. ★

"Now, MUSH ON!"

Thornton's command cracked out like a shot. Buck threw himself forward, tightening the harness with a jarring lunge. His whole body was gathered together in the tremendous effort. His muscles knotted under his silky fur. His great chest was low to the ground, his head forward and down. His feet flew, and his claws scarred the hard-packed snow. The sled swayed, trembled, and started forward. One of Buck's feet slipped, and one man groaned aloud. Then the sled slowly moved ahead.

Men gasped and began to breathe again, unaware that for a moment they had stopped breathing. Thornton was running behind, encouraging Buck with short, cheery words. The distance had been measured off, and as the dog neared the pile of firewood that marked the end of the hundred yards, the men began to cheer loudly.

The cheer burst into a roar as Buck passed the firewood and halted at command. Every man was clapping wildly, even Matthewson. Hats and mittens were flying in the air. Men were shaking hands, and they did not care whose hand they shook.

Thornton fell on his knees beside Buck, head against head. Thornton was shaking him back and forth. Those who gathered close heard him talking to Buck. He talked softly and lovingly.

"Gad, sir! Gad, sir!" sputtered the tall man. "I'll give you a thousand for him, sir, a thousand, sir—twelve hundred, sir."

Thornton rose to his feet. His eyes were wet. The tears were streaming down his cheeks. "No, sir," he said to the tall man. "No, sir. You can't buy this dog for any amount of money."

Buck seized Thornton's hand in his teeth. Thornton shook him back and forth.

The men drew back a ways, and none dared to disturb the man and his dog.

## D COMPREHENSION

Write the answers.
1. At the beginning of the chapter, why were the runners of the sled stuck to the ground?
2. Why do you think Matthewson said Buck had to break the runners free?
3. How did the tall man's offer for Buck change during the story? Why did it change?
4. Why did Buck bite Thornton's hand? When had Buck done that before?
5. Why do you think the men didn't dare to disturb Thornton and Buck?

## E WRITING

How did Buck change during the story?
• Write a paragraph that explains your answer. Tell what Buck looked like at the beginning of the story and what he looked like at the end. Also tell how his feelings changed.

## A WORD LISTS

| 1 | 2 |
|---|---|
| *Hard Words* | *New Vocabulary* |
| 1. boughs | 1. migrate |
| 2. drowsy | 2. plentiful |
| 3. lullaby | 3. volunteer |
| | 4. identify |
| | 5. spawn |

## B READING

# Trees
## by Harry Behn

Trees are the kindest things I know,
They do no harm, they simply grow

And spread a shade for sleepy cows,
And gather birds among their boughs.

They give us fruit in leaves above,
And wood to make our houses of,

And leaves to burn on Hallowe'en,
And in the Spring new buds of green.

They are the first when day's begun
To touch the beams of morning sun,

They are the last to hold the light
When evening changes into night,

And when a moon floats on the sky,
They hum a drowsy lullaby

Of sleepy children long ago . . .
Trees are the kindest things I know.

# In Time of Silver Rain
## by Langston Hughes

In time of silver rain
The earth
Puts forth new life again,
Green grasses grow
And flowers lift their heads,
And over all the plain
The wonder spreads
    Of life,
    Of life,
    Of life!

In time of silver rain
The butterflies
Lift silken wings
To catch a rainbow cry,
And trees put forth
New leaves to sing
In joy beneath the sky
As down the roadway
Passing boys and girls
Go singing, too,
In time of silver rain
When spring
And life
Are new.

## C COMPREHENSION

Write the answers.

1. The poem "Trees" gives several reasons to explain why trees are so kind. Describe at least three of those reasons.

2. How could trees "hum a drowsy lullaby"?

3. In the poem "In Time of Silver Rain," what do you think the poet means when he says, "The butterflies lift silken wings to catch a rainbow cry"?

4. In what ways are these two poems alike?

5. In what ways are they different?

## D WRITING

Write a poem about an animal you like. Tell how the animal looks, how it sounds, and what kind of skin or fur it has. Also tell what the animal does. Your poem does not have to rhyme.

## A WORD LISTS

| 1<br>*Hard Words* | 2<br>*Country Names* | 3<br>*Vocabulary Review* | 4<br>*Vocabulary Preview* |
|---|---|---|---|
| 1. tanager | 1. Colombia | 1. migrate | 1. enlarge |
| 2. salmon | 2. Ecuador | 2. plentiful | 2. mysterious |
| 3. molting | 3. Peru | 3. volunteer | |
| 4. scarce | 4. Brazil | 4. identify | |
| 5. fuel | | 5. spawn | |
| 6. scientist | | | |

## B VOCABULARY FROM CONTEXT

1. They decided to **enlarge** their house by adding a room.

2. The old castle was strange and **mysterious**.

## C READING

# AMAZING ANIMAL JOURNEYS
## Chapter 1

*During the next two lessons, you will read four short articles about four different animals. One of the animals is a brightly colored bird, another is a magnificent fish, the third is a shy mammal, and the last is a small butterfly. These animals are different in almost every way except one: they all take amazing journeys.*

# THE ALL-AMERICAN FLYER

Every year, thousands of beautiful scarlet tanagers migrate back and forth between North and South America. These small birds spend summers in the United States and Canada and winters in Colombia, Ecuador, Peru, and Brazil.

To make the long journey between North and South America, scarlet tanagers fly across the Gulf of Mexico and Central America. No tanagers get lost—not even the young ones. Yet the trip is almost four thousand miles!

## Feathers for All Weathers

When tanagers arrive in May to spend the late spring and summer in North America, they are in what scientists call summer dress. The wing and tail feathers of the male birds are jet black, and the rest of their feathers are bright red. The female's feathers are greenish-yellow.

As the summer passes, tanagers begin shedding their old feathers and growing new ones for the long flight back to South America. This process is called molting.

By August, the birds look ragged. Males lose their scarlet-red feathers and grow green ones in their place. Females don't change as much, because their new feathers are almost the same color as the old ones.

By September, both sexes are in green winter dress. Not a single tanager is scarlet now.

## Flying for Food

During September, the days grow shorter. The weather gets colder, and the insects that tanagers eat become scarce. So the birds begin moving southward.

Male tanagers leave first. After a few days, the females follow them. Flocks from

the East head toward Florida, taking a route called the Atlantic Flyway. Midwestern birds head for Texas, using a different route—the Mississippi Flyway.

Tanagers fly during the night. Each morning, the birds land and eat as many insects, fruit, and seeds as they can. Then they rest and eat some more. At dusk, their long journey continues.

The birds reach South America during the rainy season. Forest trees have new leaves, and food is plentiful.

The rainy season lasts for several months, but then the dry season begins, and food gets scarce. Before that happens, the tanagers molt and leave. Traveling in summer dress, they fly back to North America on the same route they used on their way south. Some even return to the places where they started their trip.

## Bands Tell the Tale

How do we know about the tanager's migration between North and South America? The United States Fish and Wildlife Service has been studying bird migrations for years. Volunteers in North and South America catch the birds in nets, put bands on their legs, and release them. Each band has its own number. When other volunteers catch the birds months later, they report the numbers on the bands.

Thousands of reports about scarlet tanagers are now on file. The reports show that tanagers travel about eight thousand miles a year, avoiding winter in North America and the dry season in South America. Their journey is amazing. But then, tanagers are amazing birds. ♦

Tanager in summer dress

Tanager molting

Tanager in winter dress

# WHEN THE SALMON COME HOME

People who fish have always told great stories, but none as strange as the one about salmon. About a hundred years ago, people who fished for a living said that salmon spent a few years in the deep ocean and then returned to the rivers where they were born.

Was the story true? How could anyone prove it? How could anyone tell one fish from another? Long ago, Izaak Walton, an English writer, tied ribbons on the tails of fish to find out where they went. But either he never saw the fish again, or the fish lost their ribbons.

## Clipping and Tagging

Eventually scientists discovered a way to identify salmon. The scientists caught young salmon soon after the salmon were born in spawning grounds, which are places along the bottom of a river where salmon lay their spawn, or eggs. The scientists clipped off part of each young salmon's fin, marking fish from different rivers in different ways. If some of these salmon were later caught out in the ocean, their marks would show which river they came from.

Meanwhile, scientists on fishing boats out in the ocean used little plastic or metal tags to mark salmon. When these scientists caught salmon with clipped fins, they tagged the fish and recorded where they were caught. Then they released the salmon back into the ocean.

Back in the rivers, the chance of finding any salmon that were both clipped and tagged was slight. But in time, many clipped and tagged salmon were picked up near their spawning grounds.

Here was solid proof that salmon do return to their birthplace. Their spawning ground may be located in a distant upper branch of a big river, yet somehow the salmon find their way home.

## A Long Way Home

How far do salmon travel to get home? A large chinook salmon was tagged in the Pacific Ocean fifteen hundred miles from the coast and was later found a thousand miles upstream in the Columbia River. Its homeward journey was twenty-five hundred miles! ★

Most salmon do not take such a long trip, but those that are born in long rivers like the Columbia or the Yukon in North America may travel hundreds of miles to reach their spawning grounds. Others, like the pink salmon, go only a few miles.

How long do the salmon stay in the sea? The pink, which is small, stays two years. The chinook, the largest of the salmon, stays two to five years. Food is plentiful in the ocean, and the salmon grow big and fat before they start for home. As soon as they reach their home rivers, the salmon stop eating. While swimming upstream, they live off the fat they stored in their bodies while at sea.

## Swimming Upstream

Some salmon come home in the spring and others in the fall. Before they start swimming up a river, thousands of the same kind of salmon gather at the place where the river flows into the sea. As the salmon begin rushing up the river, the water seems to boil. The fish swim so fast

Salmon swimming upstream can leap up waterfalls.

that their upstream journey is called a run. Swimming against the current, the salmon often cover fifty miles a day.

The run slows down in places where dams have been built. Since salmon can't scale the high walls of a dam, they are provided with a kind of stairway called a fishway. Water flows down the stairs, and the salmon leap from step to step until they are above the dam. Then they continue rushing upstream to their spawning grounds.

By the time salmon reach their spawning grounds, they are thin and exhausted. Yet they dig nests in the riverbed, mate, and lay eggs. When the salmon have done what they set out to do, they die. Soon afterward, baby salmon hatch from the eggs. Like their parents, they will take an amazing journey to the ocean and then come back home.

## D COMPREHENSION

Write the answers.
1. Tell what happens when birds molt.
2. Name two reasons tanagers fly south in September.
3. Explain how scientists used clips and tags to prove that salmon return to their spawning grounds.
4. Tell what salmon do after they return to their spawning grounds.
5. Compare salmon and tanagers. Tell how they are different, then how they are alike.

## E WRITING

Pretend you are a scarlet tanager.
• Describe a year in your life, beginning with your arrival in North America during the spring. Tell what you do during each season of the year. Describe the places you see and the trips you take.

# A WORD LISTS

| 1<br>*Hard Words* | 2<br>*Compound Words* | 3<br>*New Vocabulary* | 4<br>*Vocabulary Preview* |
|---|---|---|---|
| 1. marmot | 1. woodchuck | 1. litter | 1. misery |
| 2. hibernate | 2. groundhog | 2. reluctant | 2. tussle |
| 3. monarch | 3. underground | 3. limp | 3. intense |
| 4. caterpillar | 4. runway | 4. sensitive | |
| 5. cocoon | 5. homeowner | | |
| | 6. housekeeper | | |

# B VOCABULARY FROM CONTEXT

1. The baby felt great **misery**, and it would not stop crying.
2. The puppies began to **tussle** and fight, and they rolled all over the floor.
3. They wore sunglasses to block the **intense** light.

# C MAIN IDEA

1. Roses grow in the summer.
   Pansies grow in the summer.
   Buttercups grow in the summer.
2. Flowers produce oxygen.
   Trees produce oxygen.
   Grass produces oxygen.

# AMAZING ANIMAL JOURNEYS
## Chapter 2

*In the last lesson, you read about two animals that take amazing journeys: the scarlet tanager and the salmon. In this lesson, you will read about two more. One is a woodchuck and the other is a butterfly. Their journeys are just as remarkable as the tanager's and the salmon's.*

## JOURNEY TO DEATH'S DOOR

Call it a woodchuck, a groundhog, or a marmot. It doesn't matter which name you use. The animal is really just a big squirrel—one that lives on and under the ground.

Like its squirrel relatives, the woodchuck gnaws with its front teeth. You might think a woodchuck gnaws wood, but it really eats softer foods, such as clover, grass, and garden vegetables. Woodchucks eat so many of these plants that some farmers think of them as pests.

### Home, Sweet Den

The woodchuck's home is an underground den with a front entrance and a back entrance and another hole that's used for a quick escape. Like little office workers, woodchucks leave home in the morning, spend the day at work, and then come back to sleep at night.

The woodchuck's den is about three feet underground and has runways connecting separate rooms. Like many homeowners, woodchucks keep improving their dens. Every spring they add new rooms or enlarge some of the old ones.

Woodchucks are good housekeepers except for one messy thing. In the fall, they store plants and other food in their dens, just like their squirrel relatives. Some of the food gets moldy and rots because woodchucks don't eat everything they have "squirreled away."

### Winter Slowdown

Woodchucks hibernate in their dens when cold weather comes. When animals hibernate, they sleep through the winter. To hibernate, the woodchuck travels just three feet under ground; but those three feet are a journey to the door of death.

To get ready for hibernating, the woodchuck plugs the entrances to its den with dirt and grass. When the woodchuck is snugly holed up, its breathing slows down. Then its body temperature starts to fall to just a few degrees above freezing. Its heart beats only four times a minute. The

Woodchucks eat clover, grass, and other soft foods.

woodchuck scarcely moves. It seems to be dead.

In the spring, many hours of warmth are needed to bring the woodchuck out of its winter sleep. When warm weather gets underway, the woodchuck wakes up and comes out of its den. Again, it travels only three feet, but this time it takes a journey back to life. ♦

## THE MYSTERY OF THE BUTTERFLY TREES

What has six legs and flies south for the winter? The answer is a monarch butterfly. About fifty years ago, thousands of people helped discover this fact by working together. Scientists had observed that monarchs from east of the Rocky Mountains fly south in the fall. But no one had the faintest idea where they went.

### From Caterpillar to Monarch

Most of the monarch's life was well-known. In spring, it lays its eggs on milkweed. The caterpillar that hatches from these eggs eats and grows. Then it covers itself with a case called a cocoon. Inside the cocoon, the caterpillar changes completely.

When the caterpillar comes out of its cocoon later in the spring, it has changed into a lovely monarch butterfly with four orange and black wings. All summer long, the monarch flies from flower to flower in search of nectar. This sweet liquid is the monarch's food.

## On the Wing

In early autumn, monarchs start flying south. When night comes, they stop. Thousands gather on certain trees and then take off the next morning.

But where do they go? The only way to track them is to tag them. A Canadian scientist, Dr. Fred Urquhart, discovered a label that would stick to a butterfly's wings. He had thousands of these labels printed with numbers and instructions. Then he called for volunteers to help tag monarchs. ★

News of the tagging program spread, and people from Maine to Mexico became butterfly watchers. They caught monarchs in nets, tagged them, and sent them back to Dr. Urquhart in Canada. After hundreds of thousands of monarchs were tagged, it became clear that monarchs fly all the way to the Sierra Madres, which are mountains in Mexico.

## Mountain Hideout

Just where in the Sierra Madres did the monarchs go? Some Mexicans offered a clue. They told of mysterious trees covered with butterflies, high in the mountains. But they were not sure where the trees were.

Years passed before Dr. Urquhart found the trees. Led by guides, he climbed ten thousand feet to a stretch of forest where all the trees looked orange. Every tree was covered with monarchs—millions of them! Staring in wonder, Dr. Urquhart noticed a tagged butterfly that had come from Minnesota. It had traveled two thousand miles.

## Butterflies on Parade

The story of the monarchs that live west of the Rocky Mountains is different. Instead of going from north to south, western monarchs go from cool mountains to warm valleys. In the town of Pacific Grove, California, a place where monarchs spend the winter, school children welcome them with a parade. Tourists come to see the trees on which they settle.

East or west, monarchs are always welcome. Of all the animals that migrate, they are the smallest. Their journey is amazing. But then, the tanager, the salmon, and the woodchuck also make amazing journeys!

# E COMPREHENSION

Write the answers.
1. Why do you think the article about woodchucks is titled "Journey to Death's Door"?
2. Tell what a woodchuck's den looks like and where it's located.
3. How does a woodchuck's body change when the woodchuck hibernates?
4. Tell how caterpillars turn into butterflies.
5. Why did Dr. Urquhart put tags on butterflies?

# F WRITING

Write a paragraph that compares migration with hibernation.
• Tell how the two processes are alike and how they are different. Tell why animals migrate or hibernate. Tell which kinds of animals hibernate and which ones migrate.

## A WORD LISTS

| 1 | 2 | 3 |
|---|---|---|
| *Hard Words* | *Word Endings* | *Vocabulary Review* |
| 1. North Carolina | 1. incredible | 1. sensitive |
| 2. coax | 2. snuggle | 2. reluctant |
| 3. Yodeler | 3. tickle | 3. limp |
|  | 4. tussle | 4. litter |
|  | 5. tumble |  |

## B MAIN IDEA

1. Wild deer live in the jungle.
   Wild tigers live in the jungle.
   Wild apes live in the jungle.

2. Vanessa dug a hole.
   Then Vanessa picked up a tree.
   Vanessa put the tree into the hole.

# Adventure on the Rocky Ridge
### *by Donna Clearwater*
### Chapter 1

Little Martha never knew she was almost given away when she was still a tiny puppy. She didn't know she was a runt, the smallest puppy in a litter of twelve hounds. And she didn't know that her mother was a prize hunting dog owned by people who raised the best hunting dogs in North Carolina. Little Martha didn't understand that the owners kept only the best puppies from each litter. Those were the biggest and the strongest. The rest were given away.

Little Martha's first memories were of great happiness and terrible sadness. Her eyes were still closed when she was born, and they remained closed for two weeks. While her eyes were closed, Martha experienced great joy when she snuggled next to her warm mother. She also felt great de-

spair when one of the large puppies in the litter pushed her away, leaving her shivering and cold.

Martha would squeal little sounds of misery as she lay there, but her mother couldn't do much to help her. There were just too many puppies in the litter, and her mother could not take care of all of them. So during her first days of life, Martha spent a lot of time aching from hunger and shivering from cold.

Julie Owl saved Martha. Julie was the twelve-year-old daughter of the people who owned Martha. She pleaded with her father not to give away the little runt. "I'll take care of her, Dad," she said. "Really, I will. I'll feed her and you'll see. She'll be a fine dog."

Mr. Owl was reluctant to keep the runt. "Julie," he explained, "why don't you take one of the other puppies? I'll give you any other puppy in the litter. But that runt won't be as healthy as the others. It will always be . . ."

Mr. Owl stopped short as he looked at Julie's pleading eyes. He suddenly realized why she wanted the puppy. It was because she saw herself in the puppy. Like the puppy, Julie wasn't as healthy as other children, and she walked with a leg brace.

After a moment, Mr. Owl smiled and said, "Maybe you're right. Maybe that puppy will grow up to be a fine dog."

Julie's face brightened, and she threw her arms around her father's neck. "Oh, thank you, Dad!" she exclaimed. "I'll take good care of her. And I'll name her Martha."

That was a very strange name for a hound dog. Outside in the kennel were dogs named Boomer, Flash, Duke, and Queenie. There were Prince and Princess, Dodger

and Digger. But no dog had a name like Martha.

Julie mothered Martha. She got a little bottle and fed Martha six times a day. She made a warm bed for Martha next to her own bed. She held Martha and petted her and talked to her and kissed her. She loved Martha the way a mother loves her baby. ◆

• • •

All the dogs that Mr. Owl raised had a powerful sense of smell. Although Mr. Owl didn't know it at the time, Martha's nose was more sensitive than the nose of any other dog he had ever raised. In fact, it was better than the nose of any other dog in North Carolina.

Even when Martha's eyes were still closed, she recognized Julie's smell. At first, however, Martha wasn't wild about this smell. Whenever Julie's smell came near, it meant that Martha would be removed from the wonderful smells of her mother and the smells of her brothers and sisters. But after a while, Martha began to love Julie's smell. She learned that the smell meant warm milk and soft petting and a nice blanket to keep her warm.

Shortly after the puppies' eyes opened, Mr. Owl tested the puppies to see which ones would be the best hunting dogs. The test was simple. He placed all the puppies in a shallow box. He put a screen over the top of the box so that if a puppy tried to climb or jump out of the box, the puppy would bang its head on the screen. Then he put the mother dog just outside the box and waited.

Some of the puppies kept banging and banging and banging their heads. Those were the puppies that would probably make the best hunting dogs. When they grew up, they would probably hunt and hunt, no mat-

ter how rough the country was or how tired they were.

Julie put Martha in the box with the other puppies. Some of the big puppies banged and banged against the screen. They whined and cried, but they kept banging against the screen. Martha whined and cried, too, but she didn't jump up, not once.

Julie knew that her father would think Martha was no good, so she tried to coax Martha to jump. But still Martha sat there without jumping as the other puppies pushed her around. At last, Julie removed her from the box. She held Martha and said, "It's all right. You're still going to be the best dog in the world."

• • •

After the puppies learned to run and jump, they began to play. Sometimes Martha's brothers and sisters would get too rough for her, but she still loved playing.

She was happy just to be with them, even when they were rough. ★

One of them would usually start playing by grabbing another's droopy ear and taking a nip. Then the tussling would begin. The two puppies would tumble over each other and growl. Soon the others would join in. When the wrestling became too rough, one of them would run from the group, waiting for the others to follow. Then there would be more growling and tumbling.

The only experience that is more exciting to a young hound than playing is catching the scent of a wild animal, such as a rabbit or a deer. When a hound catches the scent of another animal, the hound feels delighted. The hound is so delighted that it wants more and more and more. It wants to keep following that scent forever. For the hound dog, following a scent is the greatest experience in the world.

Martha first discovered this marvelous experience when she was watching her brothers and sisters tussle in the meadow behind Julie's house. The puppies were now three months old. Martha had been wrestling with the others, but they were too rough for her. One of her brothers had knocked her down so hard that she had lost all interest in playing.

As Martha watched the puppies tussling, she suddenly smelled something that was more interesting than anything else she had ever smelled. The wind carried the scent. Martha held her nose high in the air and tried to catch more of it. Then she let out a little howl and tried to get closer to the smell.

Martha left the others and put her nose near the ground. She began sniffing very quickly. "Yes, yes," her nose told her. "Get closer. Follow it." So she did, even though she could hardly run. Her ears were so long that when she tried to run with her nose to the ground, she kept stepping on her ears with her front paws.

Just as the smell was becoming so intense that Martha could hardly stand it, she caught another scent—Julie's. Julie picked her up and said, "You can't go hunting yet. You have to stay with the others."

Martha cried and squirmed and tried to get away. But Julie held on to her and limped slowly back to the place where the other puppies were playing.

## D COMPREHENSION

Write the answers.
1. At first, why did Mr. Owl want to give Martha away?
2. Mr. Owl believed that Julie saw herself in Martha. Explain why Julie might feel that way.
3. In what ways did Julie treat Martha like a human baby?
4. Why would the dogs that kept banging their heads during the test probably be the best hunting dogs?
5. Do you think Martha will be a good hunting dog? Why or why not?

## E WRITING

Write an essay (a short article) about smells.
- Tell about the different smells you experience during the day. Describe the ones you like the most and explain why you like them. Then describe the ones you like the least and explain why you dislike them. Add any more thoughts you have about smells.

# A WORD LISTS

| 1 Hard Words | 2 Word Endings | 3 Word Practice | 4 New Vocabulary |
|---|---|---|---|
| 1. kennel | 1. ledge | 1. moist | 1. kennel |
| 2. quail | 2. ridge | 2. moisture | 2. ridge |
| 3. dwarf | 3. edge | 3. chill | 3. ledge |
| 4. Yodeler | 4. nudge | 4. chilly | 4. quail |
|  |  | 5. tearful | 5. dwarf |

# B MAIN IDEA

1. Maria looked through a lens.
Then Maria said, "Smile."
Then Maria pushed a button on her camera.

# C READING

# Adventure on the Rocky Ridge
## Chapter 2

When Martha and the other puppies were six months old, they were all interested in hunting, but they weren't allowed to run free. Julie still kept Martha in her room, but Martha's brothers and sisters lived in a kennel with the other hounds. The hounds in the kennel howled and ran back and forth, trying to get out of the kennel, but the only time Mr. Owl let them out was when he trained them.

Even though a hound has a magnificent nose, training a young hound to hunt takes two years or more. The problem is that a young hound wants to hunt everything. The hound may start out following the scent of a deer. But if it comes across the scent of a rabbit or a quail, the hound will quickly forget about the deer and follow the new scent. Young hounds must work hour after hour learning to stay with one scent and ignore the others.

Martha didn't go hunting with her brothers and sisters because Martha was a pet. She was Julie's constant companion. She slept under Julie's bed and stayed inside during the day while Julie was in school. When Julie returned from school, Martha wagged and wiggled and whined. But when Julie left, Martha felt lonely and sad. The hours seemed to drag until she caught Julie's scent or heard the sound of her voice.

One day after school, Julie had just finished cleaning the kennel when she saw her father far off on the rocky ridge. The path up to the ridge was steep and dangerous. Julie's father did not allow her to go up there because of her leg. As Julie watched her father, she knew he was returning from a training session with Martha's brothers and sisters. He had taken Leader with him. Leader was the best hound in the kennel. Mr. Owl took Leader along so that the other dogs could imitate him and learn from him.

Julie could tell by the way her father was walking that he was disappointed. When he was disappointed, his shoulders drooped and he plodded along slowly. As she watched him climb down from the ridge, she knew why he was disturbed. Ever since she could remember, he had talked about raising a dog that could track an animal over the rocky ridge. No dog in the county had ever done it because the

ridge did not hold the scent of animals. It had no long grass or moisture to hold the scent. Instead, the ridge was nothing but hard, polished rock, with tiny patches of dwarf grass here and there.

A constant wind blew over the rocky ridge, and that wind blew away what little scent any animal left on the rocks. Julie had often watched hounds try to track animals over the ridge. They would easily follow the scent through the long grass below the ridge. Then they would move upward, to places where there were more rocks and less grass. Here, they would become confused. They would whine and run in circles, trying to pick up the scent. Sometimes, the best hounds—like Leader—would run farther, almost to the edge of the ridge. But even Leader would lose the scent on the ridge and run aimlessly this way and that. ♦

As the dogs came off the ridge, they saw Julie and Martha. They ran ahead, jumped all over Julie, and began wrestling with Martha. They quickly stopped playing, however, because they were tired from their long outing.

A few minutes later, Julie's father sat down on the grass next to her. The half-grown hounds climbed on him and licked his face. He laughed and pushed them aside. Then he explained to Julie, "Around noon, I saw a large deer climbing the rocky ridge. I was hoping that one of the young hounds would be able to track it over the ledge. But . . ." His voice trailed off.

"Maybe one of them will be better than Leader," he continued, pointing to one of the half-grown hounds. "Yodeler over there did as well as Leader. But when the dogs reached the top of the ridge, they lost the scent."

• • •

Three months later, when Martha and the other dogs from the litter were nine months old, a terrible thing happened. It was late fall, and the nights were very cold, with raw winds and the smell of winter.

Julie came home from school, greeted her mother, and limped into the living room. She sat down to read a book as her mother worked in the kitchen. Then Martha jumped into Julie's lap.

"Get out of here," Julie said, laughing. "You're not a little puppy anymore. You have to stay on the floor."

Julie pushed Martha down and returned to her reading. But Martha wanted to play, so she grabbed Julie's shoe and started to wrestle with it.

"Cut it out," Julie said. "I'm busy." Martha sat down with her tail wagging and looked up at Julie.

"All right," said Julie. She stood up and walked over to a box in the corner of the room. Then she took a rubber ball from the box and rolled it across the floor. Martha took off after the ball. She caught it and began to wrestle with it. Then she began to chew on it as Julie sat down and started reading again. After a couple of minutes had passed, Martha brought the ball over to Julie and dropped it by her feet. She let out a little bark. Julie picked up the ball and rolled it across the floor again.

The game went on for a while. Then Julie played another game with Martha. Julie took one of her old mittens. She let Martha smell it for a few seconds. Then she hid it behind the couch. "Go find the mitten," she told Martha.

Martha held her head high and sniffed the air. She trotted in a circle and suddenly stopped. She turned and went directly to the mitten. Julie had hoped the game would keep Martha busy for a while, but Martha's nose was so good that it took her only a few seconds to find anything inside the house. In fact, when Julie had played the same game outside, Martha would always find the mitten in a few minutes, even when it was hidden far out in the middle of the meadow. ★

Suddenly, Julie noticed that her mother was standing by the living room door, looking outside into the darkness. "I wonder what happened to your father," she said thoughtfully, still peering into the darkness. "He should have been back hours ago."

"Where did he go?" Julie asked as she put the book aside.

"I think he went out with Yodeler and the others," her mother replied. "But I don't think he intended to stay out after dark."

Julie suddenly felt anxious. She limped over to the door and opened it. A raw wind sent a chilly blast into the room and almost pushed the door out of her grip.

"Close the door, honey," her mother said. "I'm sure your father will be home shortly."

Three hours later, the house was silent. Julie and her mother were sitting at the table, but neither had eaten very much. They sat without saying a word, trying not to think about why Julie's father hadn't yet returned.

• • •

Mr. Owl had a good reason for not returning. He couldn't walk. He had taken Leader, Boomer, and the other dogs from the litter over the rocky ridge. Two of the young dogs had picked up the scent of a deer and had followed the scent along the steep slopes, where the grass was long.

Julie's father tried calling the dogs back and followed them for over two miles. Then he came to a treacherous place where the trail went over a narrow ledge. He tripped on one of the rocks and fell more than twenty feet. He landed sharply in an awkward position. The severe pain from his right leg told him that the leg was broken.

Climbing back up the ledge was impossible. So Mr. Owl called Boomer and Leader close to him. He curled up with the dogs and tried to stay warm. Then he began to wait, trying to ignore the intense pain in his leg.

• • •

Julie looked out the window of her living room. Suddenly, she noticed some forms in the yard.

"Look, Mom," she said, pointing out the window. "There's Yodeler."

Julie's mother ran to the front door and opened it. Yodeler and three other dogs from the litter ran into the house. Usually, they weren't allowed inside, but neither Julie nor her mother scolded them. Instead, they looked outside into the darkness.

"Bill?" Julie's mother called. "Bill, are you out there?"

The only response was a howl from one of Martha's sisters. Soon, five more of the dogs were inside the house, wagging their tails and sniffing everything.

Julie's mother turned to Julie. With a worried voice, she said, "Julie, I'm afraid something has happened to your father."

## D COMPREHENSION

Write the answers.
1. Why do young hounds have trouble tracking just one scent?
2. Why was it difficult to track animals over the rocky ridge?
3. Why was the mitten game easy for Martha?
4. Why did Mr. Owl curl up with Boomer and Leader?
5. How do you think Julie felt at the end of the chapter?

## E WRITING

What is your favorite kind of dog?
• Write an essay that explains your answer. Tell which kind of dog you like and why you like that type. Describe why you like that kind of dog better than other types. Tell about any dogs of that type that you have known.

# 56

## A WORD LISTS

| 1<br>*Hard Words* | 2<br>*Word Practice* | 3<br>*Vocabulary Review* | 4<br>*New Vocabulary* |
|---|---|---|---|
| 1. Johnson | 1. gong | 1. ledge | 1. stocking cap |
| 2. receiver | 2. possible | 2. dwarf | 2. down |
| 3. alert | 3. possibilities | 3. quail | 3. receiver |
| | 4. expected | 4. ridge | |
| | 5. unexpectedly | 5. kennel | |
| | 6. operation | | |
| | 7. Whitebirds | | |

## B READING

# Adventure on the Rocky Ridge
## Chapter 3

Julie's mother pushed the door shut, closing off the wicked wind. She then walked briskly to the telephone. "I'm going to call the Whitebirds," she said as she picked up the receiver. Julie watched her mother ignore the dogs that were trying to jump on her and lick her face.

A few seconds later, Julie's mother put down the receiver and said, "The phone line is dead. The wind must have blown down the line." She went to the closet, got her coat, and threw it over her shoulders. "I'm going for help," she explained. "You put the dogs in the kennel. Then keep an eye open for your father. I may not be back for some time."

As soon as Julie's mother opened the door, the fierce wind blew it out of her hand. The door swung all the way open, making a loud banging sound as it struck the wall. Julie's mother grabbed the door, and as she pulled it shut, she smiled and said, "Don't worry, honey. Everything is going to be all right."

Julie returned Yodeler and all the other dogs except Martha to the kennel.

Then she went inside and waited. "Just be patient," she told herself. She tried to figure out how long it would take before she received some word about her father. The Whitebirds lived three miles away. Possibly, her father had stopped there to get out of the cold.

No, he would never let the dogs go home by themselves. And besides, not all the dogs had come home. Eight of the dogs from the litter had returned. But Boomer and Leader were still out.

Maybe the younger dogs had run away. Maybe they had come home while Julie's father had stopped at the Whitebirds.

Then Julie began to imagine darker possibilities. Maybe a bear had attacked her father. Maybe Boomer and Leader had tried to defend her father. Maybe they were . . . No, don't think of that.

If only the dogs could talk and tell Julie what had happened! ♦

An old clock in the living room chimed each hour. Julie sat near the window and listened to the clock. Each time it chimed, she became more anxious. When it sounded with eleven gongs, she threw her arms around Martha's neck and held her tightly. "What are we going to do?" Julie asked.

Julie knew she couldn't sleep, so she decided to try reading—but it was no use. She read the same passage over three or four times without understanding what it said. Then she put the book aside and returned to the window.

Shortly after midnight, Julie became so anxious that she opened the front door and called for her father as loudly as she could. Martha cocked her head and became very alert, glancing first at Julie and then at the darkness. Julie's voice was drowned in the sound of the wind.

At one o'clock in the morning, Julie couldn't stand it any longer. She knelt down in front of Martha, took Martha's head, and held it firmly between her hands. She looked intently into Martha's big brown eyes and said, "You've got to help me find Daddy." Martha let out a playful groan and licked Julie's face. "Please, help me," Julie said. "Please." Martha shook free and attacked Julie's hand with another playful growl.

Julie wrote her mother a note that told where she was going. She got a flashlight and tested it to make sure the beam was strong. Then she went to her room and dressed in her warmest clothes: a heavy down coat, thick mittens, a thick stocking cap, wool knee socks, and winter boots. She got a leash from the kitchen and attached it to Martha's collar. Then she found a pair of gloves her father had worn that morning. She knelt down and held the gloves in front of Martha's nose. "Daddy," she said excitedly. "These are Daddy's gloves. Go find him."

Martha grabbed the gloves and began to wrestle with them.

"No!" Julie said sharply. She then continued in a softer tone. "Don't play. You must help me find Daddy." She held the gloves in front of Martha's nose for a few moments. Then she put the gloves in her pocket and went outside.

She didn't know which direction her father had gone, so she decided to walk around the meadow that surrounded the house. Before Julie and Martha had gone three hundred feet, Martha caught a scent. Martha held her head up and let out a howl. The dogs in the kennel responded by howling back. They wanted to join her. Martha pulled on the leash and continued to howl.

A few minutes later, Julie realized that Martha was tracking something that was moving in a small circle. "It's a rabbit," she said aloud. Rabbits always circle when a hound tracks them. She bent down in front of Martha again and removed her father's gloves from her pocket. She held the gloves in front of Martha's nose and said, "Daddy. Find Daddy. Please understand. Please." ★

And for some reason, the dog did understand. It's hard to say why. Martha had not been trained to track. And for Martha, the scent of a person was far less interesting than the scent of a quail or a deer. Of course, Martha had the ability to track a person. Her nose could easily tell one person from another. It could also tell her which direction the person had been moving and how long ago the person had been in a particular place.

Martha easily recognized the scent of Julie's father on the gloves. The only thing Martha didn't understand was what Julie wanted her to do. When they had first gone out into the night, Martha had thought that Julie was giving her an unusual treat. It wasn't often that Julie let her sniff the magnificent smells that were in the meadow. But now, something was different.

Possibly, the cold wind made Martha become more serious. She really didn't enjoy being in the cutting wind, but something about the way Julie behaved told her there was important business out here. Somehow, Martha knew that neither she nor Julie would go back into the comfortable house until the important business had been completed.

Suddenly, Martha sniffed the gloves and looked at Julie with a serious expression, almost as if she was saying to her mistress, "I understand that we have a job to do."

Julie put her father's gloves back into her pocket and continued circling the meadow with Martha. When they came to the side of the meadow that was closest to the rocky ridge, Martha began to sniff the grass excitedly. Then she raised her head and gave a funny little bark. It wasn't the kind of howl that she always let out when she caught the scent of animals or birds. Each of those howls was a long "ooooo" that would sometimes last four seconds. The sound that she let out now in the bitter wind was an excited little bark, as if she was trying to say, "I found it!"

Martha pulled Julie this way and that as she tried to decide where the trail went. Julie did her best to keep up, but because of her bad leg, she couldn't move very fast. At last, she made a difficult decision. She took off her mittens and unfastened Martha's leash.

Julie realized the chance she was taking. If Martha caught the magnificent scent of a deer or some other animal, she might not come back. But Martha would be able to work faster if she were free. Before releasing Martha, Julie held her by the collar and once more presented the pair of gloves. Then she let go and said, "Go find Daddy!"

---

## C COMPREHENSION

Write the answers.
1. What do you think Julie's mother was doing while Julie waited at home?
2. Do you think it was wise of Julie to go out looking for her father? Explain your answer.
3. How did Julie give Martha her father's scent?
4. Why did Martha move in circles in the meadow?
5. Why did Julie let Martha off the leash at the end of the chapter?

## D WRITING

Continue the story of Julie and Martha.
- Tell what kind of problems they have as they look for Mr. Owl. Tell how Martha is able to help in the search, and how Julie works with Martha. Then tell whether they find Mr. Owl and what happens afterward.

# A WORD LISTS

| 1 | 2 | 3 |
|---|---|---|
| *Hard Words* | *Vocabulary Review* | *New Vocabulary* |
| 1. Mr. Taylor | 1. down | 1. wild goose chase |
| 2. hoarse | 2. receiver | 2. unexpectedly |
| 3. emotion | | 3. sprawling |
| 4. afford | | 4. cast |
| | | 5. hoarse |
| | | 6. face |

# B READING

# Adventure on the Rocky Ridge
## Chapter 4

Martha circled the place where she had first caught the smell of Julie's father. She circled it three times to find out which direction the tracks led. After completing the third circle, she knew the direction. She took off quickly, leaving Julie far behind.

From time to time, Martha raised her head and barked. Julie listened for the barks and followed them as quickly as she could, but she couldn't walk very fast. Soon she was far, far behind Martha. Julie could no longer hear Martha's barks, but she knew where Martha was heading—right up the face of the rocky ridge.

When Julie realized that her father had gone up the rocky ridge, a dismal feeling came over her. Julie had seen Leader and the other dogs with keen noses track animals to the top of the ridge. She had seen them cast aimlessly across the ridge trying to pick up the scent on the windblown rocks.

Julie followed in the direction Martha had gone. It took Julie more than half an hour to reach the steep slopes of the rocky ridge. She turned on her flashlight so she wouldn't trip over the rocks that jutted out of the grass. She was wearing mittens, but her hands were beginning to ache with cold.

She tried not to pay attention to the pain. From time to time, she stopped and called, "Martha! Martha!" But she had little hope that the dog would hear her.

Julie continued up the rocks. In some places, she had to climb the rocks the way you would climb a ladder. She had trouble holding the flashlight and going up. Once, her bad leg slipped and she crashed into a rock. She hurt her ribs, and the fall damaged the flashlight. It still worked most of the time, but the light would sometimes go out. By banging the flashlight against the palm of her hand, Julie could make the beam come on.

For nearly half an hour, Julie climbed up the side of the rocky ridge. She knew she wasn't following the same path her father had taken. She knew he would have led the dogs up a trail that was easier to climb than the one she was on. But she didn't know where that trail was. She knew only that he had probably gone to the top of the rocky ridge. She figured that as long as she was climbing up, she would get to the top as well.

At last, Julie reached the top, which was flat and smooth. The sky was clear, and the moon shone so brightly that Julie could see her shadow. She turned off the flashlight and stuffed it into her pocket. Then she cupped her hands around her mouth and called, "Martha! Martha!" She continued to call until her voice became hoarse. ♦

Suddenly, Julie saw Martha's dark form casting along the flat surface of the ridge. "Martha!" she called again. The dog stopped, turned, and ran over to her. Julie could tell from Martha's behavior that she had lost the trail.

Julie took off her mittens and tried to fasten the leash to Martha's collar. Her fin-

gers were becoming so numb that she could hardly feel what she was doing, but she finally managed to hook the leash onto the metal ring of the collar.

Just then, Julie noticed two dots of light in the valley to the south. She quickly took out her flashlight, pushed the button forward, and pounded the flashlight four times against her palm until the beam came on brightly. Then she pointed the flashlight in the direction of the lights below and waved it back and forth. Soon, the other lights responded by moving back and forth.

Julie then removed her father's gloves from her pocket, held them in front of Martha's nose, and said, "Daddy. Go find Daddy."

The young hound wagged her tail, turned away, and began to pull on the leash. She was trying to return to the place where she had lost the scent. Martha had followed the trail of Julie's father to a large, flat area on top of the ridge, but the scent had become so faint that she had lost it.

Martha led Julie back to the flat area. As Martha sniffed the ground, she pulled Julie along, first in one direction, then in another. At last, Martha caught a very faint scent. She raised her head and let out a little yelp. Then she pulled forward with so much power that Julie almost stumbled. "Good dog," Julie said. "Go find Daddy."

Martha followed the scent for about a hundred feet, but then she started to move in small circles. She had lost the scent again. She stuffed her nose into cracks between the rocks and sniffed so loudly that Julie could hear the sniffs above the wind. Suddenly, Martha raised her head and gave another little bark.

Julie turned around and noticed that the lights from the south were approaching quickly. She didn't want to stop searching, because she was afraid that if Martha lost the faint scent, she might not find the trail again. "Go find Daddy," Julie said, and Martha began pulling on the leash again. ★

As Julie continued to follow Martha, she heard voices calling above the wind. "Bill?" a man's voice called. "Is that you, Bill?"

"No, it's me!" Julie shouted, still following Martha.

Within a few minutes, the lights were very close, and Julie could recognize the voices. They belonged to her mother, Mr. Whitebird, and another neighbor, Mr. Taylor. The three of them were trying to find Mr. Owl on the rocky surface.

When the party grew close, Julie's mother shouted, "Julie, what are you doing out here?"

Before Julie could answer, Mr. Whitebird asked, "Where's your father?"

"I don't know," Julie said, "but Martha's on his trail."

"She can't be," Mr. Whitebird said as he trotted up to Julie. He caught his breath and then continued, "No dog alive can track over these rocks."

"Martha can," Julie said hoarsely.

Julie's mother threw her arms around her daughter. "Julie," she said, "what on earth are you doing out here? You'll freeze to death."

"Mom," Julie said, "Martha's on Dad's trail. She's followed him all the way up here."

Julie could see the dim outline of Mr. Taylor shaking his head. "You better get yourself back home," he said flatly. "That dog is just taking you on a wild goose chase."

"No, she isn't!" Julie protested. "She's tracking."

At that moment, Martha caught the scent of a rabbit. It was a marvelous scent, the kind that hound dogs dream about. With a great pull on the leash, she lunged forward and let out a long, "Ooooooooo."

She pulled Julie so hard and unexpectedly that the girl slipped and went sprawling on the rocks. Mr. Taylor helped her up, and Mr. Whitebird grabbed Martha's leash.

"No," Julie protested. "That's not the signal she makes for Dad's trail. She must have picked up a different scent. But I'm telling you she was on Dad's trail."

Then Mr. Taylor patted Julie on the shoulder. "You know," he said slowly, "you may be right."

Mr. Whitebird added, "I don't know what that dog was just tracking, but she sure was tracking something. And I've never seen a dog that could track anything up here. Maybe we should give her a chance to show what she can do."

"She'll do it," Julie said, fumbling in her pocket for her father's gloves. "She'll do it. You'll see." She held the gloves in front of Martha's nose again and told her, "Go find Daddy."

## C COMPREHENSION

Write the answers.
1. How could Julie tell if Martha was on the trail of her father or on the trail of an animal?
2. Why did Julie keep searching even after she saw the lights from the valley?
3. At first, why didn't the men believe that Martha could be on Mr. Owl's trail?
4. Why did the men change their minds?
5. Why is it so hard for Martha to follow a trail on the rocky ridge?

## D WRITING

Pretend you are Julie and that you are trying to convince the other people that Martha is on the right trail.
- Write the explanation you would give. Tell what talent Martha has and what she's already done. Tell why you think she's on the right trail.

## A WORD LISTS

**1**

*Vocabulary Review*
1. wild goose chase
2. sprawling
3. unexpectedly
4. cast
5. hoarse
6. face

**2**

*New Vocabulary*
1. intently
2. operate

## B READING

# Adventure on the Rocky Ridge
## Chapter 5

Mr. Whitebird was holding Martha's leash. Mr. Taylor was next to him. Julie and her mother were close behind. As they walked along, Mrs. Owl explained that she and the two men had been looking for Julie's father for several hours. Mr. Whitebird had driven to the base of the rocky ridge in his big van, and they had walked up from there.

Suddenly, Martha tried to follow the rabbit's trail. Julie shouted, "No!" and again let Martha smell her father's gloves. At last, the dog started to cast about for the scent. She went across the top of the rocky ridge, from one side to the other. Suddenly, she let out a sharp bark. "That's it!" Julie announced. "She's got it again!"

Julie heard Mr. Taylor say, "Look there! She's on a different trail now."

Both Mr. Taylor and Mr. Whitebird raised dogs, and they understood dogs well. They knew that Martha was certain about the scent she was now following. And they knew that it was not the same scent she had howled about earlier.

Martha went for another two or three hundred feet along the flat crest of the rocky ridge. Then she started down the

other side. She was right on the trail that Julie's father had left. And she was only about a thousand feet from where he was lying at that moment. But when she started down the far side of the rocky ridge, Mr. Taylor pulled on the leash and stopped her. "I don't know," he said above the wind. "I can't picture Bill going down there. This is a very dangerous place."

Julie and her mother caught up to them. Mr. Whitebird explained. "I don't know if we should try to go down there. Maybe the dog has Bill's scent, and maybe the dog doesn't. But there are some treacherous places down there. I can't imagine why Bill would go down there."

"Martha's on his trail," Julie said sharply.

"But why would Bill go down there?" Mr. Whitebird replied.

"I don't know," Julie said. "Maybe one of the dogs got away and he went after it."

During the moment that followed, the wind blew bitterly. Finally, Mr. Whitebird said, "You may be right. There's some grass down there. Maybe one of the dogs picked up a scent and Bill went after it."

Mr. Taylor shook the leash and said to Martha, "Go find him."

Martha turned around for a moment; then she put her nose to the ground and began trying to find the scent. She was on a narrow, rocky path, so there was only one direction for her to go. She moved forward, stopping every few feet to search the cracks of the rocks for some sign. But the scent of Julie's father was now quite old and was almost gone.

The party moved slowly down the trail, but Martha gave no sign that she was tracking Julie's father. At last, they came to a place where a large clump of grass grew out of the rocks. When Martha was about four feet from the grass, she suddenly tugged forward. "Yep, yep," she said. Then much more loudly, she announced, "Arrr, arrrr."

A moment later, a response came from somewhere in the darkness ahead of them. It was the long "Oooo" wail of a hound. ♦

Everybody stopped as Mr. Taylor pulled back on Martha's leash. "Did you hear that?" Mr. Taylor asked.

"I heard something," Julie's mother said. "It sounded like Leader."

"I think it came from ahead of us," Mr. Taylor said. Then he flicked the leash and said, "Get him, Martha."

Martha pulled forward to the next patch of grass. "Arrr, arrr," she announced.

Everybody stood silently and listened intently for some sound above the wind. "Ooooooooo," came the reply.

"That's Leader," Julie's mother said. "Leader!" she called. "Here, boy. Come here."

"Ooooooo," came the reply.

"Let's go," Mr. Whitebird said, and he moved forward cautiously over the jagged rocks.

"Bill! Bill!" Julie's mother called. "Can you hear us?"

Two dogs howled in response.

"That's Boomer," Julie said. Her feet were numb from cold, but she didn't even notice them. She was exhausted from all the climbing and walking, but she wasn't thinking about how she felt. Her mind was concentrating on only one thing—any sounds that could be heard above the wind. She searched every sound of the wind for a familiar voice.

At last the party came to the place where Mr. Owl had slipped. The scent was now very plain to Martha. She could smell Mr. Owl below her. She could also smell Boomer and Leader. She stood at the edge of the trail, held her head high, and announced with a very loud voice, "Arrr, arrr."

"Help," a dim voice replied from down below.

Julie held onto Martha's leash as Mr. Taylor, Mr. Whitebird, and her mother scrambled along the path looking for a place where they could climb safely down to Mr. Owl.

• • •

The trip back to Mr. Whitebird's van was long and cold. The men cut some branches and fastened them to both sides of Bill's broken leg. Then, one man got on each side of Bill, and they led him back up to the flat surface of the rocky ridge. From there, the party moved slowly along the top of the ridge until they came to the path that led down to Mr. Whitebird's van. Julie's mother ran ahead to start the engine and turn on the heat.

When everybody was in the van with the heater on full blast, Mr. Taylor asked, "How are you doing, Bill?"

Slowly, Mr. Owl said, "I don't think I would have lasted the night. It was horrible."

Julie's mother put her arms around him and held her face next to his. "It's all right now," she said. "You're going to be okay."

The van had three rows of seats. The adults sat in the first two rows, and Julie sat in the back row with the three dogs. She hugged Martha and said, "Oh, thank you so much."

Everybody turned around and looked at Julie. Mr. Taylor said, "Your dad owes a lot to you, young lady. We would never have found him without your help."

Nobody said anything for a long time. They just sat there, with the humming sound of the heater filling the van with wonderful hot air.

• • •

The story of Julie and Martha went on for many years. Martha grew up and had several litters of puppies. Once, she had a litter of fourteen. The morning after Martha delivered that litter, Julie's father picked up the smallest puppy and said, "Don't worry, little one. Nobody's going to give you away. Maybe you'll be as great as your mother."

And that puppy was great, but not as great as Martha. Many people came from far off just to see Martha track. Even Leader knew that Martha was the finest hunting dog in the pack. When Leader lost a scent, he would hold his head up and look at Martha. Then he'd follow her.

Some nice things also happened to Julie. The next year her leg was operated on. The operation helped her walk better. But the doctor told her that she would still walk with a limp.

Julie wasn't disappointed. When the doctor announced that she would still have a limp, she looked at him and said, "I don't mind. You don't have to be born perfect to be outstanding. I learned that from my dog, Martha."

---

## C COMPREHENSION

Write the answers.
1. At first, why did the men think Mr. Owl would never have gone down the far side of the ridge?
2. When Martha came to a large clump of grass, she picked up Mr. Owl's scent. Explain why.
3. Why did the men fasten branches to Mr. Owl's leg?
4. Mr. Taylor told Julie, "Your dad owes a lot to you." Explain what he meant by that.
5. At the end of the story, Julie said, "You don't have to be born perfect to be outstanding." Give an example of what she meant.

## D WRITING

Pretend you are Julie's mother. Write the story of Julie and Martha in your own words.
- Tell what you were doing while Julie and Martha were searching. Tell what happened after you found Julie. Tell how you felt about Julie doing something so dangerous. Tell what you learned.

## A WORD LISTS

| 1 Animal Names | 2 Word Endings | 3 Compound Words | 4 New Vocabulary |
|---|---|---|---|
| 1. chimpanzee | 1. extinction | 1. overhunting | 1. extinct |
| 2. rhinoceros | 2. competition | 2. livestock | 2. endangered |
| 3. grizzly bear | 3. pollution | 3. firewood | 3. species |
| 4. parakeet | 4. destruction | | 4. resources |
| 5. leopard | 5. admiration | | 5. habitat |
| 6. alligator | | | 6. reserve |
| 7. bandicoot | | | |

## B READING

# ENDANGERED ANIMALS
## Chapter 1

When a type of animal becomes extinct, every animal of that type dies out all over the earth. Among the animals in danger of extinction are the African elephant, the chimpanzee, the rhinoceros, the blue whale, the grizzly bear, and the bald eagle. Because these animals are in danger of extinction, they are called endangered animals. Each of these beautiful animals may soon vanish from the earth forever.

Extinction is nothing new. Throughout the history of the earth, millions of types, or species, of plants and animals have died out. What is new today is the rapid rate of extinction. Increasing numbers of people make greater demands on the earth for shelter, food, and fuel. As humans use up more and more of the earth's resources, other species have less and less.

In the past, people used the earth's resources with little thought to the effect on other creatures. Now people all over the world are becoming aware of the ways humans are endangering other animals.

African elephants, chimpanzees, and grizzly bears are in danger of extinction.

## Overhunting

Overhunting is one of the ways animals become endangered. Any species that has fewer babies than the numbers killed by hunters is on the road to extinction.

People kill animals they think are pests. Farmers shot Carolina parakeets in great numbers to keep them from eating fruits and nuts. This overhunting helped make Carolina parakeets extinct. Wolves have been hunted to extinction in many parts of the world because they kill livestock and because people fear them.

People often kill animals for their fur or other body parts. African elephants are killed for their tusks and rhinoceroses for their horns. Cheetahs and leopards are killed for their fur and alligators for their skin.

People also take animals from the wild to sell to pet dealers or collectors. Nearly a hundred species of parrots are seriously endangered because of this activity.

## Messing with Mother Nature

Wild animals that have lived in a particular area for a long time are called native animals. These native animals can become endangered when people introduce a new species into the area. When people brought rabbits to Australia, they upset the balance among native animals. Now the bandicoot, a native Australian mammal, is losing out to the rabbit in the competition for survival.

Pollution caused by people also kills many animals. Chemicals released into the world often have far-reaching effects. Acid rain falling into lakes and rivers kills both fish and the animals that depend on the fish for food. Poisons cause similar problems. When people spray poisons over farms and swamps to kill insect pests, sometimes great numbers of fish, birds, and mammals die off as well. ♦

## Habitat Destruction

The most serious threat to wildlife is habitat destruction. For example, rain forests take up only a small part of the earth's surface. But they are home to almost half the world's plant and animal species. As people clear these forests for timber and farming, more and more plants and animals become endangered.

Habitat destruction goes on everywhere. Bulldozers clear land for houses, shopping malls, factories, and farms. They cut down trees, grasses, and bushes. The plants destroyed may not seem important to humans. But when plants disappear, the animals that depend on them for food and shelter suffer. Other species that depend on those animals are affected in turn. All these plants and animals are connected to each other in some way.

Keep this connection in mind as you read about four animals that are very different from each other but have one thing in common. They are all endangered.

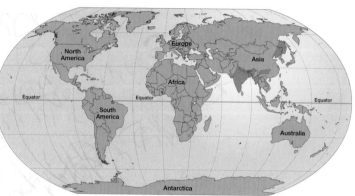

■ Where tigers live

## The Tiger

Tigers are among the most impressive animals on earth. People who see tigers in zoos find it easy to admire them. But where tigers still exist in the wild, people's admiration is mixed with fear and even hatred. Tigers are beautiful, but they are also dangerous. It is difficult for people and tigers to live together. ★

Tigers live in the grassy wetlands and forests of India and other Asian countries. They eat mainly deer and wild hogs. If farmers live nearby, tigers sometimes hunt their cattle. Tigers have been known to eat people as well.

Tigers have been a favorite target of hunters for hundreds of years. People killed them for their beautiful striped skins and to protect livestock. It was not until the 1970s that people realized tigers were endangered. The government of India banned tiger hunting in 1970 and set up fifteen large tiger reserves.

The reserves were designed to keep people and tigers safe from each other.

However, tigers require large reserves to survive, and India is a crowded country. It is hard to keep people who need firewood and land out of the tigers' reserves; and as the tiger population increases, it is hard to keep the tigers inside the reserves.

Many people agree that tigers should not become extinct. Yet conflicts between the needs of tigers and the needs of people have not been resolved. As long as these conflicts exist, the tigers' future remains uncertain.

# C COMPREHENSION

Write the answers.
1. What happens when an animal becomes extinct?
2. Why is the rate of extinction increasing?
3. Explain how overhunting can endanger a species of animal.
4. Why do animals suffer when their habitats are destroyed?
5. What kinds of problems does India have with its tiger reserves?

# D WRITING

Do you think endangered animals should be protected? Why or why not?
• Write an essay that explains your answer. If you think endangered animals should be protected, explain why you feel that way. Also explain how they should be protected. If you think they should not be protected, explain why. Also explain what will happen if those animals become extinct.

## A WORD LISTS

**1**
*Hard Words*
1. century
2. creature
3. foreign
4. European
5. primate

**2**
*Animal Names*
1. Galápagos tortoise
2. orangutan
3. peregrine falcon
4. gorilla
5. chimpanzee

**3**
*Word Endings*
1. destruction
2. starvation
3. foundation
4. population

**4**
*Place Names*
1. Ecuador
2. China
3. Java
4. Borneo
5. Sumatra

**5**
*New Vocabulary*
1. century
2. creature
3. solitary
4. confine
5. decline

## B READING

# ENDANGERED ANIMALS
## Chapter 2

In the last lesson, you learned why some animals are endangered. In today's lesson, you will read about three more types of endangered animals: the Galápagos tortoise, the orangutan, and the peregrine falcon.

**The Galápagos Tortoise**

The Galápagos Islands are located in the Pacific Ocean about six hundred miles west of Ecuador, a country in South America. When European sailors first discovered the islands in the sixteenth century, no people lived there, so the islands' creatures had never developed a fear of people. Birds and tortoises didn't even try to escape when sailors came ashore to catch them.

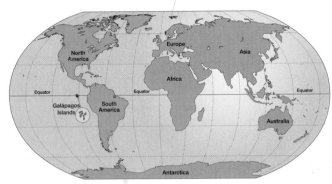
■ Where Galápagos tortoises live

Sailors killed hundreds of thousands of Galápagos tortoises for food in the centuries that followed. Animals that sailors brought to the islands caused further destruction. Many tortoises died of starvation when they had to compete with goats for plant food. Meanwhile pigs, dogs, and cats ate tortoise eggs and young tortoises. The numbers of tortoises and other native species were greatly reduced.

Little was done to help the tortoises until 1959, when the Charles Darwin Foundation was created. To help the tortoises make a comeback, the Foundation set up a breeding station on one of the islands. Tortoise eggs are brought there to hatch, and the young tortoises live in safety until they are too big to be eaten by other animals. Meanwhile, goats have been removed so that there will be enough plants for the tortoises to eat.

The eggs and the newly hatched young of the Galápagos tortoise continue to be threatened by foreign species. Fortunately, the tortoises that do survive are sturdy beasts. They weigh about one hundred fifty pounds by the age of fifteen and as much as five hundred pounds when fully grown. They can live for a hundred years or more. These peaceful giants may still be saved from extinction.

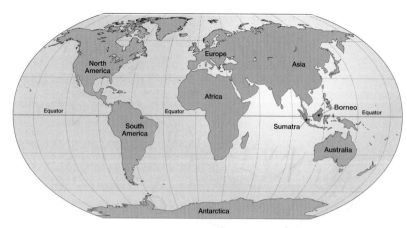

■ **Where orangutans live**

## The Orangutan

The orangutan is a solitary animal whose name means "person of the forest." Orangutans are primates, like gorillas and chimpanzees. Although most primates live in family groups, orangutans live alone. They live alone because they eat almost nothing but fruit, which is hard to find. If orangutan families stayed together, they could not find enough fruit to support the entire group.

Hunters have reduced orangutan pop-ulations. Orangutans are killed for meat or are taken from the forest to be sold as pets. But the greatest threat to their survival is the loss of their rain forest homes. Orangutans once lived in dense forests ranging from southern China to the island of Java. Now they are confined to rain forests on just two islands, Borneo and Sumatra. Unfortunately, the dense forests on these islands are being cut down for timber or burned for farmland. Shrinking areas of forest support fewer and fewer orangutans.

Efforts are now being made to save the orangutan in the wild. Special areas of rain forests have been set aside, and laws against hunting the creatures are enforced. Breeding in zoos and labs may help to keep the species alive. In the end, though, orangutans will be saved from extinction only if enough of their rain forest habitat is preserved. ◆

## The Peregrine Falcon

The peregrine falcon is one of the world's great birds of prey. Its streamlined body is built for speed and strength. It kills its prey by catching it "on the wing" or by making vertical dives at speeds up to two hundred miles per hour.

Peregrine falcons were once found in nearly all parts of the world. They were described as the world's most successful flying bird. Then suddenly there was a worldwide population crash of peregrine falcons.

Scientists noticed that the falcons were no longer successfully raising their young. They discovered that the shells of the falcons' eggs had become so thin that the eggs were breaking when adult falcons sat on them. The problem of shell-thinning was traced to a poison called DDT.

DDT was widely used in the 1950s and 1960s to kill insects. This poison does not break down when it enters the environment. At first, people thought this was a good thing because DDT would continue to kill unwanted insects for a long time. But DDT was killing many animals besides insects.

When small animals ate the insects, they ate the DDT as well. And when larger animals ate the smaller ones, the DDT became more dangerous. Birds of prey, including peregrine falcons, received the most dangerous amounts of DDT. Their populations declined rapidly because many of the birds could no longer lay eggs that would hatch. ★

When the United States finally banned the use of DDT in 1972, there were no American peregrines left in the eastern United States except in zoos. The falcon population in western states was also greatly reduced. Breeding programs were begun to save the falcons from extinction.

In the East, baby falcons in zoos were carefully raised so they would be able to survive in the wild. People used falcon-shaped puppets to feed the baby falcons so the birds would learn to expect food from other falcons, not from people. Raising falcons to live outside zoos was a difficult task, but by 1980, the birds were successfully released into the wild.

In the West, thin-shelled eggs were removed from falcon nests and replaced with plaster eggs. After the real eggs hatched, the chicks were returned to the nest to be raised by adult falcons.

Since the 1980s, more than a thousand peregrine falcons have been released into the wild. The falcon has been brought back from the brink of extinction—but it is not out of danger. It will take the efforts of many people to save the falcon and other rare creatures, all of which are important strands in the web of life.

# C COMPREHENSION

Write the answers.
1. Describe at least three ways that Galápagos tortoises were endangered by foreign species.
2. Explain how the breeding station protects tortoises.
3. What reasons do people have for destroying the orangutans' habitat?
4. Explain how DDT caused falcon populations to decline.
5. Why did people in zoos use falcon-shaped puppets to feed baby falcons?

# D WRITING

Animals are endangered for four main reasons, or causes. The four causes are overhunting, competition with foreign species, poisons and other pollution, and habitat destruction.

- Write an article that explains how one of these causes endangers animals. Give at least one example from the animals you have just read about. Explain how the animal is affected by that cause. Also show how people could help the animal.

# Glossary

## A

**abruptly** *Abruptly* is another word for *suddenly.*

**accept** When you accept a gift, you take it.

**admit** When you admit someone to a place, you let that person come in.

**advance** When you advance, you move forward.

**advantages** The advantages of a plan are the ways that plan is better than another plan.

**affection** *Affection* is another word for *fondness.*

**alert** Something that is alert is full of attention.

**amused** *Amused* is another word for *entertained.*

**apparent** When something is apparent, it is easy to see or understand.

**approach** When you approach something, you come close to it.

**approve of** When you approve of something, you like that thing.

**assignment** A task that a teacher or boss gives you is an assignment.

**astonished** *Astonished* is another word for *surprised.*

**attic** An attic is a storeroom near the top of a house.

**awkward** *Awkward* is another word for *clumsy.*

## B

**balanced** When something is balanced, it won't tip over.

**bald** A bald person doesn't have any hair on top of his or her head.

**bargain** When you make a bargain with someone, you make a deal with that person.

**barrier** A barrier is something that blocks your way.

**basin** *Basin* is another word for *sink.*

**battered** When something is battered, it is full of dents.

**blurt out** When you say something suddenly, you blurt it out.

**bondage** *Bondage* is another word for *slavery.*

**boulder** A boulder is a large, round rock.

**bounding** *Bounding* is another word for *running and leaping.*

**brace yourself** When you brace yourself, you tighten your muscles and get ready for a jolt.

**brilliant** When something is brilliant, it is bright and colorful.

**brisk** *Brisk* is another word for *fast.*

**brook** A brook is a small stream.

**bruise** A bruise is a place on your body that is sore.

**bud** Buds are leaves that are forming.

**budge** When you budge something, you move it.

**bundle** When you roll up clothes into a tight ball, you make a bundle.

## C

**cashier** A cashier is someone who takes payments at a store.

**cast** When hunting dogs cast, they try to find the scent of an animal by sniffing the ground.

**castle** A castle is a type of palace.

**caution** When you caution somebody, you warn that person about something.

**celebration** A celebration is a party.

**century** A century is one hundred years.

**charm** A charm is a magic power.

**chattering** Chattering is the sound that monkeys make.

**cheering** When something is cheering, it makes you feel good.

**chorus** A chorus of voices is a group of voices that do the same thing.

**civilized** *Civilized* is another word for *well-mannered*.

**clumsiness** *Clumsiness* is another word for *awkwardness*.

**cluster** A cluster is a group.

**clutch** When you clutch something, you hold it tightly.

**cock your head** When you cock your head, you tilt it to one side.

**coil** When something is coiled, it is in a circular or spiral form.

**comforted** When you are comforted, you feel calm.

**companions** Companions are people who keep you company.

**comrade** A comrade is a friend.

**confidence** When you have confidence, you feel sure you can do something.

**confine** When you are confined to a place, you cannot leave that place.

**congratulate** When you congratulate people, you tell them they did a good job.

**consider** When you consider something, you think over whether you should do it.

**contents** The contents of something are the things that are inside it.

**countless** If there are too many things to count, they are countless things.

**courage** *Courage* is another word for *bravery*.

**courtyard** The yard outside a castle is called a courtyard.

**coward** A coward is a fearful person.

**cozy** When something is cozy, it is comfortable.

**cradle** A cradle is a small bed.

**creature** *Creature* is another word for *animal*.

**crest** The crest of a hill is the top of the hill.

**crops** Crops are plant foods that are raised on a farm.

**crouch** When you crouch, you bend your legs and get ready to spring forward.

**cruelty** When a person acts with cruelty, that person acts in a mean way.

**cunning** Someone who is cunning is dishonest and tricky.

**cupboard** A cupboard is a cabinet.

**current** Current is the flow of water.

**curtsy** A curtsy is a kind of bow that women make.

**cyclone** A cyclone is a strong wind that spins around and around.

# D

**dangerous** When something is dangerous, it is not safe.

**dangling** When something is dangling, it is hanging loosely.

**dazzle** Something that dazzles you is so brilliant that it amazes you.

**deaf** Someone who is deaf is unable to hear.

**deceive** When you deceive somebody, you trick that person into believing something that is not true.

**declare** *Declare* is another word for *say*.

**decline** When something declines, it goes down.

**delicious** When something is delicious, it tastes good.

**delightful** *Delightful* is another word for *wonderful.*

**descend** When something descends, it comes down.

**desert** When you desert people, you leave them when they need you.

**desperately** When you want something desperately, you want it very much.

**develops** When something develops, it grows.

**diamonds** Diamonds are clear jewels.

**dilapidated** When something is dilapidated, it is broken down and in bad shape.

**disappear** When something disappears, it vanishes.

**disgraceful** *Disgraceful* is another word for *terrible.*

**disgusting** Something that is disgusting is really horrible.

**dismally** *Dismally* is another word for *sadly.*

**dome** A dome is a roof that looks like a round hat.

**domestic animals** Domestic animals are animals that live with people.

**dose** A dose of something is a certain amount of that thing.

**down** Soft feathers are called *down.*

**drawn** When something is drawn by a horse, it is pulled by the horse.

**dreadful** *Dreadful* is another word for *horrible.*

**dreary** *Dreary* is another word for *dull.*

**dwarf** *Dwarf* is another word for *very short* or *small.*

**dwell** When you dwell in a place, you live in that place.

**earnestly** *Earnestly* is another word for *sincerely.*

**ease** When you do something with ease, it is easy for you to do.

**echo** When a sound echoes, you can hear it again and again, but it gets softer.

**embrace** An embrace is a hug.

**emeralds** Emeralds are green jewels.

**endangered** When something is endangered, it is in danger.

**endurance** Somebody who has a lot of endurance can keep on going.

**enlarge** When you enlarge something, you make it larger.

**enormous** *Enormous* is another word for *huge.*

**eventually** *Eventually* is another word for *at last.*

**exchange** When you change one thing for another, you exchange those things.

**exclaim** When you exclaim, you speak forcefully.

**exhausted** When you're very tired, you're exhausted.

**expecting** When you are expecting an event, you think that event will probably happen.

**experience** Every time you do something, you have an experience.

**extend** When something is extended, it is stretched out.

**extinct** When a type of plant or animal is extinct, that type no longer exists.

**F**

**face** The face of a cliff is the part of the cliff that goes up and down.

**farewell** *Farewell* is another word for *goodbye.*

**fate** The things that happen to you are called your fate.

**feast** A feast is a large meal.

**fiddler** A fiddler is someone who plays the violin.

**field of grain** A field of grain is a field that is filled with plants like wheat and corn.

**fine** The word *fine* sometimes means "very small."

**flicker** When a flame flickers, it burns unsteadily.

**flushed** When you blush, your face is flushed.

**fond of** When you are fond of something, you like that thing.

**for** Sometimes the word *for* is used instead of *because.*

**fortunate** *Fortunate* is another word for *lucky.*

**frantically** When people act frantically, they act in a wild and nervous way.

**G**

**gallop** When horses gallop, they run as fast as they can.

**generation** A generation is a group of people who grow up at the same time.

**gingham** Gingham is a kind of checked cotton.

**glare** *Glare* is another word for *brightness.*

**glittered** When something glitters, it glistens or sparkles.

**gloomy** *Gloomy* is a another word for *dismal.*

**gnaw** When you chew on something that is very hard, you gnaw on that thing.

**gorgeous** When something is gorgeous, it is very pretty.

**gradually** *Gradually* is another word for *slowly.*

**grant** When you grant a person's wish, you give that person what he or she wants.

**grapple** When you grapple, you wrestle or fight.

**grate** When something grates, it grinds against a hard surface.

**grindstone** A grindstone is a large stone that is used to sharpen knives and axes.

**guardian** A guardian is a person who guards something.

**guilty** A person who commits a crime is guilty of the crime.

**H**

**habitat** A habitat is a place where a plant or animal lives.

**haunt** If something haunts you, it really worries or disturbs you.

**hearty** *Hearty* is another word for *large.*

**high spirits** When people have high spirits, they feel very good.

**hoarse** When your voice is hoarse, it sounds deep and thick.

**hold a horse in** When you hold a horse in, you don't let it run faster, even though it wants to run faster.

**horizon** The horizon is the line where the sky meets the land.

**humbug** A humbug is a person who pretends to be something but is really not.

**hurl** *Hurl* is another word for *throw*.

**hush** When you hush, you stop talking.

**husky** When something is husky, it is deep or thick.

# I

**ideal** *Ideal* is another word for *excellent*.

**identify** When you identify a thing, you tell what it is.

**ignore** When you ignore something, you pay no attention to it.

**imitate** When you imitate somebody, you do just what that person does.

**in spite of** *In spite of* is another way of saying *although*.

**inconvenient** If something is inconvenient, it is annoying or it requires work that is not necessary.

**injured** *Injured* is another word for *hurt*.

**instead** When you make a choice, you choose one thing instead of something else.

**intense** When something is intense, it is very strong.

**intently** When you do something intently, you concentrate on that thing.

# J

**jagged** When something is jagged, it is sharp and uneven.

**journey** *Journey* is another word for *trip*.

**jut out** When something juts out, it sticks out.

# K

**kayak** A kayak is small canoe that usually holds only one person.

**kayaking** When you paddle a kayak, you are kayaking.

**keen** If your hearing is very good, you have keen hearing.

**kennel** A kennel is a place where dogs are kept.

**kingdom** A kingdom is a place that is ruled by a king or a queen.

**knowledge** A person's knowledge is all the things that person knows.

# L

**lack** When you lack something, you don't have that thing.

**lagging behind** When you are lagging behind, you are dropping back.

**lanterns** Lanterns are lamps that burn oil or candles.

**lean** People who are lean have very little fat on their bodies.

**leather** Leather is a tough material made from animal skins.

**ledge** A ledge is a flat shelf on the side of a hill or a cliff.

**let a horse out** When you let a horse out, you let it run faster when it wants to run faster.

**limp** *Limp* has different meanings.
1. *Limp* is another word for *flimsy*.
2. When you walk with a limp, you have trouble moving one of your legs.

**linger on** When something lingers on, it keeps on going.

**lining** The lining of something is the material on the inside.

**litter** A litter is a group of puppies born to the same mother at the same time.

**lunge** When you lunge, you charge forward suddenly.

# M

**magnificent** When something is magnificent, it is wonderful or marvelous.

**maiden** *Maiden* is an old-fashioned word for a young woman who is not married.

**manager** A manager is a boss.

**marble** Marble is a beautiful rock with wavy, colored patterns.

**marvel** When you marvel over something, you think that thing is marvelous.

**mass** A mass is an area with no shape.

**meadow** A meadow is a field.

**meek** *Meek* is another word for *timid*.

**mend** When you fix something that is torn or broken, you mend it.

**merrily** *Merrily* is another word for *happily*.

**messenger** A messenger is a person who delivers messages.

**migrate** When you migrate, you travel from one place to another.

**mischief** Mischief is naughty behavior.

**miserable** When you feel very bad, you feel miserable.

**misery** Misery is great unhappiness.

**misfortune** When you have misfortune, you have bad luck.

**mistress** A dog's mistress is the woman who owns the dog.

**mock** Praise that is not sincere is mock praise.

**moss** Moss is made up of tiny green plants that grow best in the shade.

**motionless** When something is motionless, it is not moving.

**mount a horse** When you mount a horse, you get on the horse.

**moved** When you are moved by something you see or hear, that thing makes you feel happy or sad.

**murmur** A murmur is a low sound.

**mysterious** When something is mysterious, it is full of mystery.

**mystery** A mystery is a strange thing you don't understand.

# N

**nag** A nag is an old, broken-down horse.

**naked** When something is naked, it is without covering.

**notice** When you notice something, you become aware of it.

**nudge** A nudge is a gentle push.

**numb** When you have no feeling in part of your body, that part is numb.

# O

**oats** Oats are a kind of grain.

**obstacle** An obstacle is something that blocks your way.

**odor** An odor is a smell.

**officials** Officials are people who see to it that rules are followed.

**operate** When doctors operate, they fix something that is wrong with a person's body.

**orphan** An orphan is someone without parents.

**overhear** When you overhear something, you hear what other people are saying.

**P**

**passage**  *Passage* is another word for *path*.

**pasture**  A pasture is a field for farm animals.

**pattering**  A pattering sound is the sound of something that goes "pat, pat, pat."

**pave**  When you pave a road, you cover it with bricks or concrete.

**peculiar**  *Peculiar* is another word for *strange*.

**people of flesh and blood**  Real people are sometimes called people of flesh and blood.

**permit**  When you permit somebody to do something, you let that person do it.

**plentiful**  When something is plentiful, it is in good supply.

**plod**  When you plod, you move at a slow, tired pace.

**poster**  Posters are large pieces of paper that use words and pictures to advertise things.

**pounce**  When you pounce on something, you jump on that thing.

**pound**  In England, a pound is a unit of money. One pound is worth about one and a half American dollars.

**prairie**  A prairie is a grassland with few trees.

**prance**  When a horse prances, it steps around as if it wants to start running.

**prefer**  When you prefer something, you choose it over other things.

**presence**  When you're in somebody's presence, you're where that person can see you.

**prey**  Your prey is the animal you are hunting.

**promptly**  When you do something promptly, you do it on time.

**pure**  If something is pure, it is not mixed with anything else.

**push a horse too hard**  When you push a horse too hard, you try to make the horse go too fast.

**Q**

**quail**  A quail is a bird about the same size as a pigeon.

**quiver**  When you quiver, you tremble or shake.

**R**

**raft**  A raft is a flat boat with no sides.

**rapids**  Rapids are places in a river where the water flows quickly.

**ray of sunshine**  A ray of sunshine is a streak of light from the sun.

**rear up**  When something rears up, it stands up quickly.

**receiver**  The receiver is the part of a phone that you hold in your hand when you're making a call.

**recover**  When you recover, you get back your strength.

**reeds**  Reeds are tall grasses that grow on the edge of water.

**reflection**  A reflection is the image of yourself that you see in a mirror.

**refreshed**  When you are refreshed, you are full of energy.

**relatives**  Your relatives are the people in your family.

**reluctant** When you are reluctant to do something, you don't want to do it very much.

**remarkable** *Remarkable* is another word for *unusual*.

**replace** When you replace something, you put it back in place.

**represent** *Represent* is another word for *look like*.

**request** When you request something, you ask for it.

**reserve** A reserve is a place set aside for wild animals.

**resist the impulse** When you resist the impulse to do something, you don't do that thing, even though you want to.

**resolve** When you resolve to do something, you make up your mind to do that thing.

**resources** *Resources* is another word for *supplies*.

**reunited** When people or things are reunited, they are put together again.

**ridge** A ridge is a flat area on top of some long hills.

**ripples** Ripples are small waves.

**rubies** Rubies are red jewels.

**runners** The runners of a sled are two strips of wood or metal that slide over the snow.

**rust** Rust is a red material that forms on iron and steel when they get wet.

**rustling** When something moves through grass or bushes, it makes a rustling sound.

# S

**sap** Sap is a sticky liquid that is just underneath the bark of trees.

**satisfaction** When you are pleased about something you do, you get satisfaction from that thing.

**sawdust** Sawdust is small pieces of wood that fall off during sawing.

**scarcely** If you can scarcely do something, you can hardly do it.

**scarlet** Scarlet is a bright red color.

**scent** A scent is a smell.

**scramble** When you scramble, you move as fast as you can.

**seize** When you seize something, you grab it and hang onto it.

**sensitive** Something is sensitive if it can react to things that are very faint.

**shabby** When something is shabby, it looks cheap and in poor condition.

**shall** In some cases, the word *shall* means the same thing as the word *will*.

**shears** Shears are large scissors.

**shiver** When you shiver, you tremble and shake.

**shoulder an axe** When you shoulder an axe, you bring it up to your shoulder.

**shrill** A shrill sound is high and sharp.

**shrug** When you shrug your shoulders, you lift them up in the air.

**silk** Silk is a fine material.

**singed** When something is singed, it is slightly burned.

**sketchbook** A sketchbook is a notebook that artists use for drawings and sketches.

**slate** A slate is a little chalkboard.

**slightest** *Slightest* is another word for *smallest*.

**slosh** When liquid sloshes, it splashes around.

**snarl** When you snarl, you show your teeth and growl.

**sneer** A sneer is a mean-looking smile.

**snug** Something that is snug fits tightly.

**sob** *Sob* is another word for *cry*.

**sober** *Sober* is another word for *serious*.

**solemn** *Solemn* is another word for *serious*.

**solitary** Solitary animals are animals that live alone.

**sorceress** A sorceress is a female magician.

**sorrow** *Sorrow* is another word for *sadness*.

**spawn** Spawn are fish eggs.

**spear** A spear is a weapon with a long shaft and a pointed tip.

**species** A type of plant or animal is called a species of plant or animal.

**spectacles** Spectacles are glasses that you wear.

**spectators** Spectators are people who watch an event such as a horse race.

**spicy** Things that are spicy contain spices such as pepper or cinnamon.

**splendid** *Splendid* is another word for *marvelous*.

**spoil** *Spoil* is another word for *ruin*.

**sprawling** When something is sprawling, it is spread out.

**sprinkled** *Sprinkled* is another word for *dotted*.

**stagger** When you stagger, you walk unsteadily or stumble.

**stall** A stall is a small room with walls that do not go to the ceiling.

**startled** When you are startled, you are frightened or surprised.

**stocking cap** A stocking cap is a long, floppy cap that is shaped like a sock.

**strain** When you strain your body, you make it work as hard as it can.

**strangle** *Strangle* is another word for *choke*.

**stray** A stray animal is one that is far from its home.

**stretch** A stretch of road is part of the road.

**stride** A stride is a long step.

**studded** When something is studded with shiny things, it is full of shiny things.

**stunned** *Stunned* is another word for *knocked out*.

**supplies** When you go camping, the food and other items you take with you are called supplies.

**suspected** *Suspected* is another word for *thought*.

# T

**tempt** When you tempt people, you try to get them to do things by offering them something they really want.

**tenderly** When you act tenderly, you act gently and lovingly.

**terror** Terror is great fear.

**therefore** *Therefore* is another word for *so*.

**Thoroughbred** A Thoroughbred is a special breed of horse that is used for racing.

**throne** A throne is a fancy chair for a queen, a king, or a very important person.

**timid** *Timid* is another word for *shy*.

**tint** A tint is a slight color.

**tolerate** When you tolerate something, you put up with it.

**treacherous** *Treacherous* is another word for *dangerous*.

**tremendous** When something is tremendous, it is great.

**trot**  When you trot, you run slowly.

**tug**  When you tug at something, you pull hard.

**turf**  Turf is ground that is covered with grass.

**tussle**  When you tussle with somebody, you wrestle with that person.

## U

**unbearable**  When you can't stand something, that thing is unbearable.

**uneasy**  When you feel uneasy about doing something, you don't feel comfortable about doing it.

**unexpectedly**  When something happens unexpectedly, it happens when you don't expect it.

**untilled**  *Untilled* is another word for *unplowed*.

**usual**  *Usual* is another word for *common* or *ordinary*.

**utter**  *Utter* is another word for *say*.

## V

**vacation**  A vacation is time you spend away from school or work.

**vanish**  *Vanish* is another word for *disappear*.

**velvet**  Velvet is a soft material.

**ventriloquist**  Ventriloquists are people who can talk without moving their lips.

**vivid**  Something that is easy to see is vivid.

**volunteer**  When you volunteer, you offer to help.

## W

**wail**  A wail is a howl.

**weep**  *Weep* is another word for *cry*.

**whisk**  When something whisks, it moves like a broom that is sweeping.

**whittle**  When you whittle, you carve and cut wood.

**wild goose chase**  When you go on a wild goose chase, you are going after something you won't find.

**willingly**  When you do something willingly, you do it on purpose.

**witness**  When you witness an event, you see that event happening.

# Fact Game Answer Keys

## LESSON 16

2. a. East
   b. South
   c. West
   d. North
   e. South
3. a. United States
   b. Kansas
4. a. Gillikins
   b. Quadlings
   c. Winkies
   d. Munchkins
5. a. Kansas
   b. Land of Oz
   c. Land of Oz
   d. Kansas

6. a. Desert
   b. Emerald City
7. a. Cyclone
   b. Eye
8. a. North
   b. West
   c. East
   d. South
9. a. Yellow
   b. Gray
   c. Blue
   d. White

10. a. Scarecrow
    b. Lion
    c. Dorothy
    d. Tin Woodman
11. a. Kalidah
    b. Oz
    c. Toto
12. a. East
    b. North
    c. West
    d. East

## LESSON 26

2. a. South
   b. West
   c. West
   d. South
   e. East
3. a. Cyclone
   b. Eye
4. a. Land of the North
   b. Land of the South
   c. Land of the West
   d. Land of the East
5. a. Blue
   b. Green
   c. Gray
   d. Yellow

6. a. Dorothy
   b. Scarecrow
   c. Tin Woodman
   d. Lion
7. a. Kansas
   b. Indiana
   c. Maine
8. a. East
   b. West
   c. East
   d. South
9. a. Emerald City
   b. Oz
   c. Desert

10. a. Winkies
    b. Mice
    c. Kalidahs
11. Dorothy met the Scarecrow.
12. a. West
    b. East
    c. North

# Fact Game Answer Keys

## LESSON 46

2.  a. Steeplechase
    b. Liverpool
3.  a. Wild
    b. Domestic
4.  a. Dawson
    b. Yukon
5.  a. Dog
    b. Hunting
6.  a. Carrying
    b. Food
    c. Hunting

7.  a. Fact
    b. Fantasy
    c. Fact
8.  a. Cow
    b. Dog
    c. Horse
9.  a. Scarecrow
    b. Tin Woodman
    c. Dorothy
    d. Lion

10. a. Liverpool
    b. London
11. a. Land of the North
    b. Land of the East
    c. Land of the West
    d. Land of the South
12. a. North
    b. West
    c. East
    d. South